MW01037160

SQUISH THE FISH

A TALE OF DATING AND DEBAUCHERY

Dave Lundy

BOTTOMS UP PUBLISHING

SQUISH THE FISH Copyright © 2017, 2016 by Dave Lundy

All rights reserved. No part of this publication may be reproduced, distributed or trans-
mitted in any form or by any means, including photocopying, recording, or other elec-
tronic or mechanical methods, without the prior written permission of the publisher,
except in the case of brief quotations embodied in critical reviews and certain other non-
commercial uses permitted by copyright law. For permission requests, email the contact
below.

Bottoms Up Publishing
San Francisco, CA 94123
www.bottomsuppublishing.com
Contact: bottomsuppublishing@gmail.com

Publisher's Note: This is a work of fiction. Names, characters, places, and incidents are a
product of the author's imagination. Locales and public names are sometimes used for
atmospheric purposes. Any resemblance to actual people, living or dead, or to businesses, companies, events, institutions, or locales is completely coincidental.

Squish the Fish / Dave Lundy — 1st edition (082017)
ISBN 978-0-6927-8013-8
LCCN 2016953410

Edited by: Ro O'Connor www.ro-oconnor.com
Cover Design by: Mariah Sinclair www.mariahsinclair.com

#1 NEW RELEASE
IN HUNTING & FISHING HUMOR

Note: While it's an honor to be recognized in such a prestigious category, this book has nothing to do with hunting or fishing — but it is still humorous as F! Thanks, Amazon!

BILLS MAFIA APPROVED!

For *Buffalo, New York*: Never give up — "it" will happen! And when it does, we'll party for days until the city crumbles! Thank you for all the friendships and every outrageous moment.

For *Marc*: Your book was the kick in the pants I needed to write this one, so for that, I thank you. However, when there's a book-burning riot in Miami, it's clearly your fault.

For *My Friends*: Thank you for your encouragement and feedback during the writing process. Because of it, the comedy-romantic genre (heavy comedy, light romance) was born.
Cheers! This com-rom's for you!

For *Mom*: I love you, but please don't read any further.

"Insanity is doing the same thing over and over again, and expecting different results."

Albert Einstein (supposedly)

"It's better to be absolutely ridiculous than absolutely boring."

Marilyn Monroe (probably not)

Pregame

Unable to escape like a turtle flipped on its shell, a man flails his limbs through the puffy snow. As he passes out, the alcohol in his bloodstream does a victory dance. The orange glow from a streetlamp punctures the darkness like a police helicopter's spotlight and frames the casualty in a jagged snow angel.

Several hours later, a woman is walking her Saint Bernard down the quiet street at dawn. Upon noticing the body, her first reaction is to think, *What the hell?* But she quickly reminds herself of one important fact — *Of course there's an inebriated jackass lying in the snow. This is Buffalo, isn't it?* As she shrugs off the potential Darwin Award winner, the dog picks up a scent and is pulled in the man's direction. It tears the leash from the owner's grasp and dashes to investigate.

As the shaggy beast pants above the lush, it stares in wonder. The man's face is masked by a pair of pink panties like he's some sort of deranged bank robber. If the hound could form complex thoughts, it would speculate, *For what ungodly reason is he wearing that? Warmth, disguise, or some next-level form of perversion?* But it can't contemplate those things, so it joyfully wags its tail instead. Incapable of resisting the feminine undergarment's aroma any longer, the mutt enthusiastically licks the guy's noggin like it's a female-flavored lollypop.

1

A fresh line of boot prints made by an unknown third-party mark a trail up to the man and then continues past. "SUN 12-17 7:28 AM" displays on the frosty LCD of his Casio watch. As gusts of wind blow across the ground, his bare hand fuses with the frozen bottle of Genesee Cream Ale it grips. In his other hand, a tattered envelope flaps and scatters a rainbow of glitter dust.

Before the woman can retrieve her slobbering pet, it closes in for the grand finale and straddles the man. The poor victim — too drunk to realize his forehead is about to be the target of an amorous assault — remains oblivious. As the canine's pleasure-romp begins, it adds yet another disgrace to the long line of indignities that Buffalonians have become accustomed to.

In horror, the owner reaches down for the leash. Before grabbing it, she halts abruptly and scratches her scalp. Anger builds as she reads a urine scribbled message in the snow — it proclaims "GOD HATES BUF..." and ends in a wavy drizzle. Now in control of the tether, she gives it a harsh tug. As she leads the animal away, she reflects and mutters, "Maybe god does hate Buffalo?"

The First Quarter

A young couple lies asleep in silence on a saggy mattress without a bed frame. The digital clock radio's time changes to 7:30 AM and the guitar riff from "Crazy Train" begins to crackle from its mono speaker. Jennifer twists away from the noise and buries her Scandinavian blonde head beneath her pillow. Robert remains still as the inside of his skull pulsates to the drumbeat.

As the rock song fades out, the DJs take over. "Wow! Now that's how you end a *97 Rock* triple-shot of Ozzy! Don't you agree, Stout?"

"I do, Norton! And it's the best way to get going on a Thursday morning! Hell, any morning!"

"Yeah, especially when it's a balmy 15 degrees out! I love December!"

"Speaking of that — you know who's gonna get frostbit when they come to Buffalo this weekend?!"

"I sure do, and like coach Marv Levy says, 'When it's too tough for them, it's just right for us'!"

"Damn right it is!"

A prerecorded track of a deep male voice screams, "Squish the fish! Squish the fish!!" The high-pitched dolphin noises that follow sound like Flipper caught in a surprise gangbang.

Norton laughs. "That's right! The Miami Dolphins are gonna get squished by the Bills on Sunday!"

"Yep, and this is a must-win for both teams. It'll likely determine the AFC East champion."

"Hey, speaking of the Dolphins, you're not gonna believe who we have on the line. Miami linebacker, Bryan Cox!"

With his eyes still closed, a small smile grows across Robert's face. Jennifer pulls the electric blanket up to cover her shoulders and neck.

"No way!" Stout replies. "I'm shocked he'd speak with us after what he did back in '93."

"Yeah, and for those of you who somehow forgot what happened a couple of seasons back — Bryan not only gave a double-bird salute to all of Rich Stadium as he walked on the field, he also said some nasty things. To say that he's hated in Western New York is an understatement."

Jennifer rolls onto her back and grumbles, "Change this crap." Robert turns to her and puts his hand on her breast. He gently pinches her nipple and twists around it like it's a dial. She removes his hand and says, "Are you really doing that? Tuning in Tokyo?"

"What? You told me to change the channel? I was just trying to help."

Norton prepares to begin the interview. "Let's hear what Mr. Cox has to say. Who knows? Maybe he wants to make amends." There's a click. "Hi Bryan, welcome to the show. It's great to have you."

A voice that sounds like it's coming from a mouth full of Novocain responds, "Good morning, buh-beautiful Buh-Buffalo! Can you see the greeting I'm giving you?"

"Uh, no Bryan, we can't see it," Stout replies. "This is radio."

"Well then, lemme tell ya." Bryan begins. "It's two buh-big middle-fingers jus' for you, Buh-Buffalo! You're welcome!"

"Wow, again?! You really should come up with something new. Hey, let's take a step back." There's a pause and the sound of shuffling papers. "In the past you've said, and I quote, 'I don't like the Buffalo Bills as a

THE FIRST QUARTER | 5

team, I don't like them as people, I don't like the city, I don't like the people in the city.' So I guess you're telling us nothing's changed?"

"No, no. That was jus' some light buh-banter," Bryan answers with a droopy lower lip. "Honestly, I'd like to turn the page and stop looking buh-backwards. So in that spirit, it would buh-be my honor to give everyone in Buh-Buffalo an early Christmas present."

"Well, this sounds like a step in the right direction, Bryan," Norton says with hope. "What are you planning to do?"

"These people deserve the buh-best," Bryan replies. "I'm gonna give 'em something they'll always remember me by — gonorrhea!"

"What?!" Norton and Stout cry in unison. There's a crashing sound of the microphone hitting the table.

"That's just sick!" Stout yells. "What is wrong with you?!"

"You can't say that on the radio!" Norton shouts. "In fact, you can't say that — EVER!"

"I am strangely curious, but afraid to ask — how might you do this?" Stout ponders.

Norton jumps in, "Scratch that question. Thanks, Bryan, we *really* appreciate your call." A click ends the interview. "Alright, Buffalo, you heard it loud and clear, there's absolutely no love lost between Bryan and our great city. Bills fans, and I don't need to tell you this, get ready to let Bryan and the Dolphins really hear it on Sunday! Let's send them back to their pretentious town in teal body-bags!"

Robert's smile widens as he softly chuckles. Jennifer rolls across his stomach and shuts off the radio. "Those guys are idiots and not funny at all," Jennifer moans. "I'd like to think you're above all that nonsense."

"Oh, I definitely am." Robert can't constrain his sarcasm as he continues, "I never understood why anyone would want to drink beer, yell obscenities, and watch a game where grown men hit each other. It's just so juvenile, don't you agree?"

His response goes over her head. "Yes, I'm glad you feel that way." She places a finger in the dimple of his cleft chin. "Although, there are times I still wonder about you."

He turns to face her, slowly glides his hand up the back of her smooth leg, and rests his fingers on his favorite spot — a soft patch of skin where her butt and leg muscles disappear. As he aches to cross the border of her *labia majora*, a high school memory flashes in his mind, and he thinks, *Maybe Latin class wasn't a complete waste of time after all?*

She ignores his advances. "But you've made progress. You're growing up."

Robert slides his hand up her body to her ample bosom. "Speaking of growing, um, up," he whispers. "I'm *up* right now."

Jennifer's face scrunches. "*Annnnd* then you say something like that." She slaps his hand away like it's a gnat. "Don't even think about it, mister."

"*Pleeeease,*" Robert begs with puppy dog eyes. "I need some lovin'."

"No, no, not now." Jennifer gently pushes him away. "Asking all cute like that only works for girls like me. You need to get ready for work."

"Uuuugh," Robert whines painfully. "Fine." Wearing only boxers, he gets out of bed and shivers from the cold. With his back to her, his mouth opens to plead and then transforms into a wicked grin. He takes the cover off of a shoebox on the floor and pulls something out.

"What are you doing?"

Robert turns to her with his hands behind his back. "Who me?"

"Yeah, you." Jennifer pulls the covers up to her eyes like a nervous young teenager about to see a boy naked for the first time. "Seriously, what are you doing?"

"So you remember that thing I did to you when we first started dating? The night of that brutal thunderstorm?"

"Of course, it was so sweet. You made us lasagna and we drank a few nice bottles of wine."

"Yes, there's that. But remember what I did *to you* after?"

Jennifer giggles. "I was a little tipsy and not sure what got into me."

"Let me refresh your memory." Robert pulls out a black penis-shaped vibrator from behind his back. "This got into you."

"Oh, gosh." Jennifer blushes. "That was like — *wow*. I've never had org… I've never felt anything like that before. It was crazy good."

"Yeah it was," he replies like he's king-stud. "I've never heard you make noises like that before. You sounded like the monkey cage at the zoo during feeding time."

She laughs. "Stop. No, I did not."

"Wanna bet?" The vibrator starts buzzing. "Should we go again and record it? I bet National Geographic would love the audio footage."

"Turn that off immediately," Jennifer demands unconvincingly. "Just the sound of it is —"

"Come on — I know just how you like it." Robert glides the pleasure device down the sheets. As it passes over her longing loins, the vibrations make her swell and throb like she's riding a rumbling Harley-Davidson. Her steaming-geyser gushes as she imagines it pulsating directly on her. He starts to pull back the covers. "Wanna try it in your other hole? Like you said you wanted?"

Jennifer's eyes bulge, and she grabs his hand. "I did *not* say that."

"Um, yes you did."

She takes the vibrator and switches it off. "I would *never* say such a thing."

"If it wasn't you, can you introduce me to the girl that did?"

Jennifer shakes her head. "We got carried-away." She huffs. "I can't do this now — even if a part of me kinda wants to." She hands the gadget back to him. "Put this thing away."

Robert's hangs his head like a disappointed child. "Really?"

"Yeah, go take a shower."

"Fine, I guess I will." As Robert puts the sex-toy back in the shoebox, he can't block out the memory of it coming into his possession. One afternoon, an odd package addressed to his mother arrived at his front door.

His decision to open it turned out to be a disturbing mistake — that was, until a shit-ton of wine and Jennifer's naked body sparked devilish creativity in his Merlot-soaked mind. As he closes the lid on the phallic tool's home, an alternative, more alarming scenario slithers its way into his head. *Thank god it wasn't addressed to dad.*

Jennifer drags him back to reality. "What time did you get home last night?"

"Um, it was late. Work —" Robert strains to pull any details into focus from an otherwise fuzzy evening. "Work's been crazy lately. Sorry."

"I stayed up as long as I could, but finally had to crash."

"Don't worry about it."

While Robert walks to the bedroom door, he glances over at two framed photos on a tiny red bookcase next to his particleboard desk from college. Perplexed, he notices that one of the frames is lying face down. As he places it back in its proper upright position, he admires the picture of his two college buddies and him in a dark bar. Robert has bushy brown hair and sports at least fifteen extra pounds, hard earned from his collegiate bar days. His two friends round out the group like Neapolitan ice cream — one blond and one redhead. Screaming as they thrust their beers to the ceiling, the euphoria of the moment is captured perfectly. The analog clock behind them shows the time nearing quarter to four but AM or PM cannot be determined.

The second photo, which is displayed properly, is of Robert and Jennifer in formal attire and with posed smiles. If it wasn't for the dinner table and other people in the background, one might guess it was taken at a Sears portrait studio.

Robert turns on his space heater and lays out a pair of dress socks and boxers in front of the vent. In the frigid hallway on the way to the bathroom, he notices some odd clumps of snow that look as though they were brought inside on the bottom of a boot. *Is that from last night?*

Robert opens the medicine cabinet in the bathroom and pulls out aspirin and vitamin B-complex. He swallows two pills from each bottle and massages his forehead. He slides the cheap plastic shower curtain open and steps in. Soon, warm water rains over his body. He chuckles for a moment before belting out the chorus of "I Touch Myself" by the Divinyls.

Robert's singing reverberates through the wall and into the bedroom. Jennifer tries to fight it, but a quiet laugh cracks through. He finishes up his shower, towels off, and walks back into the bedroom.

Jennifer flirts, "*Sooo*, I heard you singing."

"Oh, you could hear that?" he asks with a grin.

"Yes, I could. I'll admit it — there are times you can be pretty cute and funny."

"This sounds promising." Robert pats himself on the back. "Knowing you though, there's a *but* coming up. Please prove me wrong."

Jennifer's tone turns serious. "*Buuuut*, I have concerns when it comes to your wild side. I've seen how you act around your friends. *And* there's the Barrister's Ball incident. Do I even need to bring that up?"

"No. No, you don't." Robert stretches his arms out like he's on the cross. "I've apologized for that multiple times. It won't happen again."

"Yes, I know, we've moved passed it. Hey, I'm sorry I was being standoffish earlier." She pouts and looks down at the clock radio. "I just heard those stupid DJs, and thoughts of you going and — oh, let's just forget about it. I'm sure I was just overreacting."

"Can we jump back to that stuff you were talking about earlier? About me being super cute and absolutely hilarious."

Jennifer smiles. "Yes, why don't we. Come over here." After removing the sheets and exposing her naked body, she sits on the edge of the bed. Robert moves in front of her. She grabs the towel around his waist and pulls him toward her while undoing it. He springs out as the towel drops to the floor. Surprised by her aggressiveness, he lets her do what she wants — not that he would ever consider fighting it.

His initial expression of shock quickly turns to joy as her tongue slowly and methodically works its magic. She fills her oral cavity and locks eyes with him while her nails tingle his inner thighs. A thought jumps into her mind, pausing her flow. "Don't forget — the OUTLaw Holiday Dinner is tonight at the Marriott. Meet me there at 6:30."

His rapid response is delivered as one word, "I'll-be-there."

As Jennifer continues, Robert is reminded again of how gifted she is. Her mouth and hands play his instrument like a summa cum laude graduate from Juilliard. Like a metronome, her delicious dumplings dangle and gently clap with her rhythm. While keeping a firm grip on his trom-boner, she pulls away and looks up at him. "Have you been drinking pineapple juice like I told you?"

Robert nods briskly and moans, "Yes! Yes!"

Jennifer takes him back in as far as she can before having to gobble-gag down the rest. As her spit valve overflows, she caresses his tight hacky sack and orchestrates the crescendo. While he spasms, his head tilts back and he smiles in ecstasy.

—

At a stop sign on South Beach's Ocean Drive, a red Ferrari glistens in the morning sun. With its convertible top down and "10INCOX" Florida license plate, it idles while a tourist family crawls through the crosswalk. Juan Carlos revs the engine impatiently. Still dressed in a navy blue suit and halfway-buttoned white dress shirt from the night before, he looks through Prada sunglasses into the rearview mirror and combs his fingers through his wavy black hair.

A bleached-blonde in a low-cut sleeveless green blouse is in the seat next to him. Emblazoned in silver sequins across her buxom chest is the phrase "Catch of the Day". Her seated position makes it seem like her butt has swallowed her shorts, and fully exposes her smooth legs. As the family nears the sidewalk, he takes his bronze hand off her left thigh and firmly grasps the stick shift. She holds her gold clutch as his internal clock ticks down, 3, 2, 1, and they rocket forward, pinned back into their beige leather seats.

As they head north on A1A, they pass oceanfront hotels flourishing with activity — the result of the weatherman's announcement for unseasonably warm temperatures reaching the low 80s. Cabana boys drag folding chairs across the beach to form perfect rows in the golden sand. Bikini-clad women in sheer sundresses pick spots to spread out their towels. A small group of dolphins jump playfully out of the cool blue ocean, high into the air, until gravity splashes them down.

Noticing the dolphins, the female passenger points and shouts with a voice that sounds like she just took a helium bong-hit, "Hey, look at those big fish jumping in the ocean!"

Juan Carlos responds in his Cuban accent, "Babe, those are dolphins. You must've seen them before."

"Are they the same as sharks? Minus the eating you part?"

Juan Carlos looks at her with one eyebrow cocked. "Same as sharks? No, quite different in many ways. Dolphins are friendly and are actually mammals because they breathe air."

"Oh, right!" She pokes the top of her skull. "They have that breathing asshole on their head!"

He practically chokes. "Babe, how about we just enjoy the soothing sound of the ocean breeze?" He puts his hand over her mouth. "Let's play a fun game and see who can remain silent the longest."

She removes his hand and folds her arms like a pouty child. "Why do you keep calling me babe? You don't remember my name, do you?"

Juan Carlos shakes his head in frustration. "You're not very good at this game, are you?"

"Um — what game?"

"Never mind." He fidgets in his seat. "Look, it was very loud at the Clevelander last night, and when we first met I couldn't really hear your name. I'm so sorry, what is it again?"

"Oh, I'm Bambi." She puts her hand out to shake. "Nice to meet you."

Juan Carlos grinds his teeth. "Uh, we already met hours ago, and you're in my car. You don't need to say — oh, forget it. You must get this all the time — were you named after the children's book?"

"No, I wasn't, but people always ask. So last year I finally started reading it, but I can't seem to finish it. If you want to know, I was actually named after my mom's dancing name — wait, unless my mom was in the book?" Bambi scrunches her forehead. "No, I don't think she was." She shakes her head. "When I was a kid, though, mom told me she was in a few magazines, but for some reason she wouldn't ever show them to me. She also told me she was the best out of all the dancers she worked with —"

Juan Carlos fires a finger gun into his skull. *Please make it stop.*

"I always felt bad for her, though, because she had to wear these six-inch heels when dancing. I said to her once, 'Momma, that's gotta hurt your feet.' And she said, 'Don't worry, honey, my knees get more of a workout than my feet.' So I guess she figured out how to rest 'em. One time she told me —"

"Great story, Bambi." He presses his index finger into a pulsing on the side of his head. "Really amazing. Hey, remember when we were dancing and we just let our movements do the talking?" Bambi nods her head. "Let's do that again and listen to some music until we get to my place. It's not much further."

Juan Carlos switches on his CD player and turns up the volume. The bass from The Notorious B.I.G.'s "Big Poppa" vibrates the car as they cruise down the road. To distract himself, he tries to concentrate more on what he can put *into* Bambi's mouth and less on what's coming out. After the last time he hooked-up with a girl like her, he told himself never again, but knew his little head would always trump the one on his shoulders. Like his father before him, Juan Carlos also knew the more agonizing the conversation — call it "verbal foreplay" — the crazier the sex. Thus again proving the father-son adage holds true — the asshole doesn't fall far from the tree.

Slowing the car, they take a left on West 63rd Street and drive across a short bridge onto a small residential island. A few minutes later, they arrive outside his twelve thousand square-foot mansion. He presses a button on the car's visor and the metal gates swing open. They pull into a circular brick driveway lined with palm trees.

"So what do you think, Bambi?"

"This is incredible! When you told me you had a mansion, I thought it might just be a line to get me back to your place, but here we are!"

Juan Carlos gets out of the car and walks around to open her door. "Wait 'til you see the pool," he says. "Let's go inside." She takes his hand and spins her long legs around to step out in her high heels. After she turns, he admires the assets tightly held in her white short shorts.

As Bambi walks up the marble steps to the twenty-foot mahogany front door, she grins and resists the urge to pat herself on the back. *Well played.*

—

A black Corvette with a "University at Buffalo" license plate holder is waved through the Cornwall, Canada border checkpoint. Its chained tires chew through the snow as it speeds across the bridge over the St. Lawrence River and into the northernmost part of New York State. Zabka puts the pine-scented car freshener to his nose to briefly escape the funky hobo-armpit smell spewing from the neighboring paper mills. He checks the clock on the dash — *There's not enough time to go home and change.* He figures he can manage the day, even with the eye-catching stain on his tan pants — courtesy of the impromptu lap dance he received from, as he so eloquently puts it, "last night's bang."

Route 37 takes him through patches of forest and past electrical towers to work in Massena. The parking lot of the GM Powertrain Plant is almost completely filled with pickup trucks. Several groups of plant workers clothed in sandstone-colored Carhartts walk slowly toward the entrance. The muffled thumping sound of music shaking Zabka's car draws their attention. While rolling through the lot, Zabka sings and groin-thrusts to the beat of Whitesnake's "Slide It In".

Zabka received his nickname in college, and it promptly replaced his given name, Kyle. William Zabka is an actor who starred in several iconic films in the '80s. His two biggest roles were as Johnny in *The Karate Kid*, and as Chas in *Back to School*. In both films, his characters excelled at being the handsome-yet-overly-cocky antagonist. Kyle's stark similarity in appearance wasn't the only thing that created the initial connection between the two. As people got to know him, it became clear that some characters don't just exist in movies. Now, everyone calls him by the Zabka moniker except his mother — she still prefers to call him jackass.

After finding a parking spot, Zabka opens the compartment under the armrest and fishes through it. Pushing past receipts, gum wrappers, and several Trojans, he finds his badge. He then looks in the rear-view mirror, checks his shoulder-length blond, curly hair, and winks at himself. The left side of his nose is concave as a result of three nasty right hooks to his beak. He winces thinking about the one that broke his nose in college, and how he had to pop it back into place.

In his white dress shirt, khakis, and unzipped black leather jacket, Zabka stands out from the plant workers walking in. He heads toward a different entrance and walks inside. As he struts through a room with several secretaries, their attention is naturally drawn to him.

One secretary smiles and flirtatiously says, "Good morning, Zabka."

He smirks. *It's way too easy being me. They all want me.*

Another secretary shakes her head. *What a douche.*

Zabka enters his office, hangs up his coat, and proceeds to check email on his Windows 95 PC. Red exclamation points make several urgent emails standout. Their subject lines display problems such as "Network Performance Degradation Alert" and "Backup System Failure". Quickly scanning past them, Zabka continues until he sees "The Buffalo Bills Report". He clicks on it and reads intently. Practically jumping out of his seat, he exclaims, "Holy shit! The 17th is this Sunday! The Bills are play-ing the goddamn Dolphins this weekend!" Knowing that getting tickets to a big game like this is next to impossible, Zabka puts his hands on his head and tries to think of a way.

A few seconds later, Scott, his boss, rushes into his office. Several do-nut crumbs fall off his pudgy face as he yells, "Gee willikers, Zabka! Have you seen the darn emails?"

Zabka's taken by surprise. "Um, yeah. Of course I have."

Scott pushes his high prescription round lens glasses back up his nose. "We need to fix this network problem right away! The slowdown caused Jed to go nuts this morning. He didn't mention the backup failure, but we need to get on that too, like ASAP, before he goes ballistic!"

"I know, I know. Jesus, calm down and go take your high blood pres-sure medicine. It's moments like this you remind me of a Chris Farley character. I was just figuring out how to resolve these issues when you walked in. I'll take care of things."

"Okay, okay. You're right." Scott's hyper condition subsides. "I knew you'd be all over this. I'm really lucky to have you working for me."

"Not a problem. Go relax, I got this." Scott exits, and Zabka leans back in his chair. After staring at the ceiling and considering a few options to get game tickets, a smile comes across his face. He claps his hands, stands up, and heads out the door.

—

The solitary eastern blue bird's stubbornness sealed its fate when it refused to accompany the flock south. As the frigid wind keeps it aloft, minuscule drops of moisture solidify in its feathers and a downward drag takes hold. Diving like a falling rock, flickers of sun-bleached blue and faded red wave as they appear out of the tundra. As the ground rushes closer, the bird's final sight before impact is Robert's head. THUMP!

Robert spins around. *What the hell was that?* Standing in the snow in his dress shoes and protective rubbers, he surveys the space in front of his apartment complex. Unable to find the source of the sound, he looks at where there should be a walkway to the parking lot. Instead of being shoveled this morning, it's covered by a few inches of fresh powder. Several additional feet of snow surround the path like an arctic valley — the result of the previous weekend's record drop of 38 inches in twenty-four hours. The sight of everything causes him to heave a laugh, which shoots a large white cloud from his mouth. As his nose takes in a frosty breath, his nostrils temporarily freeze stuck.

Tipping forward, he forces himself onward and tramples through the snow with a crunch from each step. He stops at the parking lot, which is shared with an adjoining apartment complex, and notices that only the other half has been plowed. "Cheapest fucking landlord ever," Robert mumbles. "I bet that son-of-a-bitch in Fort Lauderdale or something."

Snow covers his oxidized red Ford Escort Pony and each window is opaque with frost. He climbs inside, starts the car, and turns on the defroster and radio. The guitar riff from The Bangles song "Hazy Shade of Winter" blares out of the speakers as his right hand blindly searches behind the seat until it grasps the ice scraper. Robert jumps out of the car and slams the door shut. The door's frozen lock prevents it from closing and it bounces back. Accustomed to this glitch, he moves on. While circling the car, he wipes off the snow and scrapes the ice from the windows. Satisfied with his work, he looks over at the sheet of winter covering Jennifer's car and replays the morning in his head. *Fuck, she was amazing. One good servicing deserves another, right?*

After completing his task on Jennifer's car, Robert gets in his vehicle and scrapes the ice from the interior of the windows. *Another treat brought to you by Buffalo.* Driving a stick shift with a door that's frozen open requires an extra level of dexterity. Robert puts the car in reverse and guns it backward to get out of the unplowed half of the parking lot and onto asphalt. Once past the snowdrift, he slams on the breaks and jerks the wheel to the left to point the car at the road. During these maneuvers he's essentially a one-armed driver, because the sole purpose of his left hand is to hold onto his door handle so it doesn't fly open.

Exiting the little suburban neighborhood of Amherst, Robert gets on the 290 east and heads toward work in Cheektowaga. The only reason anyone in their right mind ever goes there is for the airport. The radio DJ begins to talk about the upcoming game and reads a statement that Buffalo coach Marv Levy gave to the Miami media the previous day, "It's bitter cold with high winds and arctic blasts. But it's not supposed to last. The weather is supposed to turn bad." In agreement with Marv that warmer is bad, Robert knows the Bills have an advantage in the cold. *Shit, we need what we had last weekend.*

As Robert passes many nondescript buildings, Kixx nightclub stands out from the rest and triggers a flashback. He grins as he thinks back to all the happy hours he enjoyed there during college. Turning off the road, he pulls into the Techspan entrance and back into reality. Robert stops at the guard booth and produces his Secret clearance badge. The guard checks it, lifts the gate, and waves him through. After parking, he's careful not to slip on any black ice as he walks to the entrance.

From outside or within, the Techspan building is neither warm nor inviting, which may have been entirely by design. Built in the early 1950s, the aura from its cold war birth still remains, as do most of its original metal desks and chairs. On a typical day, Robert dreads walking through its light green and piss-yellow concrete walls and across its black and white checkered tiled floors. Today he skips into his prison cell office and finds his officemate Dale. Heavyset with a goatee and a shoulder-length ponytail, Dale sits at his desk and labors intensely on his new Sun workstation.

"Good morning, Dale! Great to see you!"

Dale turns his head. "Great to see you too, Robert. Happy Thursday."

Robert takes off his jacket. "Have you ever noticed how this wall here looks like pistachio ice cream? Yum, love it! And look at the floor — we could play human checkers on it. How much fun is that?! When I can afford to buy a house, I'm hiring the same designer!"

"You sound way too happy, what's up?"

Robert's red paisley tie from JC Penney dances as he makes wide circles with his arms. "This place brings me joy!"

Dale spins in his chair to face Robert. "Okay, that's bullshit. This *has* to be the makings of the lovely Jennifer. She's one of the few things that gets you goofy like this."

"Guilty as charged." Robert chuckles.

"I take it that you had a pleasant morning?"

Robert smiles widely. "Yes, I had a *very* good morning."

"Ah, I see," answers Dale, like he's been around this block. "Well, enjoy it while you can. Us married guys don't get that kind of wakeup call anymore. I've spent fourteen glorious years of often begged for but rarely received oral! And when I do get it, it's a tongue lashing!"

"Ha! I feel for you buddy, but to be honest, it's actually been a little while for me. Things have gotten kinda, you know — routine for the most part." Robert sits down at his desk. "Jennifer's not as spontaneous and fun, which is what attracted me to her in the first place."

"So you're out of the honeymoon phase?"

Robert shrugs. "Yeah, maybe that's it. Now we spend the bulk of our time in my apartment and rarely go out — we've got one of her law school things tonight, but that's an exception. She's also way more serious since school started back up. It's been frustrating."

Robert's mind drifts back to when he first met Jennifer. During the summer, a few friends dragged him to a karaoke bar to blow off some steam. The second person to sing after they arrived was a curvy blonde. She took the stage with intoxicated fearlessness mixed with the sexy confidence of Marilyn Monroe singing "Happy Birthday" to President Kennedy. The girl's moves and the way she sang "Like a Virgin" hypnotized him. Before the song ended, Robert approached her girlfriends and asked the one with dark gravity-defying '80s metal hair for the singer's name and favorite shot. Upon acquiring the information, he went to the bar and bought the unfamiliar libation.

Robert then strode up to the vocalist and introduced himself as Bob, which was the nickname he was using at the time. "Hi Krystal with a K, I'm Bob. I thought you were amazing up there." He smiled as he held out the shot for Jennifer. "I got you a Hot Mexican Hooker. Call it telepathy or something, but I have a feeling you'll really enjoy this."

She scowled. "I'm sorry, but you're mistaken. I'm not a stripper — my name is Jennifer, not Krystal with a *fuckin'* K. And that drink you so thoughtfully got me is repulsive!"

Bob's facial expression did not hide his shock. He glanced at her conniving friend who was observing and trying to conceal her chuckling with her hand. Clearly having been played, he thought quickly and spoke into Jennifer's ear, "I apologize. I asked your friend back there to help me out, and she obviously decided to have some fun with me. So the way I see it, we have two options. One, I walk away and we never get a chance to get to know each other — which would suck — or two, we team up and fuck with her." He leaned into Jennifer and looked her in the eyes with a devious grin. "Which way do we go with this?"

"That sneaky little bitch tried to clam-jam me. The choice is easy — we fuck with her." She tugged on his arm. "Follow my lead."

They walked over to the table where her friend was sitting, and Jennifer asked in an accusing tone, "Hey Faige, you remember Bob? I understand you two have already spoken?"

Faige replied in a thick Bronx accent, "We may-a tawked briefly."

Jennifer huffed. "And you told him my name is Krystal because you wanted him to embarrass himself and strike out with me?"

"Nooo, nooo," Faige stammered. "It was a joke, *Jennifa*."

"Well, here's the funny part of your joke. After speaking with him, it's clear that Bob's real interest is in you, not me." Jennifer points a finger at both of them. "And based on what you did, obviously you must have some interest in him too."

Flustered, Faige replied, "I, I mean —"

Bob smoothly added, "It's cool. I was nervous about meeting you and, I know it's a bit unconventional, but that was the only way I could think of to break the ice. I would actually love for *you* to take this shot." He sat down next to Faige, put a hand on her thigh, and gazed into her eyes. "I feel like we have a real connection here. Salud!"

Faige's longing for companionship — compounded with three glasses of cheap wine — compelled her to gulp down the shot without further consideration. The mixture of tequila, hot sauce, and tuna fish juice made her stomach do somersaults. As she jumped from her chair and ran to the ladies' room, Jennifer and Bob laughed uncontrollably.

The loud thud from Dale's hand slamming on his solid desk startles Robert. "Hey! Hey, Robert! Snap out of it. So what was different this morning? Was she making up to you for something?"

"No, I'm pretty sure she wasn't. I don't really know what got into her this morning — well, except me of course." They laugh for a few seconds.

Dale leans in toward Robert. "To us, women can be mysterious, but there's a purpose behind what they do — especially when it *seems* out of the ordinary. Jennifer may not even know what's going on, but she senses something." Dale looks over his shoulder and lowers his voice. "Women have some sort of freak gift — or curse depending on how you look at it. While they lack the ability to combine facts with reason, that impediment is compensated by their power of perception. Anyway, she wants to bring you closer to her. It could be because she really loves you — or she's a black widow. Who knows?"

"You're crazy." Robert shakes his head. "Couldn't it be just as simple as she had the urge to give me head?"

Dale's face writhes like he just swallowed a rotten oyster. "Have you ever met a woman who's just had that *urge*?" Robert ponders the question. "Because if you have, I need her to talk my wife into it."

"Oh, come on, I'm sure over the course of time, it's happened. There doesn't have to be some crazy motive behind it all."

"I've got several years of experience on you, so trust me on this. You'll understand soon enough, my friend."

"Who are you? The vagina whisperer?"

Dale's fingers stroke his goatee. "Some have said that."

—

The mansion's enormous double-doors swing open, and Juan Carlos waits for Bambi to enter. Inside, Digby, an older gentleman dressed in a crisp, black tuxedo greets them with a slight bow and with British flair says, "Sir Juan Carlos, good morning. Miss, good morning."

Bambi chuckles softly and replies in her best impersonation of his accent, "My baby ate your dingo."

"Your baby ate? Really?" Juan Carlos bites his lip. "And he's from England, not Australia." He shoots Digby an I'm-sorry look and finishes introductions.

Digby nods courteously. "It's a pleasure to meet you, Miss Bambi."

"You too, Digby," Bambi replies. "Sorry about my mistake. Sometimes I have a brain queef."

Digby barely contains a smile while fixing his wide-eyes on Bambi. "Sir Juan Carlos, you have far outdone yourself this time. Bambi surely must be a Mensa!"

Confused, Bambi asks, "Mensa?" After a slight pause, a lightning bolt zaps her and she turns to Juan Carlos. "Wait a minute, Mensa. We talked about this at the club — I told you I'm *not* on the rag."

Juan Carlos's jaw hits the floor. Digby fails at his attempt to remain formal and releases a loud, high-pitched "HEEE!"

Juan Carlos gently grabs Bambi's arm and pulls her towards the large opening in the wall that lead to an expansive backyard. "Digby, we'll be by the pool. Bring us two Bloody Marys, pronto."

As they exit, Digby nonchalantly remarks, "Way to stay consistent, sir. However, I feel like you may have outdone yourself this time."

Juan Carlos looks back at Digby and slits his throat with his finger. The couple begins their way to the saltwater pool by following a concrete path through lush green grass. In the distance, across the Biscayne Bay, is the Miami skyline.

"Oh, sir!" Digby yells. "What do you want me to do about your appointment?" He looks down at his watch. "It's in an hour."

Juan Carlos stops and turns around. "What are you talking about?"

"Your appointment. Maria is coming by for your weekly scrotum maintenance. She had to move it today."

Juan Carlos's ears turn red. "Um, tell her to push it to this afternoon."

Bambi chuckles. "Weekly? You must grow like a weed down there."

"No, not really. I just like to keep it tight."

"If you *really* want it tight, you should get it lasered-off like me." She makes a buzzing sound and acts like she's performing the procedure on herself. "I'm like a prepubescent girl down there."

Juan Carlos wonders if his thoughts could be considered statutory. He shakes them out of his head. "No laser is going anywhere near that area."

As they approach the pool, Bambi notices a tall, slender woman lying on her stomach in a folding chair. Her mane is glistening black — a drastic change from the abundance of the frizzled bleached-blondes floating around Miami. With her hair up in a bun and her top undone, she maximizes the sun's exposure over her cinnamon skin.

As the couple nears, Bambi sizes up the sun worshiper and shoots daggers from her eyes. "Hey, who's this chick!?"

Startled by the inquiry, the woman rolls over onto her back, exposing her jiggle-resistant double-Ds. Her natural look could be mistaken for a young Cindy Crawford until she morphs into something like a mental patient off her meds. "This chick is Summer!" she screeches. "Who the fuck are you, and what are you doing with my husband!?"

Juan Carlos scrambles to say something as Bambi steps toward Summer, about to attack. She stops, pulls her hand back, spins around, and delivers a mighty slap across Juan Carlos's face.

Taken aback and with his cheek throbbing crimson with pain, Juan Carlos attempts to regain control. "Bambi, she's not my wife! Summer is dating Bradford, my business partner! And as you can already tell, she's a complete asshole!"

Summer laughs hysterically. "Oh my god that was good! Nice one Bambi! Way to give that cheater what he deserves!"

Bambi turns and gives Summer the look-of-death. "Bitch, you're dog-shit crazy!" Bambi hurls her clutch and hits Summer in the head. She then jumps through the air WWF-style and lands on Summer. They roll around and pull on each other's hair until they topple off the chair and into the pool.

From the edge of the water, Juan Carlos contemplates jumping in to break things up, but instead decides to enjoy the entertainment. The girls alternate between screaming violently and pulling each other underwater. As the girls submerge, he closes his eyes and enjoys the silence for a few seconds.

The surface of the pool unexpectedly rushes at him and a pain shoots from his neck. He splashes through and realizes an arm is around his throat. He grabs the arm and turns around to find it's attached to Bradford, who's laughing bubbles out of his mouth. Both of them burst out of the water and Juan Carlos punches Bradford squarely in the nose. Bradford, still laughing, covers his bleeding snout and yells in pain.

The girls stop fighting and release their grips from each other. Disoriented and unable to speak from exhaustion, they observe the guys. Juan Carlos gets his heartbeat and breathing under control so he can speak. "Bambi, let me introduce you to Bradford Threadgold III. As his name clearly states, he's a douchebag."

—

Zabka arrives at the main plant's expansive factory floor and soaks in the noisy chaos like he's enjoying a mountain top view. He scans the room, but can't find who he's looking for. Suddenly a forklift speeds past from behind and just misses him by inches. As it screeches to a halt, he notices the Dale Earnhardt number 3 in red spray-paint on the side.

A tall, brown-bearded man with a medium-sized beer gut jumps off the forklift. "Hey Zabka! What the hell is going on with IT this morning?! You guys are like a bunch of monkeys fucking a football over there!"

"Jed, just the man I've been looking for." Zabka tilts his head and stretches out his arms. "Listen, I've been working on this all morning and there's not much we can do until corporate finishes the network upgrade. It's literally out of my hands." He alternates a few times between showing his palms and making fists.

"Bullshit!"

"I know you conduct a lot of important business on your PC, and I understand how big a problem this is for you. So what specifically has your panties all up in a wad this time?" Zabka pauses with a shit-eating grin. "Downloading NASCAR highlights or midget porn?"

"Screw you, asshole! You know I can't go a day without my NASCAR! Even if Yahoo keeps pointing me to the same stuff."

"Are you ever gonna get the Internet at home?"

"Dial-up? Are you kidding me? It's too damn slow."

Zabka inspects Jed's face. "Wife won't let you because you can't get enough of watching miniature people boink, right?"

"Oh come on, man," Jed pleas. "That's not — shit, you know me too damn well."

"Forget about the network issues." Zabka pounds his fist into his palm. "This weekend we've got bigger fish to fry."

"What's going on?!" Jed asks, barely able to contain his excitement.

"We're going to the Bills game. We leave tomorrow."

"In Buffalo?" Jed ponders the proposal like a chess move. "Football and beer?"

"Yeah, in *the* Buffalo. And of course there'll be football and beer! And a bunch of other nonsense! It's gonna be awesome!"

"I can't say no to that. I just gotta give the wife a heads up."

"Not that she'd even notice you're gone, but okay." Zabka laughs. "We'll stay with my buddy, Bob. Remember me telling you about him?"

"Yeah, he's the guy whose balls were detached by his girlfriend and are now a trophy on her mantle."

"Yep, you do remember him. His bitch-face girlfriend Jennifer turned him from 'fun Bob' into 'pussy Robert,' and I don't like it one bit. We seriously gotta do something about it this weekend." Zabka clenches his fists. "If we remove her from him, that means death to Robert and his nuts will be liberated! Then they can triumphantly return and reattach to Bob!"

"Viva la nuts!" Jed shouts. They both glow as they consider their plan.

"Oh, one other thing. We're taking your Bronco, or your truck, or whatever you're calling it these days."

"Normally I would like that plan, but why don't we just take our snowmobiles?" Jed swivels and points in the direction he believes is correct. "We head southwest towards Toronto, cut across Lake Ontario and we're in Buffalo in no time?" He pauses for a split-second after seeing Zabka's chastising look. "I mean *the* Buffalo."

"*Hmmm*, let me think about that, Jed. Something to do with the lake not completely freezing over kinda makes that idea shit." Zabka starts walking backwards towards Scott's office. "I'll talk to ya later. I've got BIG plans for the game, so we have some prep work to do tonight."

After leaving the factory floor, Zabka walks back through a maze of hallways until he reaches Scott's door. He pauses for a second to regroup, and then storms in to find Scott with beads of sweat on his forehead, frantically typing an email.

Scott looks up from his keyboard. "Zabka, did you fix things? Are the guys in the plant pissed? Please tell me it's not slowing down the line."

"I told you to relax, and the way you are acting is far from it."

Speaking quickly, like he just drank a pot of coffee, Scott responds, "I know, I know. I'm trying."

"Okay, breathe. Slow down." Zabka waits as Scott calms himself and his breathing returns to a normal pace. "I spoke with Jed — and I'm not gonna lie — he was pretty pissed off. *Buuuut*, I managed to cool him down and explain the situation. He's working with the rest of his Union guys to make sure this isn't a big deal and they can get their work done. Bottom line is, it's gonna be alright. However, we have to smooth things over with him. We don't want this to come back and bite us somewhere down the line. We need an ally in there."

"Yeah, yeah, agreed. Any ideas?"

"Not really off the top of my head. Um, let me think." Zabka pinches his chin. "Oh, I know! Jed really likes the Buffalo Bills."

"Well, is there a game anytime soon?"

"As a matter of fact there is! There's one this weekend. Holy shit, Scott! That's a great idea!!"

Scott smiles, feeling quite proud of himself. "Thanks!"

"You're a genius, Scott. Every day I learn something new from you. You'll be in charge of tickets. You can handle that, right?" Scott nods. "Good. We'll need four total for you, me, Jed, and my buddy, Bob — he lives in the Buffalo."

Scott grins like a young boy who just plopped his first unsupervised shit in the toilet. "I got it covered." He blows on his knuckles. "This is gonna be a swell time."

"Great! We'll cut out a little early tomorrow and hit the road." Zabka starts to leave Scott's office. "Okay, gotta run. You the man!"

Scott thinks through the details. *Buy tickets at the box-office on Sunday and expense the receipt. Done! Easy as pie.* He raises a hand above his head and slaps it with his other. "High-five!"

———

With Robert gone, the apartment is quiet except for the soft howl of wind outside. Jennifer dries herself with a towel and stands naked before the bathroom mirror. She inspects her body like a gay fashion designer figuring out how best to hide flaws with a custom tailored outfit. Jennifer sucks in her belly and then frowns as she lets it plop back out. Wings, pizza, and beer, which replaced her diet in Southern California of salad and lean turkey, have been efficiently converted into an extra winter layer. After turning her backside toward the mirror to check out the junk-in-the-trunk, she lets out a high-pitched scream. As she moves closer to the mirror to get a better view, Jennifer hopes her eyes are deceiving her. She scrutinizes her butt and scans what looks like a patch of miniature divot-holes made by a pocket-sized golfer. Growling, she turns away and goes into the bedroom to change.

As Jennifer pulls herself into tight blue jeans and an off-white turtleneck sweater, she thinks about the cute sundresses and sandals she'd wear back in Orange County. She wonders how, of all the places in the world, she ended up here. She's thankful she met Robert, but at the same time bitter that Buffalo was her only law school option — the result of average college grades, some bad boyfriend decisions, and poor finances.

Bundled up for school, Jennifer exits the apartment complex. Three hollering kids across the street grab her attention. She stops to see what they're doing and examines their unusual snow structure. To her it looks like a freakish penis with a large side-tumor and a disturbingly thin needle-head.

The kids line up on all fours about ten-yards from their phallic creation. One kid notices Jennifer and flashes her a smile. After white steam jets from his crimson nose, he squeals, "Squish the fish!" Like a starting pistol just fired, the kids jump from their downward position and race at the disfigured-snow-cock. Just before impact they leap through the air and annihilate it into chunks of snow and white flurries. The kids laugh with joy as they wiggle around on their backs. They look over at Jennifer expecting an ovation or praise of some sort. She apathetically shakes her head and tramps down the snowy path to the parking lot.

One of the boys yells to her, "Hey! Are you a stupid Dolphins fan or something?"

Jennifer stops. "No. I just think you're all acting childish."

The kids look at each other cross-eyed, and one responds, "Well I think you're acting like a fat fatty!" The other two kids are knocked over with laughter.

She scowls. "I'm not acting anything! And I'm not fat! This is just an oversized coat!" Jennifer takes a few angry steps forward until her foot awkwardly lands on what feels like a fist-sized Tootsie Roll Pop. She cracks through the outer shell and squashes the inside. Her foot slips forward, sending her into an uncoordinated cheerleader split and crash-landing. The kids shriek with glee and start replicating her split and fall, each time cracking up the others. Jennifer, her face red with anger, gets up and brushes herself off. Ignoring the kids as best she can, she searches for the culprit that dropped her. Kicking around the snow, she grimaces upon uncovering a frozen dead bird. *What the fuck?* She shuffles cautiously through the snow for the rest of her journey.

As Jennifer nears her beat-up VW, she finds a smiley face scraped in the frost of her passenger side window. She throws her arms up in the air. *Christ! Couldn't he have just cleaned off the whole thing?* After clearing the windows, she gets in her car and drives a few miles down the road to school. She pulls into the huge parking lot with the University at Buffalo School of Law sign, but can't find parking anywhere near her building. After happening upon a spot about a quarter of a mile away, she grabs her oversized leather carrying case filled with large law school textbooks. While walking to her destination, a giant gust of wind picks up a sheet of snow and throws it onto her. She curses a few times and fights through until she gets inside.

Pulling open the entrance door, the warm air welcomes Jennifer as she enters the lobby. She spots Faige sitting by herself drinking coffee at one of the café tables. Faige is an average looking brunette with above average hair — blown out in every direction like a lion's mane with a can of Aqua Net from the previous decade. She's wearing her winter padded-bra for extra warmth.

Faige glares at Jennifer as she approaches, and in the same dialect of a guy selling peanuts in Yankee Stadium, she asks, "*Jennifa*, where youz been?"

"Sorry." Jennifer sits down with a thud. "What am I, like five minutes late?"

Faige puts her hand on Jennifer's shoulder. "I jus' wanted ta have some time ta tawk befaw class. We've both been so busy wit' finals and everyting, dat we haven't had a chance ta catch up in a while." Faige pouts. "I missed youz."

"I know, I know. I've missed you, too."

Faige resumes her interrogation. "So, where were youz?"

Jennifer crosses her arms. "I was at Robert's place."

Faige's right eye shuts halfway and twitches. "So ya still seein' 'im?"

"My god, yes. It's been about six months, and sure, we've had our ups and downs, but what couple hasn't? Why do I always feel like I have to defend myself when we talk about him?"

Faige sips her coffee. "I know it's like two months ago, but I thawt dat afta what happened at da Ball, he'd be history by now. I jus' figga'd it was takin' youz extra time ta kick 'im ta da curb."

Jennifer's mind fades back to autumn and the Barrister's Ball. The women wore cute dresses and had on makeup that took them an hour to apply. The men were dressed in sharp suits and fancy ties. Jennifer had only been dating Robert for a few months, and so her friends were still being introduced to him. There was good music and dancing, and also an open bar, which led to over-indulgence. Having recently discovered the beauty of free bar booze at a few weddings and formal events, it didn't take long for Robert to become a big fan. That night his enthusiasm was at an all-time high, and his judgment was at an all-time low.

Faige snaps her fingers. "*Jennifa*, where-ja-go?"

In a daze, Jennifer responds, "I'm still here, sorry."

"Youz rememba what he did?! It was totally inappropriate!"

"Yes, it was. I agree." Jennifer nods her head a few times. "And I know I told you this before, but Robert had a few too many and was just *trying* to be funny. After everything went down, we had a long talk about it. Believe me, he knows not to pull a stunt like that again."

"*Tryin'* ta be funny?!" Faige bellows like a livewire zapped her. "What he did was disgustin' and rude! Do youz really wanna guy like dat? I mean — does he take anyting seriously? Youz gotta tink about all his traits and if dey align wit' youz kareeah goals. How youz gonna become a Supreme Court Justice? He can't publically embarrass youz like dat."

"It's not a problem — I've been working on him." Jennifer raises her chin up. "He's been really good lately and understands that things had to change from how they were. Actually, we've both toned things down considerably. We've both matured."

"Yeah, but what's he really wan' outta life? Ta drink and go ta strip clubs?"

"No! Why would you even say something like that? He wants what I want. For everyone to be able to be who they are and not have to worry about it." Jennifer grins. "Plus, I know how to get him to do whatever I want. Which equals him taking care of me, and me being happy."

"Are youz sure abou' dat?" Faige asks skeptically.

"Yes! Just this morning, he cleared *all* the snow and ice from my car. *And* I didn't even have to tell him to do it this time." Jennifer makes a slam-dunk motion. "Hey, why are you giving me the third-degree?"

"Sawree, I know I can be protective. I jus' wan' da bes' fa youz, *Jennifa*."

"I know, but please, *please* don't worry about me. I've got things totally under control — believe me. He'll be at the OUTLaw dinner tonight, and you'll see how he's different. Give him a chance, okay?"

Faige answers as though she's being asked if she'd like a rotten tooth pulled. "Yeah, I guess. Fa youz, I'll give 'im anotha."

"Thank you. But enough about me." Jennifer leans-in and looks at Faige sympathetically. "Let's talk about you. Have things gotten any better in the men-department?"

"*Hmmm*, how do I say dis politely? Men suck. Sometimes I tink dey mo trouble dan dey worth." Faige's eyes twinkle. "I'm considerin' takin' a break. Wanna join me?"

Jennifer laughs. "No — like I said — I'm good right now."

"I know. I was jus' kiddin'." Faige jokingly brushes Jennifer away. "Anyway, if youz decide ta get me a Christmas gift, please make shua it's big, phallic, and vibrates. Cuz dat's da only ting I wan' hurryin' down my chimney."

Jennifer laughs and tilts back in her chair. She regains her composure and says, "I'll make sure to jot that one down on my naughty-shopping-list. Now let's get to class."

—

Still damp from the pool mayhem, the two Miami couples soak up the sun and enjoy freshly made habañero Bloody Marys — the kind that light your tongue on fire. Bambi sits on the edge of the pool and kicks the water. Nearby, a group of pelicans fly over Biscayne Bay, searching for their breakfast. Bradford watches with a sharp eye as they slow to near suspension in the air, tilt their long beaks down, straighten their bodies skyward, and transform into dropping darts. Piercing the water, they open their beaks and take several fish into their enormous throat pouches. Climbing upward through the water to the surface, they fly away to enjoy their morning prize.

Bradford hops up onto the diving board to boost his 5'4" stature. He unbuttons his damp white linen shirt and throws it on a chair. With his hairy, tan, chiseled chest exposed, he addresses everyone, "In this world." He points to the sky. "You either hunt." He drops his arm and points down. "Or you are the prey. *I'm* a hunter, and I take what I want. Those that don't hunt end up on the wrong side of the next meal."

Bambi shakes her head slightly so it's not noticed. *My god, these guys are pricks.*

Juan Carlos asks, "Bradford, where are you going with this?"

Summer interjects. "Let him finish. He's the brains of your business. You just had daddy's money to start it."

Juan Carlos scoffs at her. "Like you have either brains or money!"

"Oh, I've done alright for myself." Summer laughs and pokes her chin in Bambi's direction. "And I've got more brains in my tits than she has in her whole head!"

"You've got brains in your tits?" Bambi asks. "I just thought it was a couple bags of silicone?" Her verbal punch stuns Summer.

Juan Carlos chuckles. "Good one, Bambi!"

Bambi elects to save cross-examination of *Summer's mysterious tit-brains* for another time, and she savors the moment.

Bradford takes back the floor. "So as I was saying before you idiots interrupted me — we must be hunters. With that being said, I have a proposition for this weekend — so listen up!"

Summer responds eagerly, "I am!"

Bradford smirks. "I know you are, because you do what I tell you." He points north. "Gas up the jet, cuz we're going to Buffalo this weekend!"

"Are you out of your fucking mind?!" Juan Carlos shouts.

"No." With crazy eyes, Bradford points at his skull. "I'm *in* my fucking mind! Remember the war of northern aggression? Well now it's time for some southern aggression! We're going to the Dolphins game — but that's not the only thing we're gonna do."

—

Robert and Dale are reviewing their code when a knock on the door twists their necks. Their visitor, his head only inches from the top of the doorframe, is Tommy Janks.

Janks's grandfather, Bolek, grew up in a small city in Poland, and discovered that because of his abnormal height, he was able to lurk behind walls outside, elongate his neck, and peer over at unsuspecting females. He quickly became known around town as "masturbować żyrafa" — in English that roughly translates into "the masturbating giraffe." If he were caught before completing a quick hit-and-run, he'd throw an angry fit. At age seventeen, Bolek was 'encouraged' by the community to immigrate to the New World. Upon arrival, he found work in the Bethlehem Steel mills in the Buffalo Southtown of Lackawanna. After receiving a fair amount of ethnic discrimination in his blue-collar circle, he changed his family name from Jankowski to Janks.

Robert greets him, "Hey, Janks. What's up?"

"You boys wanna go hunt deer this weekend? Me and a couple of other guys from downstairs are gonna go south and bag a few trophies."

"Who? Guys on the radar project?" Dale asks.

"Yeah, we do it every year." Janks closes one eye and looks down the barrel of the imaginary riffle he holds in his hands. "We use our muzzle-loaders to track those sons-a-bitches and take 'em down. It's a hell of alotta fun!"

"Sounds like a fair fight to me, but sorry, it's not really my cup of tea," Robert replies. "However Dale, you love that sort of thing, right?"

Dale turns his head toward Robert and sends him a raised eyebrow glare. "Yeah, sounds fun, but I don't have a license or really hunt."

Janks stares at the floor. "Well, that sucks." He sulks for a moment until a lightning bolt seems to hit him. "Hey! What about this, Dale? What if we get you a license tomorrow and I teach you how to hunt over the weekend? I even have an extra gun. Boom! Problem solved!"

Robert gives his two cents, "Sounds like a no-brainer to me, Dale."

Dale's glare pleads to Robert. "Shit, I totally forgot. My wife is making me go to her knitting show this weekend. I know it's really lame, but I gotta do what the lady says."

Janks frowns. "Oh, well. Next time then, for sure?"

Dale forces out a fake smile. "Um, yeah sure. I'll do my best."

Janks turns to leave, but something strikes him. "Wait, I forgot! On the way back on Sunday we're going to the Bills game! I got a couple extra tickets and you know these babies ain't easy to come by." He takes a big sniff of air and closes his eyes. "We'll barbecue up some deer at the tail-gate! You guys in?!"

Robert and Dale reply with phony pouts and shake their heads no. After Janks exits and mopes away, Dale throws a pen and hits Robert squarely in the stomach. Looking back to make sure he's out of Janks's earshot, Dale whispers, "You asshole. I'm not going anywhere with that guy, especially if weapons are in the same general vicinity."

Robert looks at Dale with compassion. "Oh, you'd be fine. He's just trying to bring you closer. Ya know, like Jennifer's trying to do to me."

"Yeah, ha ha, very funny. Yeah, closer so he can kill me. Have you seen that axe in his office?"

"I have. What the heck is that all about?" Robert asks.

"Apparently it's from a black program a couple of years back — top-secret stuff downstairs. Each of those programs has an axe assigned to it. If there's ever a fire or any way that the hardware could be left unpro-tected, the axe is to be used to destroy the equipment. After one of the programs he was on completed, Janks asked for the axe and those idiots let him have it. I can't believe the damn thing is hanging in his office!"

"So he's got an axe — it's not like he's crazy enough to use it." Robert waits for Dale's agreement, which he doesn't receive. "Wait, is he?"

"Really? You didn't feel like something was a little off there? Plus, I've seen other episodes where he's flipped out. You know how great choco-late and peanut butter are together? Well, he's the opposite. He's a combo of irrational temper and dangerous weapons — *not* so great to-gether. In fact, terrifying!"

Robert shivers. "I'm glad you sit closer to the door."

"Why?"

"Because when he loses his shit, he'll take you out first. While that's happening, maybe I'll have a chance to escape before he chops me into little pieces too."

Dale thinks about it for a moment. "Yep, I'm fucked, but your odds aren't so good either." Robert nods in agreement.

Silence fills the room for an entire two seconds before there's another knock on the door. Robert and Dale cringe as they wonder if Janks was eavesdropping them. Turning slowly, they're relieved to find Pete in the doorway — a kid fresh out of grad school. Robert motions for him to enter and addresses him by his surname, "What's going on, Sametta?"

"Hey, did I just see Janks leave here?" Sametta asks.

"Yep," Dale replies.

"Did he tell you what's up?" Sametta questions.

Robert answers, "If asking us to go slaughter deer and then grill them at a tailgate is what's up, then yes, he told us what's up."

Sametta looks surprised. "Oh wow, he doesn't know yet, or he would've said something for sure."

"Can you please just tell us what's going on?" Robert commands.

Sametta sticks his head into the hall and looks around before completely entering the office and closing the door. "There's major rumors floating around that the radar program downstairs is gonna be killed. I fear this could be really bad."

"Why the hell would they do that?" Dale asks. "That's this company's showcase program. We know that technology space better than anyone."

"Agreed, but let's face facts. The cold war is over," Sametta states bluntly. "Budgets are scaling back and some of these military programs aren't really necessary anymore. Personally I disagree with cutting that particular program, but I'm also a tad biased since I work down there."

"Fuck, that sucks." Robert tries to become hopeful. "But remember it hasn't played out yet, so maybe everything'll be fine. Sorry, and I'm not trying to be insensitive, but are guys like Dale and I safe up here?"

"Not to alarm you, but I've heard whispers that all military contracts are under scrutiny. They could be trimmed or cut completely."

"Fucking fuck, I've seen this type of fucking shit before guys," Dale spits out like he has Tourette's. "Everybody gets super tense and walks around on eggshells. Something could happen — I've been furloughed before — but there's also a chance that nothing happens — I've seen that too. My advice is to keep your head down."

Robert nods. "And keep our mouths shut. No need to alarm anyone else."

Dale agrees before saying with a touch of panic, "I gotta tell you, the thing I fear the most, above a layoff — is Janks. That motherfucker has a screw loose. If he gets the axe," Dale uses his index finger to mock slit his throat, "*we're* all getting the axe! That axe from his office!" They cringe as images of Jack Nicholson in the *The Shining* pop into their heads.

"So when will we find out what's happening?" Robert inquires.

"Based on the past, if they're gonna do it, tomorrow will be judgment day," Dale replies. "They almost always do it on a Friday, but you never know. It could be today."

"Fuck. Now I'm super motivated to work," Robert cries.

"Actually, you should be," Dale answers. "They could be narrowing down who stays and who's out as we speak."

"I may just take matters into my own hands," Sametta says.

Thrown off, Robert asks, "What's that supposed to mean?"

"You'll see tomorrow." Sametta smiles like he's got a trick up his sleeve. "I'll see you then."

—

After briefly considering Bradford's Buffalo trip proposition, Juan Carlos shares some feedback. "This seems like a bad idea. It makes no sense."

Bradford replies, "Let me explain further. First of all, our business needs to establish a larger presence in the Northeast. We've talked about expanding our market share up there — well, now we have an opportunity to do that with a large set of our target audience. Second, we love our Miami Dolphins and love going to games, right? So let's go watch them crush the Buffalo Bills! We'll fly up tomorrow."

"You realize it's the middle of winter, right? Their winters are harsh."

"When you say things like that, you're just making excuses. Don't you want more money? Don't you love the Dolphins?"

"Yeah I do, but come on man, look around you." Juan Carlos gestures to the sun and girls.

Bradford cups his ear with his hand. "You hear that?" He pauses dramatically. "That's the sound of weakness! *Never* be satisfied with what you've got, because someone else is always waiting to take it. Always push forward, improve, and overcome obstacles. If you're going to let a little thing like bad weather stop you, then what are you?" He looks at the group for an answer and receives silence. "I'll tell you. You're a big *pussy*, that's what! This is a big opportunity and a big game. Let's go make some dough and have some fun!"

"Alright, alright, you've made your point," Juan Carlos surrenders. "Fine. When should you and I fly out?"

"Oh, it's not the two of us." Bradford extends his arm, points his index finger, and circles it in the air. "It's gonna be all four of us this weekend."

Juan Carlos's eyes look like they're going to pop out of his head. "You're kidding, right?" He gives Bambi the side-eye and discretely shakes his head no. "I don't think the girls would enjoy the snow or football — or Buffalo, for that matter." He addresses Bambi. "It's okay, you don't have to come. I completely understand, and I'm not offended."

Before either of the girls can speak, Bradford interjects, "Stop it. The girls will have a great time. Plus, we need their help with our marketing campaign. Honestly we can't do it without them. Ladies, you're going on a little trip this weekend. Naturally, we'll take care of all expenses. And throw in a nice gift — which I know you'll love, and will be very fitting for our destination. You in?"

"Sure, why not? I'm bored and always looking for a good time," Summer answers. "You guys better entertain the hell out of me."

Bambi shrugs her shoulders. "I guess so. I don't know where Buffalo is, but I imagine you do. I'll bring my passport."

Summer throws her hands up. "Wow! Another brilliant response!" She eyes Bradford and Juan Carlos. "You know what guys? Your company takes the hiring process pretty seriously, right? I think we should ask her one of those special interview questions before deciding if we bring her along. May I?"

Juan Carlos squirms. "I don't really think that's necessary. We're clearly not judging her on her cognitive abilities."

Bradford interjects, "No, we're not. But this could be interesting." He can't contain his grin. "Summer, please continue."

Summer stares down Bambi. "Tell me why manholes are round?"

Without hesitation, Bambi answers, "Oh, that's easy — so no one gets injured." The others look at each other like they just witnessed an eleven-year-old correctly spell "prophylactic" to win a Spelling Bee.

Summer composes herself. "That's actually a good answer — so far. Please explain further."

Bambi acts as though she's teaching class. "Sure, no problem. It's purely a shape thing." She uses her index finger and an okay-hand-gesture to poke and demonstrate. "The manhole has to fit inside the woman-hole, else there could be an injury."

Summer erupts with laughter and can barely speak. "See, goddam-mit! She fooled us all for a second!" Juan Carlos looks like he's holding in a wet fart and stressing his sphincter's contraction capabilities.

Bambi asks, "So did I get the job?" The looks on the others' faces worry her, so she doesn't wait for an answer. "Since I don't have my resume with me, I have something to add." She turns to Juan Carlos. "I'd like to highlight my unique talents as a contortionist and sword swallower." She pauses to flash him a playful smile. "I haven't tried both at the same time yet, but there's a first time for everything."

Juan Carlos imagines Bambi as some kind of sexual circus-freak and straightens up in his chair. "You and I will continue *that* part of the interview process later." To everyone else he declares, "Okay, fuck it, let's do this! Bradford, take care of the arrangements."

Bradford grins. "Not a problem." He yells towards the house, "Digby!!!" and looks back at Juan Carlos. "That's why we have a butler."

———

Inside Robert and Dale's office is a keyboard-pecking frenzy that sounds like Irish tap dancers hopped-up on cocaine. An echo of clomping wooden heels bounces down the corridor, and within a split-second their typing halts. The officemates eyebrows raise in alarm.

"Fuck, I just know she's coming to see us," Robert whispers to Dale. "I'm almost done with this new subroutine. Delay her."

Dale dashes to the doorway and almost runs into a troll-sized woman in her late-50s. Her clomping stops abruptly. She's dressed in a black suit-coat and skirt, and her short silver hair is pulled back tight. Dale tries to act nonchalant while blocking her from entering. "Hey, Dr. Cramps. Good morning." Having earned her doctorate degree in aerospace engineering, she demands to be addressed by her formal title.

"What is zis?" she asks in a harsh German accent. "Where do you zink you're going?"

Dale leans against the entrance frame. "I was just gonna get some coffee. Nothing better than caffeine to get work completed, right?"

"Actually, having your butt in zat chair wiz your fingers typing away would be much better. How about you do zat instead?"

Dale's head droops as he turns to sit. "I suppose you're right."

Robert swivels in his chair to address Dr. Cramps. "Hey, I'm making great progress. I—"

She interrupts him, "Show me what you've got."

Dale, sensing that Robert needs more time, cuts in. "Can I show you what I've done with the splash screen first? I'm pretty proud of it."

"Sure, fine." She turns to Dale. "Zis is our user's first impression of zee software. It's critical zat it looks superb."

Dale points to his monitor. "So as you can see, I took the three logos of the different Air Force agencies backing the program and laid them out evenly across the top. Then I put the acronym of the software here." He leans back to admire his work. "It's been a very gratifying project."

"First of all, your blue background is *complete* garbage," Dr. Cramps chirps. "Zat's not professional at all — I want an entirely different shade." She smudges her finger on his display. "It looks like zee blue Play-Doh my grandkid barfed up zee other day."

In shock, Dale replies, "Um, o-kaaay."

She reaches into her jacket's inside pocket and pulls out a foot-long ruler. "Also, zee layout of zee logos is off." She places the ruler on the screen and begins to measure. "See what I mean? Zee space between zee logos is two inches here and here, but two-and-a-half inches from each side. Zat's unacceptable — fix it." Like an army sergeant inspecting her platoon, Dr. Cramps moves behind Robert. "Okay, now you."

Robert straightens up in his chair. "Take a look at this. Let's say an intelligence analyst wants to research, say, 'evil dictator.'" He gives Dale a sly smile. "They type it in the search-box like this and —" He hits the enter-key. "Voila!" Several types of graphs appear that are labeled with the original search words and several related words.

Dr. Cramps puts her head down next to his to scrutinize the data. Her coffee-laced-with-mothballs aroma nearly chokes him. "Why are zair words like 'delightful' and 'boss'?" She asks. "It doesn't make sense."

"Actually it's pretty straight forward." He points at the screen. "The search algorithm looks for both synonyms and antonyms. A synonym of 'dictator' is 'boss.' And an antonym of 'evil' is 'delightful'."

She stands upright and puts her fist under her chin. "Zis needs tweaking. I want zee analysts to be able to remove any of zeez related key words — store zem in zair own personal do-not-search list for use in future queries. Understood?"

Robert sputters, "But, but the requirements document —"

Dr. Cramps halts him with a Nazi salute. "Zee requirements are what I determine zay are. I need zis —" She waves her hand at his monitor. "Changed by five o'clock Friday — not a minute later. I've got a big demonstration for zee General on Monday zat I need to prepare for zis weekend. Lucky for you, you have zee rest of today and tomorrow to work on zis if necessary. Is zis going to be a problem?" She places her hands on her hips and waits for his answer.

Flustered, Robert replies, "Um, I mean — no — um."

"Correct. I look forward to seeing zeez improvements completed by you both. Dale, I'll create a professional blue — somezing noble, like cornflower blue, but better. I'll get it to you in an hour. Zat needs to be done by tomorrow as well." Dr. Cramps stomps out of the office in a horse trot and leaves a wake of panic.

Robert waits until she's safely out of earshot. "*Zat* mother-F! *Zeez* are brand new requirements! *Zeez* are major changes!!"

"I understand, but first can I commend you on the 'evil dictator' thing?" Dale chuckles. "That was brilliant."

"Thanks," Robert replies as if it's little consolation.

"So, is there any way you can possibly finish that stuff on time?"

"I gotta think this through —" Robert continues slowly, "One, I need to change a major data structure. Two, change the way I compile search-results. Oh, AND THREE, add in personalization. Son-of-a-bitch! And I can't work late tonight because of Jennifer's damn event later."

Dale looks over his shoulder. "You know what really frightens me?"

Robert nods. "As a matter of fact, I do. She's demanding for all this to be done by *five* tomorrow, which means we could be doubly fucked. We kill ourselves to complete things, and then they lay us off."

"Yep, the timeframe is no coincidence." Dale pokes his forehead and thinks. "Another nightmare scenario is they pull our budget and give it to the radar guys. Fuck, who knows?"

"While Cramps is worrying about 'professional blue' — whatever *the fuck* that is — we all hang-on by our fingernails." Robert jams his palms in his eye sockets. "This turned out to be one *hell* of a shitty day."

—

The top of a palm tree partially obstructs the apartment's view of the peach house across the street. Inside the rental unit, a master's degree hangs on the wall, and a framed photo of a mother with her young teenage girl sits on the desk. Both women have long brown hair and, by the way the girl is bursting out of her *Like a Virgin* album cover t-shirt, it's clear she's following in her voluptuous mother's brassiere-steps.

An open folder's contents are spread out across the desk. There are a dozen photographs of Bradford and Juan Carlos, all taken from a distance and without their knowledge. Some of the photos show them outside an office building downtown, while others show them coming out of a warehouse. There's a snapshot of Bradford and Summer walking on the beach, and lots of pictures of Juan Carlos in South Beach with an assortment of blonde bimbos.

Several pages of research on Juan Carlos's and Bradford's past are marked up with yellow highlighter. At three years old, Juan Carlos's mother and father took him and left Cuba on a homemade raft powered by a lawnmower engine. They braved the 90-mile, shark-infested stretch of water to Florida and escaped to Yankee Paradise.

The family settled in Little Havana, a Miami neighborhood that is home to many Cuban immigrants. They started off broke, but Javiero, Juan Carlos's dad, was determined to give his family a better life. He used his exceptional intelligence and people skills to flourish in real estate and shipping. After almost twenty years, his businesses grew to the point where they had immense wealth.

Juan Carlos has been given every opportunity in life — the best education and management positions inside his father's companies. His performance was adequate, but never up to his father's high-standards. Each month, Juan Carlos receives a healthy family allowance — one that enables him to live a life of luxury. He views the business he started with Bradford as a means to prove himself to his father.

Bradford Threadgold III's given name at birth was Peter Short. This "distinguished title" combined with his less than average height made him an object of ridicule as a child. On his eighteenth birthday he legally changed his name and began his transformation. He chose his new persona to give the impression of status and wealth. From there, craftiness and manufactured charm helped Bradford develop the relationships he needed and eventually led him to Juan Carlos.

Also on the desk is a document containing the past three years of non-public financials for The Growth Firm — Bradford's and Juan Carlos's business. The records were obtained via an unscrupulous contact on the inside and show the company's revenue has increased by nearly 100% year-over-year.

The door to the apartment opens and in walks Bambi. She moves to the desk, places her gold clutch down, and sits. On a blank piece of paper, she meticulously writes down the details of the last twenty-four hours. Pausing, she puts the end of the pen in her mouth and analyzes her notes. She scribbles over "Juan Carlos is a tool," and writes, "Juan Carlos is someone that can be manipulated to get information."

Bambi grabs the financial documents and scans them until she lands on profits — a number just north of $4.5 million through November of this year alone. She leans back in her chair and puts her hands behind her head.

—

Zabka's Corvette, coated in gray rock salt, chases Jed's white Ford Bronco through the dark evening. A light snow falls as Jed's house comes into view. To get from the road to Jed's garage requires ascending up a driveway until it levels off at the top. In the summer, this does not present an issue, but in the winter when the driveway has not been shoveled in two days, it requires an additional set of skills. Approaching slowly, Jed presses the remote to open the door to an empty garage. He turns his SUV 90 degrees to face the driveway, accelerates hard, spins the wheels, and shoots upward. Near the curvature at the top, he slams on the breaks, fishtails to the right, and slides into the garage at nearly a 45-degree angle, barely missing both of the opening's sides.

Zabka takes the same approach pattern — slams the brakes halfway up, digs the chains through the snow and into the driveway, and anchors his vehicle in the middle of the driveway. While his location makes it impossible for anyone else to park, he doesn't really care.

Zabka and Jed grab the bags from K-Mart and a case of Genesee Cream Ale from the Corvette. As soon as they enter Jed's place, a large black Doberman Pinscher nearly knocks them over from excitement.

Jed wrestles the dog. "Hey Earnhardt! You remember Zabka? I want you to bite his balls off if he tries to steal my beer again!"

Zabka grins. "Hey, you passed-out! There was one left, so I took it!"

"Whatever. Anyway, welcome to our workroom," Jed says with his arms outstretched. "Are you ready to get down to business?!"

"I sure as hell am, but I'm way too sober!"

"Great minds — or maybe it's livers — think alike! I can't start work on this arts and crafts project until I've warmed up with at least a 6-pack. My creativity needs inspiration!"

"Well then, let's crack open a couple. And turn on some tunes."

"Yeah, will do, but first things first," Jed replies as he grabs two beers.

"Remember, our final product needs to be top notch. This will make us legends on Sunday!"

Jed laughs as he opens and hands Zabka a bottle. "You're like a diabolical Martha Stewart."

Zabka nods back with a proud look. "I'll take that as a compliment."

They clink their beers together and nearly finish them off with their first guzzle. "Damn, that's good!" Jed exclaims.

"Love that Rochester water." Zabka cherishes the taste. "Um, um, good!" He grabs another beer and hands it to Jed. "Alright, finish what you got and chug this one. We've got work to do."

—

Robert glances at the digital clock on his workstation and realizes it's already 6:00. He rapidly punches-away on his keyboard, then stops and waits. After staring nervously at his screen for a few seconds, he claps happily. "Finally, Dale! I updated the data structure and the document retrieval comparison algorithm. This subsystem's almost done."

"Way to go." Dale gives him an air-high-five across the room. "Sounds like you made some good progress today."

"Yeah, thanks. All I need to do tomorrow is update the user interface." Robert pauses. "And fuck —" He pretends to bang his head against his desk. "Add in personalization too!"

"And don't forget about the other shit that could happen tomorrow."

Robert replies jokingly, "Damn, you really don't want me to sleep tonight, do you?" But his underlying angst comes through.

"Hang in there. I'm almost pretty-sure everything will work out fine."

"Almost pretty-sure? You're not instilling much confidence."

"Anyway, you think you can complete your stuff tomorrow?"

"I sure hope so — but man, the pressure of all this is really getting to me," Robert moans. "I wish I could stay here longer, but I've gotta run to Jennifer's law school dinner thing."

"Try to have fun and relax," Dale tells him. "Hey, can we talk about one last thing before you go?"

Robert puts his rubbers on over his dress shoes. "Yeah, what is it?"

"We talked about Jennifer and women in general this morning, but you've never really told me how much experience you have. I hope it's okay to ask — like how many girlfriends have you had?"

As Robert thinks, he ticks off numbers with his fingers until he hits ten. "Naw, I'm just joking around. To be honest — and I know this sounds weird — I kinda had one before, but I think with Jennifer it's more real."

"I see." Dale pulls on the hairs of his goatee. "If I may, I'd like to offer you some unsolicited advice." Robert nods for him to continue. "Women have an inherent nature to improve us — to make us better. Not necessarily for your benefit, but for hers. Although you may not believe it, her motives are often justified."

"Sorry, but this doesn't sound like advice. It sounds more like something your wife implanted in your brain."

"Ha, ha, very funny." Dale pumps his palm at Robert. "Let me finish."

Robert shuts down his workstation. "Proceed."

"Men — you and I — we're just too stupid to realize what they're doing." Dale looks into the hallway, then leans toward Robert and lowers his voice. "The thing is — women are smarter than us — like way smarter. They know how to play chess with our minds *and* our dicks. They're always thinking two or three steps ahead of us."

"Come on, really?" Robert cocks his head. "What's your guidance?"

Dale pretends to knock over the king chess-piece. "This is a game you can't win. You can't beat a woman — they're tenacious and never give up. They're the most complex creatures in the world — no, universe."

"I agree with you whole-heartedly on their complexity."

"It all stems from evolution." Dale indicates a timeline by chopping his hand downward while moving it from left to right. "Throughout history, women have had to worry about protection, shelter, clothing, sustenance, procreation, nurturing, the future — the list goes on and on. Men on-the-other-hand have really only worried about two things — hunting and fucking. That's it, to put it bluntly. In today's world, money has taken the place of hunting, but you see where I'm coming from?"

Robert squeezes his brow, bounces his tilted head, and shrugs his shoulders as if to reply, "Kinda."

Dale continues, "A woman views it as her responsibility to bring the male and female strengths together. Once a symbiotic relationship has formed, she'll do everything in her power to protect it. If she fails and it dissolves, neither one of them will survive. Get it?"

Robert scratches his head. "I think so."

"So my advice is this — pay attention and listen to her very carefully. I know it's tough, because it's a skill we weren't born with, but work on it.

And remember, it's not only *what* she says, but also *how* she says it. If you do this and follow her direction, your life will be much easier."

Robert looks at Dale like he's trying to sell him a house on the beach in downtown Buffalo. "So what you're telling me is — I need to do what she says *and* interpret any additional underlying meaning based on her tone, sentence structure, and the context of where and when she says it?"

"Well, yeah, that's the gist of it." Dale raises a finger. "But if she's a complete nut-case, there's another set of rules you should follow for your safety. But that's a whole other can-of-worms."

"Oh, man. Okay, we'll save that lecture for another time. I gotta go."

"You said you're going to one of Jennifer's events, right?"

"Yeah."

"And why is that?"

"Because she —" Robert stops himself. "Because she told me to."

Dale smiles. "See — you're already following my advice." He swivels back to his keyboard. "I'll be here a little longer. See you tomorrow."

Robert puts on his coat and walks out. "See you in the AM."

—

Scott walks down a submerged flight of stairs to the door of his basement apartment. He chuckles while wiping his boots clean of snow on his "Hi, I'm Mat!" welcome mat. As he enters his tiny dark apartment, he flips on the overhead light, exposing barren walls and old dank furniture. He stops and inspects the room from side to side.

"Where are you? Come out, daddy's home!"

The door to his bedroom creaks open and an obese orange cat mopes out. A black cat, just as overweight, crawls out from beneath the couch. They approach, stop at Scott's feet, and lay down panting.

"Pumpkin and Ace, there you are! Have my girls had a tough day?" He asks with a frown. "It sure looks like it. Come with me, and I'll get you your dinner."

Scott's two cats are the only reminders of his brief marriage. Four years ago, when Scott was thirty-three, his parents worried he would never find a wife. He was always book smart, but lacked the social skills to meet and attract women. After his parents watched a *60 Minutes* story on arranged marriages in India, they hatched a plan to set him up. As hard as they tried to find other parents in America or Canada in the same virgin-child-boat, they were unsuccessful. Then one day Scott's father saw a personal ad in the paper from a "young and attractive" Russian woman looking for love. Her name was Misha-Labia. Misha thought adding dash Labia to her name was a nice touch and would help her stand out from the competition — and it worked. She exchanged letters and photos with Scott's parents, and when both parties were comfortable, they bought her a plane ticket to nearby Montreal.

On the day of Misha-Labia's arrival, Scott and his parents drove for an hour-and-a-half across the Canadian border to pick her up. As they waited at the gate for her to depart the plane, Scott's forehead, chest, and armpits soaked from anxiety. The anticipation was unbearable, and as he held his mother's hand, he knew at that moment he was ready to become a man. When they first saw her is what they now refer to as the "*kinda* moment." They *kinda* thought it was her, but weren't sure because she *kinda* looked like her picture. She also *kinda* had the same shape and *kinda* the same number of teeth. Nevertheless, Scott was excited and couldn't wait to get married.

On their wedding day, after sharing a late night Moons Over My Hammy breakfast, they climbed into the backseat of Scott's car behind the Denny's to consummate their marriage. Years of self-pleasure couldn't properly prepare him for the feel of her warm borscht, and just as their awkward intercourse began, it abruptly finished. That was the first time *and* last time Scott had sex.

Misha-Labia turned her attention to cats and they ended up buying seven altogether. Scott grew to care for a few of the cats, but constantly dreamed about reenacting the lovemaking event they had after their nuptials. Then one day he came home after work and found a note she had left for him. As he read it to himself, he could hear her talking in broken Russian English, "Scott, marriage over. Now citizen. I leave with cats. Leave you ones that are ass pains." That was the last time he heard from her. Of all the cats, she left him with the two he disliked, but over time they grew on him like growths that feel good to pick.

As Scott walks to the kitchen, the cats lethargically follow behind him. The kitchen's cream color painted walls chip from age and a Lake Placid calendar hangs above a short bookcase filled with cans of cat food. A photo of the snow covered ski jump used in the 1980 Winter Olympics is displayed for the month of December. He stops in front of it, puts his hands on his hips, and peruses the weekend's upcoming activities.

"Well, gosh darn it, this is ridiculous!" Scott blurts. "There's absolutely no way I can go to Buffalo. My weekend is totally packed." He rubs his forehead. "But I have to go. This is business, and it's really important. Let's think through this." He picks his nose and flicks it randomly — hitting Ace between the whiskers. "Maybe I can rearrange a few things."

Scott scans his calendar again — a red "X" crosses out each day up to yesterday, Wednesday the 13th. He takes the red marker and puts an "X" over today. All the days are blank except each Friday is designated for "Laundry" and every Saturday is labeled "Masturbate".

"I hate to mess up 'date night', but here's what we're gonna do."

Scott puts red lines through the coming weekend's events and writes, "BUFFALO" across Friday, Saturday, and Sunday. He then writes, "Laundry" and "Masturbate" on the following Monday and Tuesday. Impressed with himself, he folds his arms and looks at the calendar with a big grin. He steps back and shakes his head. "Gosh darn it, Scott! Now next week is gonna be super busy!"

He bends down, grabs four cans of cat food, and takes them to the kitchen counter. Scott opens each one with a manual can opener and grabs a spoon. He squats down to the cats where they wait in front of empty bowls. As he dishes out a slimy, puck-shaped meat by-product dinner, the cats nearly inhale it from the spoon before it reaches their bowls.

After a few scoops he stops, feeling the need to drop the bomb that's suffocating his chest. "Kids, I don't really know how to say this, so I'm just gonna say it. I have some bad news. Daddy won't be around this weekend."

The cats stop eating whatever has made it into their bowls and stare up at him.

"I know, I know. Please don't look at me that way. Sometimes with this job I have to do things I don't want to do. Okay, so maybe there will be a little fun sprinkled in too. You want daddy to have fun, right?"

Pumpkin and Ace's eyes squint a little, their tails raise, and their fur stands up. Scott squishes his head and neck inward like a turtle protecting itself. "Hey, it's mostly work related. Please don't be mad. I'll leave out plenty of dry food for you."

Suddenly, like there are springs underneath the floor, Pumpkin jumps forward with her claws out and wraps her fat legs around Scott's face, knocking off his glasses. Blinded, Scott twists, screams, and falls onto his back while attempting to rip off the clawing cat. Ace then leaps onto his man-boobs and tears at his shirt and flesh. Scott, desperate for the attack to stop, rolls onto his side, simultaneously squishing Ace and a can of cat food with his stomach. Ace lays stunned on the ground.

Scott leaps up with Pumpkin's claws firmly locked into his head, and they spin around in place like a figure skating pair. "Get off me! Daddy loves you, you son-of-a-gun!!" Pumpkin's grip is no match for the centrifugal force, and she shoots across the room like an orange meteor. After a crash landing, she wobbles away sideways from dizziness. Veering to the right, she misses the opening to the living room and bangs headfirst into the wall.

With his hands on his knees, Scott arches over in pain and through his blurry view of the room, spots his glasses. Crawling over, he grabs his spectacles and restores his vision. "Are my babies alright? Frickin'-A, this hurts! Why did you stinkers do this!? Frick!!!"

Dazed, with pain shooting from multiple locations on his face and upper torso, Scott carefully walks to the bathroom, trying not to replicate Pumpkin's accident. He flicks on the bathroom light and looks in horror at himself in the mirror. Claw marks and blood are on his left cheek and the right side of his neck. Scott's shirt is soaked in cat food and his own bodily fluid. His hairy belly mound, along with one oversized areola and nipple combo, are exposed through his torn shirt.

Scott winces as he cleans his wounds with rubbing alcohol and bandages them with gauze pads and medical tape. Satisfied with his patchwork, he puts the medical supplies back into the cabinet. While doing so, he spots his bottle of Huge Member pills, takes it out, and inspects the label. He vents to Pumpkin's blank stare, "Dagnammit, I've been taking these things for two months now and haven't seen any results. Right here it even says, 'Guaranteed, one or more inches in the first 30 days.' What in heaven's name could I be doing wrong?" Scott grabs his toiletry bag, throws in the pills, and begins to pack for the weekend.

—

Thanks to the roads being relatively clear of snow and traffic, Robert arrives at the Marriott in record time and with five minutes to spare. He walks into the lobby and sees the "University at Buffalo Law School OUTLaw Holiday Dinner" sign. An arrow points to the right, directing him to the Knox Ballroom.

Robert struts into the expansive room in step with the disco beats of "I'm Coming Out" by Diana Ross. After unsuccessfully finding Jennifer among the forty or so people there, his attention is drawn to the bar in the far corner. On a mission, he walks across the room to it. As he passes the dinner tables and dance floor, his eyebrows scrunch with curiosity as he notices that almost every shorthaired woman is wearing either a suit and tie, or a tux. He brushes off the strange looks a few of the women give him as he passes. Reaching the bar area, he sneaks around a few people so he can get closer and make eye contact with the bartender.

The bartender notices him and approaches. "Sir, what can I get you?"

"Hey man, I'd love a beer and a glass of merlot, please."

"Whoa, been one of those weeks?" the bartender asks.

"Ha! Yeah, it has. But I'm not really double fisting. The wine is for my girlfriend."

The bartender looks behind Robert. "Girlfriend? Where is she?"

"Um —" Robert quickly scans the room. "I'm actually surprised she's not here yet. She'll be here soon."

The bartender hands him the drinks with a sly expression. "I see. Well, most of the guys here don't have girlfriends. So if your *girlfriend* doesn't show for some reason, you can probably make," he continues by using air quotes, "a 'new friend' tonight. In fact, I see a few prospects checking you out right now."

Robert can feel sets of eyeballs burning holes in his backside. Leaning forward with his elbows on the bar, he wipes a few beads of sweat from his forehead. "Oh um, yeah no, I'm not really looking for any more *friends*. I'm kinda all-good in that department, thanks. Plus, the *girlfriend* keeps me really busy."

Robert feels a tap on his shoulder from behind. He jerks upward and turns slowly. "Jennifer! Oh, thank god! So good to see you, gorgeous."

"Good to see you too." Jennifer kisses him. "Are you alright?"

"Um, yeah. Yeah totally. I just had a bizarre conversation."

"Oh yeah? About what?"

"Oh, it's nothing, I'll tell you later."

Robert turns around to the bar, grabs the glass of wine, and turns back to Jennifer. "Well, look at this. There just happens to be a glass of merlot here for you."

"Oh Robert, you're the best!" Like a proud pet owner, she continues, "I've trained you well!" Jennifer takes the glass and gives him a kiss on the cheek. They look each other in the eye, clink their glasses, and take a sip. Jennifer savors hers, while Robert takes a healthy swig.

"That's *soooo* good," Jennifer says joyfully. "Yum!"

"I'm glad to hear that. I know what you like."

"Yes, you do. Speaking of what I like, do you have anything else for me?" Jennifer puts a hand on her hip.

"Um, no. What are you talking about?"

Jennifer pouts, but it doesn't spark the reaction she's looking for from Robert. She then proceeds to speak to him in the same tone that she scolds her family's dog when it's on the furniture. "Robert, we've had lengthy discussions about this before. I have certain expectations when we go out to formal events together. You need to —"

Robert holds out his hand to stop her. "Oh, sorry. I forgot, I have this for you." He reaches inside his sports coat and pulls out a red rose.

"You bad boy!" Jennifer takes it from him and lightly slaps his arm. "It's a good thing you did that." Her tone turns serious. "Or you'd be back in the dog house again."

"Believe me, I'm don't wanna go back in there. Woof!"

"You know what?" Jennifer judges his attire. "You look very nice tonight, and I really like your tie. I didn't notice it this morning when you put it on, but way to class it up a bit."

"Thanks. I got this new one and changed into it. I know how much you like red and how important it is to you for me to look good."

"That's right. Part of the impression I give is the way you look and behave." Jennifer sighs. "I'm relieved you haven't screwed up lately."

"Well, thanks — I guess. Hey, I had kind of a stressful day. Can we talk about it?"

The music's volume softens, and a woman in a black pantsuit approaches the stage. "Yeah, maybe later," Jennifer whispers. "We better go take our seats. Things are gonna begin soon. Oh, and there's Faige at our table." The two wave to each other. "Let's go."

They walk over to Faige and find that she has saved two empty chairs for them. Jennifer greets her with a big bear hug and says, "So good to see you. I've missed you terribly since this morning."

"Yeah, me too!"

Jennifer shows off her rose and beams. "Look at what Robert got me."

With a cold expression, Faige responds, "Oh, wow. Dat's nice."

Robert comes up to Faige, and they exchange a half-hearted ass-out-hug — the kind where only shoulders touch. Giving his best effort, Robert says, "Faige, it's so nice to see you again." He steps back and looks her up and down thoughtfully. "Is it okay if I tell you that you look stunning?"

Turning a little flush, Faige stammers, "Why, um, yeah. Tank youz." Robert half smiles, knowing he threw her off. As the music ends, the three of them take their seats.

The woman behind the podium on stage speaks into the microphone, "Good evening, my name is Pat Spanks. I'm the President of the OUT-Laws, and I'd like to thank you all for *coming out* this evening — pun intended." She waits for the light laughter from the crowd to dissipate before continuing. "Thank you for supporting our organization as we advocate for the recognition of lesbians, gays, bisexuals, and trans-genders as equals under the law." She gives the audience a big air hug. "We have some outstanding speakers —"

My lord, tonight's all about this? Robert takes a double-sized gulp of champagne and spies on Jennifer out of the corner of his eye. As she listens intently to the speaker, his mind races. *Don't think about getting drunk. Don't think about getting drunk. Don't think —*

———

Metallica roars through the stereo and a NASCAR highlights video-tape plays on TV as Jed and Zabka work on the middle of the living room floor. A self-made enclosure of empty Genny Cream Ale bottles surrounds them. Between them are their materials and tools, which consist of a large sheet of blue Styrofoam, scissors, XXL white t-shirts, and cans of teal and orange spray paint. The end product that's made its way through their inebriated assembly line lies off to the side.

Zabka admires his work. "Sometimes I even impress myself."

"I have to say, this is one of our better ideas. The Bills fans will love us! LOVE US!" Jed exclaims.

"Dolphin fans will hate us! That is, if any are actually stupid enough to go to the game."

"Ha, ha! Screw 'em! They'd have to be complete idiots to do that! We don't treat Dolphin fans too kindly."

The front door slams open against the wall. BOOM! They turn just in time to see Brandy, Jed's wife, collapse to the floor in the foyer. Earnhardt sprints from the kitchen and barks over her.

Unfazed, Jed shouts, "Hey, I'm going to the Buffalo this weekend."

After struggling to her feet, Brandy squints at them with a bombed-out-of-her-mind look of confusion. It's the same look she had when she was once handed a full can of beer with no pop-top opening. As she points outside behind her, she slurs, "Who's da arse-hole in my drive-way who can't farking park?" They follow her finger and notice her car is jammed into the front yard snow about ten-feet from the door.

Jed responds. "Hey Zabka, you want to answer that question?"

"Sure, Jed," Zabka replies. "Brandy, I have to admit that *arse*-hole would be me. Obviously I didn't realize your front yard is a more acceptable place to park. My apologies."

She wobbles, leans forward, and blows an enormous raspberry, "THHHHBBBBTTT." Mid-response, her spittle transforms into a stream of yellow vomit, which triggers Jed and Zabka to erupt with laughter.

"Wow Jed! Your wife Brandy really is *a fine girl!*"

"I know. Keep your mitts off! She's all mine!"

They continue laughing as Brandy shrugs and begins stumbling upstairs to bed. The dog sticks his nose in her puke and licks it up.

Jed yells to her, "Sweetheart and love of my life!" Brandy pauses without looking back. "You just gonna leave that there for Earnhardt to clean up?" Unresponsive, she continues onward by pulling herself up the stairs with the railing.

Like a couple in Lamaze class, they focus back on meticulously preparing their brainchild for its scheduled Sunday delivery. Jed stops drawing to take a swig of his beer and asks, "May I voice a concern?"

"By all means. Communication is important in any healthy relationship. Fire away — just don't say anything idiotic."

"No guarantees. So I know we're staying at your friend Bob's this weekend, but is he gonna be any fun? I mean with him being a eunuch and all?"

Zabka laughs. "That's a fair question. And also a solid ball-bust — keep up the good work." They tap the bases of their beer bottles together. "Bob and I lived in the same house for a couple of years in college. I told you some stories about the crazy shit we used to do back then, right?"

"Yeah, I remember. He sounded fun in those stories."

"But you're right. Like we discussed before we want Bob, not Robert."

"Okay, so tell me about how all this Robert shit came to be," Jed asks.

"I'm not completely sure, but what I can tell you is what happened this summer when I visited him."

"The floor is yours."

"Long story short, Bob and I had a *minor* incident with the law." Zabka leaves a small gap as he pinches his thumb and index finger together. "Bad timing led to an unfortunate mishap. Ya know, the usual."

"Okay, and?"

"And after it happened, he called me a few weeks later and told me things like he was 'changing his ways' and that he needed to 'grow the fuck up' or some crap like that. It was the most annoying phone call I've ever had in my life."

"Where did all that come from?"

Zabka finishes cutting a large square out of the Styrofoam sheet. "I asked the same thing, and he said that the *fun police* — that's his girlfriend, in case it wasn't obvious — gave him a serious talking to. I told him he shouldn't listen to bad advice, and then he had the *gall* to tell me that she was *right*."

"No way! He said she was right? Fuck. This guy really needs our help. He needs — what's it called?" Jed itches his forehead. "An intervention?"

"Exactly. But it gets worse. He said a few things like," Zabka changes to a slower, listless voice, "Jennifer is good for me, and I'm really starting to care about her."

"Disturbing on so many levels." Jed shakes his head. "So disturbing."

"I know, right?! I'm the guy who understands Bob the best." Zabka points to himself. "*I'm* the one that's good for him."

"Obviously Zabka knows best."

After Earnhardt finishes the last of Brandy's liquid dinner off the floor, he staggers briefly before tipping over. The clock on the wall gongs once, shifting their attention. "Anyway, I suppose I should call him and let him know we're coming." Zabka stands up and walks to the phone. "That would be the proper thing to do."

—

Jennifer tries to drift off to sleep on her side of the bed, but Robert's light snoring counteracts her attempt. Her mind keeps replaying the night's dinner as a half-conscious dream. She smiles thinking about how Robert went out of his way to be attentive to Faige when she was surrounded by horny lesbians on the dance floor. He swooped in and rescued her with a dance, even though she was somewhat resistant.

Drifting back to reality, Jennifer feels the space that surrounds her. It's dark and quiet except for a trace of moonlight and the howling wind through the window above their heads. A sharp ring from the kitchen phone breaks the silence. Jennifer opens her eyes anxiously and checks Robert's clock radio. It's 1:03 AM. After the second ring, Robert tosses back and forth a little, but his eyes remain shut. After a couple more rings, the answering machine picks up.

The outgoing message plays, "Hi, you've reached Robert's. I'm not available right now, so please leave a message."

The machine beeps and Jennifer's ears perk up like a dog's.

"Robert? Who the fuck is Robert? I know Bob. I wanna talk ta Bob! This is Zabka! Put Bob on the phone right now!"

Jennifer's eyes widen like they are going to pop out of her head and her lips purse tightly. Robert rolls over and hugs his pillow.

"Hey Robert, give Bob this message." Zabka slurs his words. "We're coming to the Buffalo tomorrow *furr* the Bills game. We're gonna stay at *yrrr* place and party! Party like never before! Get ready!!! Oh, one last thing. Robert, go *fuuuuck* yourself."

Jennifer shakes with rage and her attempt to calm down has little effect. She sits up and checks on Robert. Seeing he's still asleep, she carefully gets out of bed so as not to wake him. As she enters the kitchen, the answering machine's blinking red light acts like a beacon that draws her closer. Hovering over the machine, her face changes from darkness to the color of the devil with each passing second. She moves her finger above the erase button and pauses to look over her shoulder. Confident that Robert has not awakened from his slumber, she turns her head back around and presses her finger down. The machine beeps loudly, the tape rewinds, and the light stops blinking.

Feeling satisfied with her decision, Jennifer returns to the bedroom. Without stirring Robert, she sneaks back into bed. With his back facing her, she rolls onto her side, inches closer, puts her arm around him, and makes him her little spoon.

The Second Quarter

Sprawled across the reclining chair, Jed sleeps like a dog without a care in the world. A stream of saliva oozes from the corner of his mouth, through his beard, and into a puddle on the headrest. His forearm, which got stuck inside a Pringles tube five minutes before he passed-out, is completely numb. His chest is caked with broken potato chips.

Zabka is sleeping upright on the couch — one hand tucked inside his pants, and the other holding an empty beer. His indented nostril remains silent as an obnoxious snore radiates like a foghorn out of its quivering counterpart. The rising sun shines through the window, reflects off a wall mirror, and creates an intense point of light just above his head. As the sun arcs higher, its laser beam cuts down through his forehead and pops beads of sweat to the surface.

Zabka awakes with a painful squint. He blocks the light with his hand and moves his head away. Lost in a bizarre flashback dream, he says, "Officer, it wasn't us! It was those other two dipshits!" After coming to his senses and a hopeless attempt to coerce a drink from his dry beer, he tosses the bottle on the ground with the rest. "Jed! Wake up, dumb-ass!" Unable to get even a twitch in response, Zabka walks over and flicks a finger into Jed's forehead. "Come on! Get up!"

Jed's eyes crack open, and he peels his face from the recliner's fake leather upholstery. "Are we late for the Bills game?"

"No, shithead. It's Friday and we're still in Massena — in *your* house!"

Jed looks around. "Oh right, I thought I recognized this place."

"Come on, get with it."

"Whatever. You get with it." Jed pulls the Pringles can off of his limp arm and flings it at Zabka.

Zabka dodges the projectile. "Nice try. Hey, just so you're aware, Scott's coming with us this weekend."

Alarms flash in Jed's eyes. "And why the hell is that?"

"How do you think I got us Bills tickets? This is to make up for network issues you guys suffered through yesterday. Get it? Make sure to give him shit, but not too much."

"I'll need guidance. I'm not good at reducing my shit-giving output."

"Don't worry, I'll be your shit-giving regulator. However, I kinda have my own issues in that department, so we'll see how that goes."

Jed reviews the mess on the floor. "So what now?"

"Well, mister genius, we need to pack and go to work for a little bit. Then the three of us will take-off in the afternoon." As Zabka turns to depart, he remembers something. "Oh, and don't forget to bring the gear for the game that we made last night. It's *extremely* important."

Before Zabka can reach the door, Jed shouts, "Hold on! I'm coming with you!" Jed rolls off the recliner and falls on the floor. He then crawls military-style on his stomach through a platoon of green dead-soldiers belonging to the Cream Ale army. "I'm late for work." From his knees, he scoops up the pile of gear and stands. "Okay, I'm ready to go!"

At first, Zabka looks at him in disbelief, but that state of mind leaves rather quickly. *Of course Jed's ready. As long as there's beer later, he'll be happy.* He opens the door, steps back, and waves Jed through. As Jed exits, he returns a courtesy nod.

———

Robert senses the patriot's musket pointing at the back of his skull as he pulls the colt's blue reins across the AstroTurf. With a thundering roar, a jet streaks across the luminous sky and disappears in a flash of green. He's pushed into a barren, bleached room. *Are those dolphin noises?* Dazed, he stands in front of a wall with a waist-high hole until instinct takes over. He plops his junk inside and feels a warm summer breeze. With jitters, he dangles and waits. Behind him, a buffalo snorts. His neck begins to tingle. A firm tug from the other side jolts him — pulling his mind, and crumbling away this bizarre world.

Jennifer releases her grasp from Robert's shaft and continues kissing the back of his neck. He wakes with a smile, but his eyes remain shut. He says, as if to himself, *"Mmm, I must be dreaming."*

She butterfly-kisses him with her eyelashes. "Maybe. About what?"

"About this really hot blonde."

"With a great butt?"

"With an *amaaaaazing* butt."

She whispers in his ear, "Oh, yeah? You know what she's thinking?"

"No. Do tell."

"Well — she's really into you, and —" Jennifer pecks Robert's cheek. "She thinks you guys should get away for a romantic weekend."

"That sounds nice — when can I meet her?"

Jennifer nudges him and giggles. "Stop that, silly-boy. I *really do* want to get away." She snuggles into his back and slides her hand halfway down his stomach. "Niagara on the Lake would be just perfect."

Robert ponders for a second. "Canada? Instead of our usual Blockbuster run and movie rental binge?"

"Yeah." She squeezes him into her. "We should celebrate us — our relationship. We need some good quality time together."

Robert replies in a little girl's voice, "I feel just like a princess that's been swept off her feet. You're *soooo* amazing to take me away like this."

"Oh honey, you know I would love to do that, but this poor law student just can't right now. Will you be my prince?"

"As much as I would like to — I obviously didn't plan for this." Robert rolls a few inches away from her. "I don't know how much it'll cost and, as you know, I have student loans. There's also this thing going on at work that's kinda majorly bad. I tried telling you about it last night —"

Jennifer slides her hand further down his stomach, just past his belly-button. She nibbles on his earlobe, then whispers, "I'll —" She breathes warmly in his ear, "I'll do whatever you want. Anything you desire will be yours this weekend." She slides her hand down a little further, stopping it short of where he so badly wants it to go.

Robert gulps and rolls onto his back. His voice cracks, "I want you so bad right now."

Jennifer looks at him with expectant eyes. "Are we going away this weekend?" Her fingers creep a downward.

Teetering on the edge between agony and ecstasy, he gasps, "Yes — oh yes, we will."

Jennifer brings her teasing hand up to his cheek and pulls his head close to give him a soft, wet kiss. He twists to face her. As they make out, she can feel how excited he is for her. Bending back, she looks him lovingly in the eyes. "Robert, we're going to have the best time this weekend, and I can't wait to take care of you in every way possible. I want you so bad right now, but it's best that we wait so tonight can be perfect."

This turn of events brings both of Robert's heads to the brink of explosion. One is left crazy with anticipation, while the other is shocked by how easily its more powerful counterpart controlled it. Frozen and wide-eyed, he stares at the wall.

Jennifer senses the need to press forward and close the deal. She gives him a big hug. "I love you so much. We'll leave right after you're done with work. I can't wait!"

As Robert's eyes move to their picture, he notices the photo with his college buddies is face down again. *What the fuck is going on?*

———

Bradford pulls the satin sheets aside and exposes Summer, asleep on her back and completely naked except for a tiny thong. He admires her body like it's a soft copper sculpture, and grins as he crawls backward to the foot of the bed. After positioning a hand on each side of her bottom, he surveys her hipbones and slender waist.

His mouth salivates as he draws closer to her — his morning wood matched by her morning dew. Like an all-you-can-eat buffet, he decides to first nibble on a few appetizers before diving into the main course. He gently kisses a circle around her bellybutton and then leisurely moves south. Navigating to the left, he continues down her inner thigh before shifting over to her right and pecking back up.

Summer's legs spread apart and holler like a downfield receiver without coverage, "I'm wide open!" As Bradford's lips press against her skin, moisture rises from the depths of her hot spring. He slides her intimate undergarment down an inch and uncovers the only non-laser-clean part of her pelvic girdle — a small square patch of short curly black hair that is the spitting image of Hitler's mustache. If that distraction wasn't enough, another requires serious concentration to ignore — the cursive tattoo to the left of her vaginal afro that lovingly reads, "Fuck you daddy!" Like it's Medusa, he averts his eyes. As he slowly removes her thong, his teasing makes her squirm. He skims his slippery tongue around the barren sides of her passageway three times before plunging inward and licking her open. *I need to make her cum.*

Bradford savors Summer's succulent flavor and feels as though he could graze the rest of the morning on her kibbles-n-bits. She moans as her hands clench the sheets. He finds the slightly metallic taste of her tuna-juice oddly enjoyable, and laps it up like a thirsty dog. As he slides a finger inside her and makes the come-hither motion, her body quivers. While gliding his other hand up to her breast and clamping onto her thimble-sized mammilla, he flicks his tongue across her love-button like a Komodo dragon trying to get to the center of a Tootsie Roll Pop.

Summer's hips rock, and her back arches to the point where she would see the wall behind her if she opened her eyes. A cry of pleasure and pain builds inside her throat, begging to be released. Then it happens — her pink opening flaps like the tiny end of a squeezed whoopee cushion as a fart-like expulsion smatters liquid across Bradford's chin. His body reflexively propels backwards — almost knocking him off the bed. In a daze, he wipes off the fluid with the back of his hand, and they identify the fresh red smudge at the same time.

Summer pulls Bradford by the hair back into the dining area. Her thighs grip his head like a suffocating vise as she commands, "Don't be a pussy! Finish me off!" Strangely turned on, he eagerly continues — dipping and stirring his index finger like a celery stick into her Clamato cocktail. After noticing that her bleached starfish is self-lubricating with sweat, he slips his pinky inside a place where nature most likely never intended it to go. His tongue picks up where it left off and doesn't stop until her screaming and convulsions subside.

—

As Robert walks down the long hallway to his office on Casual Friday, he passes several excited coworkers. Most don attire only appropriate for Sunday football, while he's dressed in his typical work clothes minus the tie. Close to half of the people are wearing Bills' Zubaz pants, which are loose-fitting cotton and zebra-striped in Buffalo's blue, white, and red colors. Most wear a game jersey of their favorite player, with the bulk being Kelly, Smith, or Thomas. *Why are they acting like there's no impending doom? Has the layoff situation somehow remained under the radar?*

Robert walks into his office and finds Dale wearing Zubaz clothing from head to toe. "Holy crap! They make Zubaz hats and shirts too?" Robert can't hold back his smile. "You look utterly ridiculous. Please tell me they don't make Zubaz thongs."

Dale laughs as he inspects Robert's corporate uniform. "Good morning to you too! Way to get into the spirit! Jesus, you've lived here long

THE SECOND QUARTER | 65

enough so you know how this works. Why don't you join the fold like the rest of us — especially before a huge game like Sunday's? You do remember that football's the only goddamn thing this town lives for, right?"

Robert sits down at his desk. "Yeah, yeah, I know. Well, I used to go to games and had some cool Bills gear from my college days, but it has since left my possession."

"How does something leave your possession?" Dale asks curiously. "Did your stuff get shipped to Africa along with four years' worth of prematurely printed 'Buffalo Bills Super Bowl Champs' t-shirts?"

Robert shakes his head. "No. Let's just say that someone found them in my closet one day and decided I didn't need them anymore."

"Now why would Jennifer do such a thing?"

"Great friggin' question. It's like a switch flipped one day, and she took over my life. Now — god knows why — I'm taking her to Niagara on the Lake this weekend!"

Dale cups his hand like he's holding a pool ball. "Dude, she's so got you by the testies."

"Yeah, no shit, right?" Robert glances at his desk, notices an envelope, and picks it up. "Hey, what is this? Fuck, tell me this isn't a pink slip."

"It's not. That's your Christmas bonus. Prepare to be blown away."

"Oh, thank god." Robert turns the envelope over as he inspects it. "Will it help me pay for this weekend?"

"Oh yeah, definitely." Dale chuckles. "Go ahead, open it."

Robert smiles and tears into it. "Okay, here we go." He pulls out a check and his expression goes south. "What the hell is this? A check for $12.73? Is this some kind of a joke?"

"Oh, wow. Yours is even less than mine. I wonder why that is?"

Robert reads aloud the fine print on the paper the check is attached to. "Your check has been prorated to $25 because you have been a full-time employee of Techspan for less than half a year. Have a very Merry Christmas." He tosses it back on his desk. "What the fuck? Less than half a year? Let's see — I worked here as a *non-paid* intern my last semester and was a temp through the summer. Then I was hired full time in September. Goddammit, that's a full year of work!"

Dale laughs. "Yep, you obviously haven't contributed enough to the company, so they cut your amount in half. I got fifty bucks, so don't be too jealous. Well, minus taxes and 401k it didn't amount to much either."

"My god, so because I only 'officially' worked here since September, they did that?" Robert scratches his forehead. "Oh, what's the difference? It's nothing either way, which I guess is my point. I can barely buy a decent dinner entree for that."

"Hey, look on the bright side," Dale says half-jokingly. "That may be more than any severance package we might receive."

"A shitty Christmas bonus on the day I get shit-canned." Robert shakes his head. "Thanks a lot, universe. For a Friday, you really suck."

As they begin to work, Sametta enters their doorway and knocks. He's wearing a white Bills jersey with a big blue number 11. "Can I come in?"

"Only if you're gonna tell us good news," Robert responds.

"Well, it's good news for me," Sametta claims. He walks in and puts his arms up like he just won a race. "Boys, I'm moving to the land of fruits and nuts — California! I've had enough of this shit."

"Oh, crap! Did they lay you off?"

"Nope. I told you yesterday I was going to take matters into my own hands."

"So you just up and quit?" Dale asks.

"Ahh — get them before they get you, right?" Robert adds.

"Yeah, it's partly that." Sametta smiles. "The other part is these rat-bastards wouldn't give me the raise I wanted, so I'm outta here. I just handed in my two weeks notice — I'm driving out west come the new year!"

Robert leans toward him in his chair. "Oh, man, I know you're crazy, but what did you ask for?"

"I've been putting in some outstanding work downstairs on the radar program, and so I feel like I deserve a significant raise and promotion. I told them I want $70k a year."

Robert and Dale look at each other and start laughing. "Oh my god, you're kidding, right?" Dale asks. "That's gotta be about double your current salary. Your boss's boss, who's been here about fifteen years by the way, probably makes $55k, maybe $60k tops a year. You're insane!"

Sametta chuckles. "Yeah, maybe so, but I figured either way I'd come out a winner. Either I get a huge raise or I move to friggin' sunny California, baby! I couldn't lose!"

"I'll admit, I'm jealous," Robert tells him. "I'd love to join you. Heck, this spectacular Christmas bonus might fill half my gas tank!"

"Yeah," Sametta laughs. "Seeing my check this morning was the cherry on top."

"You realize if there's a layoff, you probably would get a severance package of some sort," Dale states.

"What? Two weeks?" Sametta scoffs. "Fuck 'em. I go out on my own terms."

"Good for you," Robert says. "I'm gonna miss you, buddy. We've had some fun, but I can't say I blame ya. Before you leave, we're definitely gonna go out big-time for a proper sendoff."

"You know it!" Sametta shouts. "That would be great!"

"If I may selfishly switch the topic to those of us with our heads on the chopping block," Robert requests. "Have you heard anything more about what's going on?"

"I haven't heard anything, but I did just see Muhammad wandering the halls." Sametta hangs his head and shakes it. "He was mumbling to himself and slapping his forehead with a pamphlet. I think he's losing it."

"He's a manager," Robert adds. "That doesn't sound good *at all*."

"He's a new manager." Dale's eyes pop like he's seen a ghost. "Oh fuck, he's Janks's manager!"

"Are you shitting me?" Robert says in a panic. "No you're not, that's right! Sametta, what was the pamphlet?"

"Not exactly sure. It said 'How To' something. Looked official."

Robert pushes back his hair and holds it. "Listen to this, guys. Yesterday I heard a rumor that HR hands out a pamphlet that instructs new managers how to layoff people. Can you believe that?"

"No, that can't be," Dale states. "You can't learn how to fire someone like Janks from a pamphlet. You don't need tact — you need *protection!*"

"Yeah, like *heavily armed* protection," Robert adds.

Dale pulls on his ponytail. "Guys, I can't think about this anymore. Running through these scenarios is stressing me out."

"Everything will be fine," Sametta tells them half-convincingly. "Hang in there. Sorry, but I gotta go."

Robert stops him. "One last thing before you leave. I absolutely love that on the day you give notice, you wear a Scott Norwood jersey — the kicker who missed the field goal that would've won the Bills their first Super Bowl. What a kick in the nuts! Brilliant!"

Sametta bows as he walks backwards out the door. "I like to go out in style, boys. Now excuse me as I exit *wide-right.*"

—

Red and green Christmas lights snake around palm trees trunks and wait for dusk to illuminate. A rainbow of umbrellas shade customers as they sip their late morning espressos and lattes. In her favorite corner of the outside part of the cafe, Summer sits and digests the front page of the Wall Street Journal. After her initial investments in Dell and Starbucks paid off handsomely, she decided to postpone college and invest in herself by getting breast enhancement surgery.

A bead of sweat trickles down Summer's cleavage and into her tank-top. She grabs a piece of ice from her water and rubs it around her chest. While she does this, she senses lingering eyes and catches two mesmerized men. *Why are they looking at me? Do they think I'm some kind of circus freak?* She holds up her paper and opens it to hide from their view.

While reading an article about Netscape's recent IPO, Summer notices a familiar face out of the corner of her eye. She watches a handsome man her age walk into the cafe and hustles inside to catch him. Upon reaching him, Summer taps his shoulder. "Hey Johnny, how you doing?" She smiles brightly. "It's been years since we've seen each other."

"Oh, hey. Things were great at Florida State until my injury this season." Johnny whirls his arm around once and then throws a mock-pass. "I'm getting better though." He squints his eyes at her. "Um, who are you again? Did we hook up?"

She blushes as she looks at the floor. "No, I wish," she mumbles. "I mean, no. We uh, we went to high school together. I'm Summer."

"Summer?" He scratches his head. "Did you look different back then?"

"Yeah, I had short hair, um, played softball. I used to come to all your football games. You were the best."

"Oh, shit!" Johnny responds like he just got clocked in the head. "Pancakes! I remember you!" He points at her chest like it's some absurd balloon animal. "Yeah, you definitely look different."

"Yeah, um, I blossomed after graduation." Summer puts her arms out and wiggles her chest. "No more pancakes — only melons."

"Sorry, but all I see is that gawky nerd who *I let* strike me out once in Little League," he stabs. "A new set of cans doesn't change who you are."

"I didn't know the other boys would make fun of you, I swear." She interlocks her fingers as if she's going to pray. "I told you I was sorry about that a million times. Why won't you forgive me?"

"There's nothing to forgive." Johnny raises his chin sanctimoniously. "I was just being nice." He brushes her away. "You can go now."

Summer cries, "But let me buy you a coffee or something. It's the least I can do." Johnny turns his back to her without a response. She waits a few awkward seconds before returning to her table outside. *One of these days I'll win him over. I'll do whatever it takes.*

As Summer is finishing a newspaper article, she becomes distracted by a gorgeous woman jogging across the street. Men turn and watch her perfect baby-milkers rise and fall in what seems like slow-motion as she bounces down the sidewalk. *What the fuck? That's goddamn Bambi!* As Johnny pauses mid-sip to study the runner's form, Summer uses all her restraint to not throw her coffee mug at Bambi's skull.

A hand waves in Summer's line of sight, breaking her absorption. She shades her eyes while looking up and immediately makes recognition. Still wearing thick glasses and the same "Weird Al" Yankovic t-shirt from tenth-grade, the man says, "Hey Summer, what's going on?"

"Oh hey, George." She looks back down. "Just reading my paper."

"I hope you don't mind, um —" With his hands behind his back, he kicks the ground. "I wanted to tell you that I, um, I think you're beautiful. Remember that day after AP Chemistry when you were crying on my shoulder over that jerk you liked? I wanted to tell you back then."

"Okay, please stop." Summer's metal chair scrapes the ground as she rearranges her sitting position. "I knew you had a crush on me, but I figured it was because I won the science fair that year."

"No, that's not it." His face burns. "Um, can I get you another drink — or anything?"

She points at her half-full coffee. "I'm good."

George waves his hand again to get Summer's attention. "I got you this." He pulls a red tulip from behind his back and gives it to her. "It's almost as pretty as you are."

"I don't understand." She takes the flower and throws it on the ground. "Are you trying to make fun of me?"

"No, no. Not at all," he replies painfully.

"Did Johnny put you up to this?" She asks on the verge of tears.

"Uh, uh — no." George stammers.

Summer gets up from her chair and leaves.

—

Zabka stares impatiently at the clock on his desktop. After it changes to 2:52 PM he says to himself, "Fuck it. We're leaving." He grabs his bag for the weekend and speed-walks to Scott's office. Zabka enters to find Scott flipping through some papers. "Put those down. It's time to roll."

"Hey Zabka, just give me a second to finish this up," Scott replies.

"Jed's waiting for us in his truck," Zabka presses. "It would be rude to be late — and we don't want to be rude, do we?"

"Yeah, you're right. I'm sure this weekend will be refreshing, and I'll have plenty of energy to finish up these year-end reports on Monday."

"Sure, whatever you say." Zabka taps his watch. "Let's get out of here."

Scott grabs his extra-large suitcase from the corner of his office, and they walk outside to the parking lot. Zabka spots Jed's two door white Ford Bronco parked nearby in a designated visitors spot. Dirty exhaust fumes fill the air behind the vehicle as Jed sleeps in the driver's seat.

Zabka knocks on the passenger side window and opens the door. "Jed, wake up! It's go time!"

Without opening his eyes, Jed lifts the beer resting between his legs and takes a swig. "You guys are a little early, but I'm flexible."

Zabka pulls the passenger seat forward for Scott and motions to him. "Get in the back." After they're all aboard, Zabka slams his door shut.

Jed opens his eyes. "Take it easy boys." He looks in the rearview mirror and notices the dry blood encrusted paw scratch on Scott's cheek. "Hey, what the hell happened to you?"

Before Scott can respond, Zabka jumps in, "I wish there was a better answer, but he was attacked by his cats last night. The damn things figured out he was leaving 'em for a few days."

Jed scoffs, "So that story sucks. Come up with something better while we're on the road." He puts the Bronco in reverse, backs up, and flies out of the parking lot. "Grab a beer for yourselves. And while you're at it, grab me one too, but make mine a lite. I'm driving and have to be the responsible one in this crew."

Zabka opens the lid of the cooler that is on the armrest next to him and fishes through the ice for beers. "Okay, here's a Genny for Scott. And here's a Genny for me." He puts the beers on his lap and searches down to the bottom. "Hey Jed, I don't see any lite beer in here."

"That's weird." Jed pauses to think for a second. "Oh that's right, I don't drink lite beer because I have testicles. Gimme a Genny too."

Zabka laughs and cracks open a can for Jed. "Here you go." He then turns around to hand a beer to Scott in the backseat.

Scott puts his hands up as if the police had just told him to. "I'm okay. I need to continue reading about Buffalo history in my encyclopedia."

Annoyed, Zabka gestures at Jed with his eyes and head, and silently mouths to Scott, "Drink it."

"So you're a teetotaling history professor that gets torn-up by kitty cats?" Jed asks. "Do I have that straight? Or are there additional pussy-repellent facts about yourself that I should know about?"

"Gimme that darn beer," Scott steams. Zabka smirks, winks, and tosses the can back. Scott catches and opens it. "Cheers, fellas. Let's have a most pleasurable time this weekend."

All three of them put their cans together and yell, "Cheers!" as they merge onto the freeway heading south.

After chugging his beer, Zabka crushes the can and throws it over his shoulder. It whizzes past Scott's head and ricochets off the back window. "One down!" Zabka shouts as he opens the cooler to replenish. "Hey Jed, how many cases of beer did you get?"

"I got five or something," Jed replies. "I figure we need at least a case for the drive, another case for breakfast and late night cravings, and then a few for the game."

"Yeah, that sounds reasonable," Zabka confirms. "Plus we can always get more if we need to."

"God bless America!" Jed shouts.

After a healthy gulp, Zabka demands, "Scott, tell us about the tickets you got for the game."

Scott stumbles, "Well, I um, I was thinking —"

"They better be good." Jed bounces in his seat. "You guys really screwed the pooch yesterday, so my expectations are high this weekend."

"Hey, this is my boss you're talking about. He's got *everything* under control." Zabka shifts around to face Scott. "Go ahead, tell him how you got us tickets to the sold out game. It's cool, you can brag about it."

Scott's face turns as red as it did when as a twelve-year-old he was caught in a closet at the lake cabin watching his college-bound cousin take off her bikini. As Zabka's eyes burn holes into Scott's skull, he works to compose himself, now aware of how screwed he is. While delivering an off-the-cuff response, the distinct aroma of bullshit floats from his mouth, "Sorry, but this is a little embarrassing. Not to boast, but I have some connections in the Bills organization and was able to land us some pretty cool seats. I think you'll like them."

"See! What did I tell you, Jed?! This is gonna be an epic weekend! Only thing left now is to go get laid! Let's get some drunk bitches!!"

As Jed and Zabka chant, "Laid! Laid!" over and over, Scott wishes he could shrink into a cocoon between the seats. With the weekend just beginning, he wonders if he can possibly unfuck his fucked-up situation.

———

With the setting sun at their backs, the foursome follows their shadows across the tarmac of Miami's Opa-Locka Executive Airport. The length of their bodies projecting across ground exhibits the sharp contrast between Bradford and Summer's heights. A jet with a polished black exterior and sparkling gold trim windows waits for them. The impression that Arab royalty might be boarding dissolves upon noticing the registration identifier of "10INCOX" on the tail-wing. The co-captains and leggy flight attendant welcome the sharply dressed passengers aboard as they finish climbing the plane's stairs.

Juan Carlos gestures at the four chairs surrounding a stylish oak table. "Pick whichever one you like, Bambi." They sit, strap on their seat belts, and prepare for take-off.

Once at cruising altitude, the flight attendant serves champagne and sets the bottle in a bucket of ice on the table. Bradford raises his glass in the air and the rest follow suit. "Here's to a Dolphin's victory and making more of that," he sings in tune with The O'Jays song, "money, money, money, mun-nay!" They clink glasses and take a sip.

Bambi gulps her drink down like a shot. "I love that bubble juice!" She brushes the excess from her lips and chin with the back of her hand. "So I keep hearing about all this money we're gonna make. Can someone explain how?"

Bradford answers, "Bambi, what we sell gives men what they want to have the most. You may think it's fortune, power, love, but —" Bambi raises her hand. "This isn't a trivia contest. Let me continue."

Bambi puts her hand down. "Oh sorry, I was just gonna guess that all men wanna have a big fat dick. But go on."

Bradford points at her like she's a winner. "Correct! You got it!"

"Great! What do I win?!"

"You win the opportunity to promote and sell our Huge Member male enhancement products! The more you sell, the more money we make. Summer, tell her how it works."

"You and I are the eye candy." Summer pushes her boobs together. "The bait and hook so to speak. While promoting, we make the guys feel desired, but shall we say, *inadequate* to get with us. We sell them the product that gets them what they want. Get it?"

"Sure, I get it," Bambi replies. "You sell them huge cocks to replace their puny wieners."

"No, you imbecile! You can't sell someone a new dick. That's physically impossible! We sell them special growth pills and cream!" Summer thinks, *I can't believe guys buy into this crap. If they do, Bambi surely will.*

The others watch Bambi as she imagines the magic beans in *Jack and the Beanstalk* are real — and, just as she wants, she projects amazement.

Summer begins to explain, "There's a scale that ranges from one to five. Our products will grow you one to two levels. One is 'Where is it?' Two is 'Close but no cigar.' Three is 'That'll do the trick.' Four is 'Intimidating.' And five is 'Oh, hell no!' That's how it works."

Bambi's world mutes as she peers through the window at a cloud formation, lost in her thoughts.

Summer whispers to Bradford, "Look at her. I bet she hears things that no one else does."

"I should be afraid to ask, but I wonder what?" Bradford replies.

As Bambi stares at a puffy white mass, another plane's contrail grows and penetrates the cloud brain. *Looks like a mind-fuck. How appropriate.*

—

The sound of Robert's rapidly tapping foot on the tile floor fills the office. Sweat coats his forehead as the latest revisions of his code compile.

"Hey, Robert," Dale says. "I understand you're a little freaked out, but I can't concentrate with you making that noise."

Robert's foot stops. "I'm sorry, but I'm so close. If this works, I should be good with all the changes Dr. Cramps wanted. I'm trying to not even think about the other thing."

The clock on Dale's monitor displays 4:59 PM. "So, here's the good news. I've always heard that if you don't get a call by 5 o'clock, you're in the clear. I think it's safe to say we can relax on the whole layoff thing."

Robert closes his eyes and breathes a sigh of relief. As he does, the phone on his desk shakes from a loud, RRRINNNGGG!

In a panic, Robert pushes away from the sound and rolls backwards in his chair.

—

At the tail-end of dusk, the Massena crew cuts through Syracuse on Interstate 81, and the sparkle of city lights takes over the surrounding horizon. What appears to be an illuminated white cloud hanging low above the street catches Scott's eye and he points at it. The beginning stages of intoxication have taken over and increased the volume of his voice. "You know what that is!? That's the Carrier Dome! Syracuse University built it in 1975 and both the football team and basketball team play there. It's pretty awesome from what I've seen on TV."

"Oh yeah, well is it as awesome as the Bruce Dome?" Jed asks.

"Um, I'm not familiar with the Bruce Dome. What's that?"

"We're going to the Bruce Dome. How can you not know it?"

Zabka softly chuckles. "Yeah Scott, you mean that's not in your history book? Everyone knows about the Bruce Dome."

Scott pages through his book like a teenage boy looking for the nudie pictures in a Playboy. "No, it's not in here. Come on, tell me what it is."

"Well Jed, since you're the one who brought it up, I'll let you explain."

"I'd be happy to. The Bruce Dome, ya see, well that's where the Buffalo Bills play. I assure you it makes the Carrier Dome look like an igloo made of frozen blocks of polar bear feces."

Scott sips his beer. "You sure? I've never heard of the Bruce Dome."

"Don't question me. If there's one thing I know about, it's domes."

Zabka slaps Jed on the back of his skull. "You shit-head! If there's one thing you *don't* know about, it's how to drive. You missed the exit for the 90 to get to the Buffalo! Take the next exit and turn around."

"Hey, there's something I've been wondering." Scott inquires, "Why do you say, '*the* Buffalo'?"

"Why do we say, '*the* Buffalo'?" Zabka asks like an eight-year-old smart-ass. "We say, '*the* 90' and '*the* Buffalo Bills.' Why *wouldn't* we say, '*the* Buffalo?' You tell me, Encyclopedia Doo-Doo Brown."

"Flippin'-A, I can't have these conversations with you. It's a no win situation." Scott shakes his head. "I'm hungry. Can we stop at *the* Burger King? I really need some BK."

"I'm pretty sure you don't really *need* it, Scott." Zabka munches on an invisible hamburger. "But alright. Plus, I gotta take a wicked piss."

"Do you think there's a Burger King on the Erie Canal?" Scott asks. "The canal will kinda parallel our route and checking it out totally fits in with our trip. Did you know the canal made the Buffalo a major trade hub as America expanded west? It was completed way back in 1825 and would be cool to see. This way we could kill two birds with one pit stop."

Zabka turns around and tells Scott. "Burger King mixed with a history lesson!? Are you fucking kidding me? Here's your two birds." He flips Scott off with both hands. "We're not going to some mythical Burger King on the Erie Canal. We're gonna find the next fast-food rest-stop on the freeway and then get our asses to the Buffalo. Knowing Bob, he's probably already at The Base waiting for us."

"Okay, okay. As long as we eat, that's the most important thing. I don't fare well without food."

"Oh no, what tragedy will strike you? You'll lose a few pounds?"

"I don't know, but what does happen is I get light-headed."

"Don't you worry about that grumbling stomach of yours." Zabka reaches back and pats Scott's belly. "Soon enough it will be enjoying double cheeseburgers. In the meantime, you need to understand the Bills rivalry with the Dolphins. I don't want you embarrassing me this weekend, so listen up."

"Okay, teach me, football master."

"I like the sound of that — call me that anytime." Zabka fetches a fresh beer from the cooler. "Basically, the rivalry goes like this. Each season, Buffalo and Miami play each other twice because they are in the same division — the AFC East. When you're in the same division, rivalries often develop naturally. Back in the '70s, the Bills sucked and the Dolphins were great. If you can believe it, we lost every single game against them that decade. That's twenty fucking losses in a row! When we finally beat them in 1980, the Bills fans stormed our field, tore down the goalposts, and ran around the turf with the broken pieces."

Jed interjects, "Can I stop you for a second?"

"Yeah, I guess. What's so important?"

"I just saw a sign and it reminded me of something. What's a woman's favorite group of lakes?"

"I feel like I should know this." Scott scratches his head. "But I don't."

"Yeah, me either." Zabka tells Jed, "Just give us the answer."

"A woman's favorite lakes are —" Jed puts up his hand and wiggles his digits. "The Finger Lakes. Get it?"

Zabka laughs. "Real mature joke, buddy." He slaps Jed's palm down. "So now you think you're a comedian, huh?!"

"I'll be here all weekend!"

"Sorry, but I don't get it," Scott tells them.

"Why am I not surprised?" Zabka shakes his head. "So back to what I was saying. In '83, Dan Marino began playing quarterback for the Dolphins, and the Bills drafted our quarterback, Jim Kelly. It's ironic now, but back then Jim didn't want to play for Buffalo because he hated cold weather. Instead he went and played for the USFL in Houston. After that league folded in '86, he ended up back in the Buffalo. Soon after, both teams improved and the rivalry with Miami intensified. From '88 through now, we've been fighting them for the divisional championship and have won five times."

Jed chimes in, "And in '85 they made the Dome that Bruce built."

"Thank you, guys," Scott says with sincerity. "I feel much better prepared for this weekend."

"I hate to break it to ya, but nothing can prepare you for the weekend we're about to have." Zabka laughs. "If you know anyone with a spare liver, you should call dibs on it before we get there."

———

Robert's frozen stare fixates on his phone as it rings for the third time. Nervously, he asks, "What should I do?"

"Fuck, I don't know." Dale shrugs his shoulders, as the phone's ring seems to get louder. "I guess you better pick it up."

Robert gingerly reaches for the receiver like he's going to pet a dog that may well bite him. He slouches in his chair. "Hi, um, this is Robert."

The person on the phone says, "Hey, it's five o-clock — I wanted to check on your ETA." After initial confusion, he recognizes Jennifer's voice and puts his hand on his chest. "You think you'll be leaving soon?"

"I'm so glad it's you." Robert gives Dale a thumbs-up. "I'm trying to wrap things up here." He cups his mouth and lowers his voice. "I need to tell you something. My friggin' boss dropped a bomb on me yesterday. She added new requirements that have to be completed for a very important demo on Monday. If my office window wasn't so miniscule, I would've thrown her out. Also I'm stressed from —"

"Stop right there. Do not — *do not* tell me this is going to ruin our weekend plans. This is very important to me — I mean us."

Robert straightens out of his slump. "Pardon me, but I'm under a lot of pressure here and *really* don't need this from you." He takes a breath before continuing, "I've been working my ass off for the past two days, and I'm close to being finished. I just need to test some stuff and make sure it's working properly. Is that okay with you? This is my job I'm talking about, you know. The one that's gonna *pay* for this weekend."

"Yeah, okay, calm down. Don't take things out on me."

"Pack your stuff, and I'll call you within an hour. Worse comes to worse, I'll work all night to finish this — if Cramps let's me — and we'll leave in the morning. Does that work for you?"

Jennifer's pouting transmits through the phone wires. "Well, um, I'd really like to go tonight, ya know? I, um, I've been feeling extra frisky after this morning. Remember that?"

Robert whisper-yells, "No, Jennifer, I don't remember that. It completely slipped my mind that on my way to work I had a hard-on that could cut diamonds. It took the sight of Dale to finally bring down my soldier's salute."

Dale chuckles and quietly says, "Glad I could help."

"I don't really need all the details," Jennifer replies. "But I'd like you to finish soon, so we can go. Call me in a little bit. If we can't hit the road tonight, we'll stay at my place."

"Whatever, I need to get back to work. Thanks again for the blue-balls. Bye." Robert hangs up the phone. "Dale, can you believe this? I'm catching shit from all sides."

"First I gotta ask, are your balls a professional shade of blue? Would Dr. Cramps approve?"

Robert laughs. "Oh man, they're the darkest of blue."

"Anyway, after hearing your call, I need to tell you something." Dale faces Robert like he's about to unveil a secret. "Women want what women want, and sometimes, we're just a roadblock. They'll either gently move us aside or, when that doesn't work, slam on the accelerator and bust through. Either way, they're getting what they want on the other side. It's your choice whether to comply or end up as collateral damage."

"But I feel all these expectations and pressure — it's difficult," Robert moans. "To the point where I think I'm gonna lose it."

"Take a few deep breaths and relax. Oh, here's a valuable side tip — never tell an angry woman to relax. Anyway, you'll be fine."

They fall silent while Robert closes his eyes and slows his breathing. Calmness sets in temporarily, until a faint noise from down the hall perks-up his ears. Like invisible hands are grabbing Robert and Dale's earlobes, their heads are pulled toward their open office door.

Robert whispers, "Fuck, that's her. I think everyone else is gone."

"Shit. It feels like *The Terminator* is speed-walking here to slaughter us."

"That mini-German robot frightens me more than any machine from the future. Dale, our judgment day is now."

The sound of clomping wooden heels gets louder until it stops. Dr. Cramps swivels and marches into their office. "Zis is it. Zee time to show me what you've done is now."

"Would you like to take a look at the new splash screen?" Dale asks. "The Bill's royal blue was a good call. It looks ultra-professional."

"Yes, I know," Dr. Cramps replies. "Zat's because I gave it to you. I'll assess your work after I see Robert's. My expectations are high."

Robert warns her, "I'll show you, but first I need to let you know that I spent the last three hours writing a personalization engine to use with the other foundational changes I made. I just compiled it, but haven't tested it yet." Dr. Cramps crosses her arms and nods for him to proceed. He says a silent prayer before showing off the new functionality. To his surprise, everything works flawlessly through his demo. "Well, there it is. What do you think?"

"Nice work. I'm actually impressed wiz zis." She turns to Dale. "Now, it's your turn. Let's see if you can match Robert's high standards."

Robert grins. "I'm sure the splash screen he's about to show you is the best you've ever seen. I know Dale isn't one to be a *roadblock*."

"Good to know, because more work is on its way," she informs them. "We just got word zat additional budget has been approved."

"That's awesome!" Robert shouts a little too loudly. "And how's the radar program?"

She realizes he had heard the rumors. "Zey will be fine for a while. I gotta hand it to Senator D'Amato, he saved the day. He's a true ally."

—

The pilot's voice bellows from the overhead speaker, "Please buckle your seat belts. We're about to begin our descent into Buffalo and will be landing shortly. The current temperature is a steamy 12 degrees."

A light frost covers the passenger windows, diffracting pinpoints of orange on the black ground below. The pink and green neon lights in South Beach have been left far behind. In the distance, white lights outline the airport's runway and flicker in the landing direction for guidance. The mechanical sound of the plane's wheels deploying alerts the four passengers that landing is imminent.

Meanwhile on the street below, Robert drives along a barren edge of the airport guarded by barbed-wire fence. Looking up, he sees a black jet on its landing approach over the neighboring warehouses. If it weren't for the difference in elevation, the two would be on a collision course. As he passes underneath the jet, something hits the right side of his car and jolts him. He glances in the direction of the sound and sees what appears to be a blue slushy with a chocolate chunk streaking across the passenger window. "What the fuck was that?!" His eyes follow the jet. "Are you fucking kidding me?!"

A strong gust of wind tilts the jet to one side just before its wheels slam onto the slick blacktop. As the plane's wing flaps go up and speed diminishes, the passengers release their grips from their armrests.

Bradford announces to the cabin, "We made it! Not smoothly, but we made it."

"Do we need to get out our passports now?" Bambi questions.

"Juan Carlos, I'm gonna let you handle this one."

Juan Carlos's facial expression makes him appear like he's trapped in an elevator with a stranger suffering from rambunctious flatulence. "Bambi, I told you several times that we're not leaving the country — we're in Buffalo, New York. We're still in the United States."

"How come when I look out there it feels like another country?" Bambi points outside. "Maybe even another planet. Like the planet Turkey."

"Can we please get rid of her?" Summer begs. "I'm sure the nearest dump would reject her, so let's just toss her on the side of the road."

Bradford attempts to contain the two cats. "Now, now, let's remember why we're here. It's not only for pleasure, but also for business. So we're gonna have to find a way to make this work." As they taxi to a stop, he tells the flight attendant, "Get the ladies their gifts."

The flight attendant takes two long, brown fur coats from the closet and hands them to the men so they can assist. As the girls slip into their presents, Summer moans like she does when Bradford slips his tongue into her. She rubs her hands through the fur. "I really like the feel of this. Great selection."

"Bambi, what do you think? Pretty nice, right?" Juan Carlos asks.

Bambi gushes, "I love it. Is this a down coat?"

"You mean like goose feathers in a pillow? No, this is a mink coat. We spare no expense."

She eases up close to him. "No, I mean —" She clutches his arm and whispers in his ear, "Is this a *down* coat?" She gently bites her lip. "Because while I'm in it, I can see myself going *down* on you."

Juan Carlos smiles like St. Peter just allowed him to enter the pearly gates, as he dreams of his peter entering her pearly smile. The flight attendant brings him back to earth as she announces, "We're all set to deplane. Your limo has arrived." The flight attendant helps the men into their suit jackets before leaving.

The pilots stand near the exit to see them off. As they leave the plane, one of the pilots says to Bradford, "I think I nailed a car this time."

Bradford smiles like he just hit a double bull's-eye in darts. "Are you kidding me?! That's amazing! What a great way to start the weekend. We are gonna dominate this piece-of-shit town!"

———

Robert enters his apartment to find Jennifer sitting Indian style on his living room couch and both of their suitcases on the floor.

Jennifer jumps up. "Welcome home, honey! I packed for you, so we're all set to hit the road."

"That's great, but do you mind if I sit down for a second? I've had one hell of a day."

"Sure, but just for a second." She playfully slaps his butt a few times. "Niagara on the Lake isn't gonna wait all night for us."

"Oh, I think it will." Robert sits down on the couch with her. "Aren't you gonna ask me about my day?"

Jennifer replies with a long face, "Yes, of course I am. I was just about to — please share."

"Well, first off, my buddy Sametta quit today and is moving to California. He's one of my few local friends, so I'm pretty bummed." Robert frowns. "There's also what we talked about on the phone with the requirements changes, which stressed me out all day. In addition, budgets were almost cut, so I didn't know if I'd have a job come Monday."

"Oh my god," Jennifer exclaims. "Is everything okay?"

"Yeah, things came together at the last minute, so everyone's fine."

She sighs and gives him a hug. "Thank goodness."

"Then on my way home — and you're not gonna believe this." He uses his hands to simulate the intersecting paths. "As I was driving past the airport, this goddamn private jet empties its fuckin' toilet onto my car! Some is still frozen on the side too!"

"God, that's really messed up! I'm so sorry."

"Yeah it is. Oh, I almost forgot — I received my Christmas bonus today. Wanna take a wild guess at how much it is?"

"That actually sounds like good news! Sure, I'll guess." She thinks for a moment. "Will it pay for our weekend!? Is it like $500?"

Robert reaches into his pocket, pulls out the crumpled check, and hands it to her. Jennifer unfolds it. "What is this? $12.73?"

"Congratulations, you're officially dating a sugar-daddy."

Jennifer laughs. "It's okay. For your first job, you still have an acceptable salary. It's only upwards from here."

"Yeah, I suppose, but it still kinda seems insulting to me. I guess it's better than nothing — not much better though."

Jennifer looks at her watch. "We do need to get going kinda soon, but while we're here —" Jennifer grabs his hands. "I'd like to talk to you about something for a minute, okay?"

Robert laughs nervously. "Do I have a choice?"

She raises her eyebrows. "No, but don't worry, it's a light subject — like cotton candy." She squeezes his hand. "I'm very excited."

Robert gulps. "Okay, let's hear it then."

"So here it is — I put a lot of thought into this. So we've been dating almost six months — Oh gosh, I'm just gonna come out and say it." She wiggles his hand with hers. "We're gonna work on moving into Phase 2 of our relationship." Jennifer's face becomes one huge, over-the-top smile. "Doesn't that sound awesome!?"

"Um, yeah?" Robert feels his nuts scurry up and inwards for safety. "Sorry, but am I supposed to know what Phase 2 is?"

"Well, I kinda feel like you should already be aware, but I can explain." With the same rehearsed confidence she uses in mock trial during closing arguments, Jennifer continues, "Phase 2 is *us* taking it to the next level as a couple. This is an important next step. I've seen the changes you've made and it gives me faith that we can go there. Not to bring up any of those incidents again — well, it's just — I know now you're not the same person you were back then. You've improved so much, *and* you can be even better."

For a moment, their minds drift back to mishaps surrounding the Ball. Robert, after being over-served at the bar, noticed Jennifer huddling up with her friends to take pictures. He thought it would be funny to creep up behind the group and pop into their photo just before it was snapped. At that moment he would make a V-sign with his fingers, and wag his tongue between them. After the photo was taken, he'd sneak away and wait for the next opportunity.

Jennifer's memory replays the girl's night a week after the Ball. Everyone went to Faige's place for wine and to share their newly developed photos. As they looked through Faige's, the gruesome aftermath of Robert's photo-bombing skills was exposed. Jennifer was completely mortified and fell into shock. She excused herself and cried in the bathroom in private.

Robert thinks about the fight they had after she saw his handiwork. He didn't think that his natural inclination to be goofy would be something that could break them apart. At that moment, he knew he'd have a continual internal battle to keep his true self in-check.

Robert breaks the silence. "Thanks for acknowledging my progress, but really it's been no big deal. I've done it for you."

Jennifer leans in and kisses him. "I want you to know that it means the world to me to know that I am that special to you. We can have some more fluffy conversations about Phase 2 this weekend, but ultimately it boils down to the next level of dedication, honesty, and trust."

"Sounds like some fun topics to tackle this weekend."

"I agree." Jennifer claps her hands together. "And with that, let's get going. We just need to make one quick stop on the way. I have to give my part of a final group project to Faige. She lives near the South Campus."

——

Anyone traveling west on Interstate 90 from most parts of New York State will eventually be stopped by Exit 50 — a barrier that must be crossed to reach Buffalo and its surrounding suburbs. Some look at the freeway toll as just another way for the state to take beer money from their wallet, while more perverted individuals see the toll as an amusement park entrance fee to the land of mustache rides and Tilt-A-Cowgirl thrills. However, don't expect your money back when you wake up next to a girl who's a cow with a mustache.

Jed slows their Bronco as they come to a stop in the toll line. Scott surveys the vehicle and asks, "Hey, you guys think that maybe we shouldn't stop at a toll booth in a car that has empty beer cans everywhere?"

Zabka surveys the garbage pile around Scott. "Yeah, I suppose you're right for once. Start being responsible and clean up that shit, pronto." Jed and Zabka toss back the crushed beer cans they find at their feet.

Scott gathers the rubbish with his arms and shoves it over the back of his seat. After consolidating everything in the rear, he hides their contraband with a dirty blanket. "All clear back here," Scott proudly tells them. "Just in time too — we're almost to the toll." He scoots up and leans on the cooler between the two front seats. "Hey, did you guys know that I-90 is the longest interstate in the US? From Boston to Seattle, it's over three-thousand miles long."

"Oh really?" Jed replies. "Extremely valuable info, Scott. Does it take us to the bar?"

"Bar? I don't know. Which bar?"

"Third Base, baby!" Zabka shouts. "That's where we're going! And no, the 90 doesn't take us to the Base, so nobody gives a shit about your random fact babble."

Jed pulls up to the tollbooth, rolls down his window, and hands the attendant his toll ticket. "Honey, how do I get to Third Base from here?"

The attendant detects an odor of stale beer and meat-farts. "Sir, have you been drinking?"

Jed covers his mouth. "Sorry, ma'am, it's embarrassing. I realize I have pretty bad breath, but do you have to rub it in?"

Zabka slants across in her direction. "Yeah, he actually suffers from a super rare case of expialidocious halitosis. Imagine what it's like for us to have to go on a road trip with him. You're lucky you only have to deal with him for one transaction."

"My apologies," she replies. "It's $6.85 for the toll, and sorry, I don't know where Third Base is."

Jed hands her seven crumpled dollars. "Well, you've been a lot of help with directions and improving my self-esteem. I really appreciate it." She reaches out to give him a few coins. "Keep the change and have a great night. Oh, and by the way, third base is in your pants." The tires spin as he presses hard on the accelerator. Upon catching the pavement, their vehicle jumps forward.

"Don't worry about it," Zabka tells Jed. "I obviously know how to get to the Base. Just follow the 290 up here and get off on Main Street."

"Hey, Zabka," Scott yells from the back. "We're going to meet your friend Bob, but I know nothing about him. What's he like?"

Jed throws out, "Yeah, tell 'em about this character. An entertaining story — something I haven't heard yet."

"I love to tell stories," Zabka says with a shit-eating grin. "First off, Bob and I were housemates for a couple of years in college — back when we used to drink like fish. Anyway, he's a great guy and a lot of fun. His choices of women on-the-other-hand, are questionable at best. So let's start there."

"This sounds good," Jed tells them. "But I need a fresh beer to go along with story time."

Zabka grabs the last two beers out of the cooler and gives one to Jed. After a sip, Zabka begins his tale, "I'm gonna tell you about Tammi — I think that was her name? Anyway, she was a girl Bob hooked up with at a Buff State party after drinkin' too much Wild Turkey. She had one of the most bizarre tramp-stamps I've ever heard of."

"Was it a tattoo of a midget stripper?" Jed asks.

"Are you kidding? A midget stripper? No one has that. But get this bizarre shit — on her lower back was a tattoo of a grizzly bear with a clown head fucking a unicorn under a rainbow."

"If I may put on my psychologist hat for a second. I think she *might* have a few mental issues."

"Ya think?!"

Scott leans forward between them. "Hey, so you said it's a grizzly bear with a clown head, right? But how do you know it's not a clown in a grizzly bear suit? That would make a lot more sense."

"Would it really?!" Zabka shouts. "You guys are unbelievable. There are so many disturbing layers with that tattoo, I don't even know where to begin."

Jed pushes for more. "Okay, so what else happened?"

Zabka proceeds. "So come to find out, she's a screamer — and not like a hot, moaning type of screamer. She's more of a, I'm-getting-eaten-by-piranhas-type of screamer. Oh, and we were crashing at a friend's, and they were not happy at all. The noises I heard her making sounded like a felony." He shakes his head and puts his hands over his ears. "I kinda wish I could un-hear it, because sometimes I have horrific nightmares. But then there are other times that I wake up with a massive hard-on." Jed raises an eyebrow and Zabka adds, "Yeah I know, it's fucked-up."

"Hang on," Scott tells them. "Does this mean Bob put his P in her V?"

"What? Yeah, of course. He banged her!"

"Cool! Tell me more."

"It would be my pleasure. So after they completed the deed, she wouldn't leave. She said she'd, 'bite Bob's nuts off' if they didn't cuddle. All night he said he couldn't sleep — he had terror sweats. Once the sun came up, he told her he had to drive home and asked her if she wanted a ride. Her response to his kind gesture was to tell him to 'fuck-off'."

"Is that it?" Jed asks. "Seems like an average Tuesday night for me back in junior college."

"No, that's not the end of it," Zabka replies. "About five minutes after I heard her slam the bedroom door, I was getting hungry. So I walked downstairs to the kitchen, and who do ya think I found there? With her pants off making pancakes and hotdogs like an insane chef?!"

With his hand up, Scott shouts, "I know! I know! Crazy-sex-screaming, clown-in-a-bear-suit-tattoo chick?!"

"Bingo! I told her to 'get-the-fuck-out,' but she refused. So I went and grabbed Bob."

"And did Bob handle things?"

"Yep — after I threatened to kick his ass. That's when she told him she loved him about ten times. Eventually he got her to leave — well, at least for that day."

"Meaning she came back?" Jed asks.

Zabka laughs. "Remember, we weren't at our house, so she didn't actually know where Bob lived. That's where the story gets really interesting, but I'll leave it for another time. Third Base is on my mind!"

Scott says with excitement, "Maybe some crazy stuff like that will happen this weekend?!"

Zabka grips an imaginary sphere in his hand and shakes it several times. He stops and looks down at it. "The magic 8-ball tells us, 'IT IS CERTAIN'."

—

A black limousine with miniature Miami Dolphin flags on its two front corners, exits I-290 onto Main Street and heads west. A limo driving around Buffalo in the winter will always attract some attention, but one with head of state looking flags colored teal and orange will attract everyone. Bradford sits at the front with his back to the driver, while the others are on the side seat facing the mini-bar. They drive through a neighborhood filled with small, antiquated houses. Hints of a metropolis are nowhere to be seen.

Bradford turns his head to the driver. "Hey Julio, are we going the right way?"

"Yes sir, um, I'm just taking you the scenic route. Giving you a feel for the city."

"That's great, but we've seen more than enough of this crap. We had a long flight and want to get to our hotel downtown ASAP."

"Understood, Mr. Threadgold. I'll get you there as quickly as I can." As Julio accelerates aggressively, Bradford slides off his seat to the floor.

The group laughs as Bradford picks himself up. "Jesus Christ, don't go overboard! Get us there in one piece!"

"So sorry, sir. We had the car completely detailed for your arrival and I know those seats are slick. That won't happen again."

"It better not or you're fired. Now put on some music." Bradford turns to the girls. "Can I interest you in some champagne?"

"Hell yeah! I've been waiting for you to ask!" Summer yells.

"You know it! Pop that cork!" Bambi shouts.

Julio cranks the radio and everyone sways their arms from side to side as they sing the chorus of "Hip Hop Hooray."

Bradford cries out, "We're gonna destroy those Bills and market the shit out of our products!!"

Bambi requests, "Hey! Can I ask a stupid question?"

Summer jabs, "Those are the only types of questions you ask!"

Bambi looks at Summer like she just gave her the sweetest compliment. "Thanks, Summer! My question is this — what are the Bills? Is it something I gotta pay?"

"No, dummy! That's the Buffalo football team we're playing on Sunday!"

"Yeah, I know that! But what's a Bill?"

Summer sneers. "That's obvious, a Bill is — um, a Bill is —"

Bradford interjects, "A Bill is a slimy turd in a helmet. I don't give a damn what a Bill is, I just know that Jim Kelly and the rest of those pussies are gonna get physically and mentally abused on Sunday!"

As if it's been rehearsed, Juan Carlos and Summer yell, "YEAH!!"

Bambi, still searching for clarity, asks, "Let me make sure I got this all figured out. A Bill is a slimy turd in a helmet and a Dolphin is a fish?"

Summer rolls her eyes. "Oh god, she really is a special kind of stupid."

With the calmness of a parent potty-training their child, Juan Carlos says, "Bambi, remember when we saw the dolphins jumping in the ocean?" She nods her head yes. "I explained to you then that dolphins are mammals, not fish. Do you think you can remember that from now on?"

Bambi nods with assurance. "I won't forget now, I promise. I just need to ask one more thing —"

As the end of "Hip Hop Hooray" fades out, high-pitched dolphin noises blare through the speakers and someone imitating Sam Kinison screams, "Oh! Oh!! OOOOH!!! Squish the fish! Squish the fiiiiiiish! Oh! OOOH!!!!" Everyone looks at each other with confusion.

A white Ford Bronco drives up beside them from behind and honks madly. They turn and find they're on the receiving end of a visual and verbal assault. From the Bronco, Zabka dishes out double-barreled fuck-you-fingers and yells, "Screw you, Miami!! Squish the fish!!" While at the same time, Scott wedges his large, hairy, pale ass out the window and moons them. As verbal insults are fired, Scott moves his butt-cheeks in sync so it looks like his ass is shouting the words. Then, to the horror of animal-toy rights activists everywhere, Scott inserts a miniature rubber dolphin, tail first into his man-gina hole.

Zabka points two middle-fingers at Scott's creative expression and yells, "Hey, look at what your mom showed us! Your Dolphins are gonna get ass-fucked in the ass too! Squish the fishes, bitches!!"

Bambi points at the hecklers and cries out, "See! See! I was right! Everyone knows they're fish!!!"

Bradford yells, "Enough of this bullshit!" He turns to Julio and commands, "Run that mother fucker off the road!"

—

While Robert drives south on Bailey Avenue towards the Main Street intersection, a large gust of snow temporarily hides the stoplight from view. He slows to a stop and puts on the car's right turn signal. "Hey, Third Base is right around the corner," he informs Jennifer. "Maybe we could stop in for a quick beer? I miss that place."

Jennifer looks at him like he just said the Supreme Court isn't supreme. "Your old college bar? Yeah, I don't think so."

He replies with his tail between his legs, "Oh, okay. Just kidding."

Although the light is red, the light cross-traffic permits the cars in front of them to turn right without much hesitation. As Robert is turning, a horn wails from the left and grabs their attention. The culprits, a black limo and white Ford Bronco, race through the intersection.

Robert curiously follows the road-rage from a distance. "Jennifer, what the hell is going on? That looks like O.J.'s getaway car. And —" He squints ahead. "Are there flags on that limo?"

Jennifer looks. "Yeah, I think so. I can't read what they say, but they look orange and some hideous shade of blue."

"Naw, that's teal. Those are Miami Dolphin colors. Maybe it's Dan Marino in a mad dash to pick up some wings?"

"I don't know, but let's just stay clear of those idiots."

Robert lets off the gas to create more separation from the chaos ahead. The two vehicles continue to honk and begin to dangerously swerve at each other across the two lanes that go in their direction. The limo moves ahead by a car length in the right lane and starts to move into the left lane where the Bronco is. Before it can be pushed into oncoming traffic, the Bronco slams on its brakes and is sent into a spin.

Robert exclaims, "Holy shit! This is fucked-up!"

The Bronco crashes backwards into a snow bank on the right side of the road. Jennifer points at a side street. "Look, there's a cop." The police car turns on its lights and siren, and takes off after the limo.

Robert slows down to about 15 mph to check on the crash and make sure the passengers are okay. As he approaches, a guy jumps out of the vehicle, takes off his flannel shirt, and yells obscenities at the limo like a madman. Robert pulls over just past him and stops the car. "This is gonna sound crazy, but I think that's Zabka back there."

"That's ridiculous, you're seeing things." Jennifer looks back nervously. "The cops will handle this. Come on, go."

Robert looks in the rearview mirror at the shirtless nutcase as he jumps up and down like a baboon with a beet red face. Up ahead, the police pull over the limo. The screaming gets louder as the psychopath runs up from behind, heading towards his adversary. Robert gets out of his car just as the bare-chested guy passes and yells, "What the fuck!? Zabka!?"

Zabka skids to a stop on the slick ground and walks back to Robert. "Bob! Did you see that shit?! I'm gonna kill those assholes!"

"Yeah I saw it. What the hell are you doing here?"

"What do you mean, what the hell am I doing here? I left you a message last night — about us coming for the big game on Sunday!"

Jennifer gets out. "Hi, Zabka. I see you're acting sane and levelheaded as usual. Come on Robert." She waves him to the car. "We gotta go."

Robert cocks his head and puts a hand out at her. "Hang on a second, I'm really confused. Zabka's saying he left a message, but I didn't see any this morning."

Jennifer jabs her finger in Zabka's direction. "Look at him. Obviously he just escaped from the mental ward. He doesn't know what he's talking about."

"Don't insult *me*, Jen!" Zabka yells. "Because I can surely throw insults back at you. I *absolutely* know what I'm talking about. And something tells me you know that." He sniffs the air. "Something smells fishy here." He turns his nose in Jennifer's direction. "Smell that, Jenny? Is that coming from a *certain body part* of yours? Or is it the lie you're telling?"

"Robert, this is ridiculous! Are you gonna let him talk to me like this?"

As Robert looks up at the full moon, his body hair rises and seems to grow — transforming him into Bob. "As much as Zabka is an arrogant asshole who makes inappropriate, yet funny, remarks, he's not a liar." Zabka smirks and throws his hands up as if to say, "Yep, that's me in a nutshell." Bob finishes, "Well, except for when he says stuff about how great he is."

"Hey!" Zabka shouts. "In my mind it's all true, so it's not a lie!"

"I know for a fact that he wouldn't just show up in Buffalo without telling me first. Come to think of it, now I feel like I heard the phone ring last night. I thought I was dreaming, but maybe not. Add all that together with how *coincidentally* this morning you suddenly came up with this idea for us to leave town. Now, I'm not a lawyer, but I have to agree with Zabka's sniff-test. So — are you gonna answer his question?"

Jennifer fumbles for the right words. "Very imaginative conspiracy theory, but none of it proves anything." In Bill Clinton style, she empha-sizes each word with a thumb-on-fist gesture. "There. Is. No. Message." Pausing to give Zabka the stink-eye, she adds, "Case closed. I did nothing wrong other than want to spend a nice weekend with my boyfriend." She turns her head to Bob. "By the way, the longer this interrogation contin-ues, the less frisky I feel."

"Remember the conversation we just had back at my place?" Bob raises his eyebrows. "The one about dedication, honesty, and some other shit? Can you be honest?" As Jennifer's mouth opens to reply, Bob stops her. "Before you answer, you should know that I can call my answering machine from that payphone over there and listen to all my messages — new *and* deleted. Knowing that, go ahead."

Zabka interjects, "As much as I enjoy listening to relationship babble, I already know she's full of shit. Also, because my incredibly toned body doesn't have much fat, I'm freezing. So I'm gonna go put my shirt back on. Then I'm gonna take the other two guys I'm with over to that cop and make sure those Miami fucks are fucked! See you in Third Base after you take care of your, ahem, mess here." As Zabka leaves for the Bronco, his curled lip sends a message to Bob to, "Ditch this bitch."

Bob surveys Jennifer and says, "Okay, the ball's in your court. What do you have to say?"

Jennifer, on the edge of a raging tantrum, manages to compose herself before pleading her case. "Robert, this is very important, so I need you to listen with an open mind, okay?"

He folds his arms. "By all means."

"Good, so here it is. Robert —" She takes a deep breath and closes her eyes during a dramatic exhale. "This is real scary for me, but I need to be totally honest and share something with you."

His expression tells her, "It's about time."

"The thing is — I'm already *fully and completely* into Phase 2 with you." She pauses and smiles bashfully, waiting for his response.

"Is that it?" Bob taps his foot. "Nothing about Zabka's message?"

"Can we please get in the car?"

"No. Tell me about the message."

Jennifer frowns. "Well, let's just say that *if* there was a message, I was hoping the significance of what I just said and the connection between the two would be crystal clear."

Bob is no longer able to conceal his annoyance. "No! No, it's not! You're gonna have to walk me through it."

"Sure, honey. As you know, there are three components to Phase 2. Please hear me out completely before responding. The first component is honesty. As an example, I was just *honest* with you about already being in Phase 2. I'm sorry that I held that information back, but I wanted to surprise you and tell you during dinner tonight. The second component is trust. I need you to *trust* that I will do what's right for our relationship. I hope I can trust you to trust me." Bob looks at his watch as Jennifer continues, "The third component is dedication. My entrance into Phase 2 means I am fully *dedicated* to our relationship. Actions I take are to strengthen and protect it. That being said, I admit, without regrets, that I did delete Zabka's message. For the good of the relationship, it was more beneficial for *us* to be together, then for *you* to regress into a drunken dimwit."

Bob's head shakes like it's about to explode. "Are you fucking kidding me?! What makes you think you have the right to be the decision maker on what's good or bad for me or us? This Phase 2 crap is nonsense! You just twist words so they suit you! I'm not gonna be manipulated anymore! If I want to hang out with my friends, I'm gonna do that. You don't own me. This is bullshit!" Bob hyperventilates as he huffs and puffs like the wolf from *The Three Little Pigs*.

Jennifer walks towards Bob. "Robert, you need to calm-down. Relax. You're not thinking rationally."

"You know what? You're wrong. This is the most clarity I've had since we've been dating." Bob points at his car. "Get your bag, we're taking a break. I need some time to process things."

Jennifer starts to cry and pleads, "Noooo! Things have been so good with us lately. Please, you can't do this!" Tears run down her cheeks. "If you hang around those guys, you're gonna act like an idiot again. Don't give up all the progress you've made. You're a much better guy now after I've helped you. A guy who can *actually* have a girlfriend."

Bob walks around to his trunk, takes out her bag, and places it on the sidewalk. He shakes his head. "Give me a call. We'll see if I get the message this time." As Jennifer begs him to stay, he marches past her with new purpose — his mouth watering for a beer.

Jennifer screams at his back, "You're making a HUGE mistake! Don't think you're gonna find another woman like me out there!"

——

On the side of the road, Officer Radzikowski of the Buffalo police huddles with the limo driver and his Miami passengers. The officer looks at his notepad and addresses the group, "Let me recap what I have so far. Julio says that he was trying to switch lanes and that the Bronco was in his blind spot. He says it was an honest mistake that he almost ran another vehicle into oncoming traffic and ultimately sent that vehicle spinning into a snow bank. Do I have that correct so far?" The group nods yes.

Radzikowski flips to the next page. "Let me continue with my observations. From the corner of Main Street and Capen Boulevard, I witnessed two vehicles, side-by-side, heading south on Main Street. The first vehicle was a white Ford Bronco. The second was a black Lincoln stretch limo adorned with two Miami Dolphin flags on the front corners of the hood. Both vehicles were speeding at approximately 60 mph in a 30 mph zone. They were also aggressively honking their horns." He looks up. "Have I missed anything?"

Zabka approaches from behind and yells, "Yeah! You missed the part where these assholes deliberately tried to kill us!"

Bradford shouts back, "Well look at what just crawled outta the woods! A packa *Hee Haw* rednecks!" He fondles his chin. "Do you guys shop exclusively at the Pearl Jam flannel outlet? And the way you drive, you should stick to riding your shitty snowmobiles."

Jed gives Zabka a backhand slap to the gut and says, "See, I told you we shoulda taken our snowmobiles."

Zabka puts his hands on his hips and looks over the Miami group. "Let's see what we've got here." He points his index finger at Bradford and over-exaggerates a pout. "When your mom takes you to a restaurant, do you have to sit in a booster seat?"

"Holy fuck!" Jed yells. "You know what he just said?!" He squats down and reaches his hand up. "He just said you're too tiny for the adult table!"

Zabka directs his pointer to Juan Carlos. "This guy keeps a silver-spoon stuck in his rectum at all times because it reminds him of how *close* he is with his dad."

"Oh, shit!" Jed shouts. "The silver spoon is a euphemism for your rich dad's cock!" The police officer holds in his laugh.

Zabka slides his hand to the right and extends two digits to point at both girls. "And these, of course, are your run-of-the-mill Miami bimbos. I probably wouldn't even let them kiss my dolphin, if you know what I mean. Sorry, but fur coats can't disguise trailer trash."

Before Jed can spit out a follow-up jab, Bambi unleashes a shrill response, "These aren't fur coats, they're mink! So who's the bimbo now!?"

The boys from the Bronco chuckle. "Obviously you're the queen bimbo!" Jed shouts. "It's an honor to have royalty in our midst!" He finishes with a Japanese bow.

With tensions escalating, the officer uses the radio attached to his shoulder to call for backup. The officer then says to the group, "Alright everyone, let's stay calm. I just want the facts of what happened."

Bradford steps out from the group. "Let me explain what happened. We just arrived from Miami and were doing some sightseeing around your fine city, when these guys pulled up next to us and began honking and shouting insults. We saw a sign that said, 'Welcome to The City of Good Neighbors', but we sure haven't felt a warm welcome. Those juveniles were making obscene gestures and yelling 'squish the fish' — whatever the hell that means? Then one of them," he scans and points at Scott, "I'm guessing that fat guy. He took a toy dolphin and simulated an act of bestiality so grotesque that I cannot repeat it. The girls began crying, and we all feared for our lives."

Zabka slow claps, and Jed joins in unison. While wobbling like a Weeble, Scott tries to match their timing, but his inebriation makes the attempt futile. Zabka stops clapping and walks into the space between the groups. "Great storytelling. Pulitzer prize winning stuff. Blah blah blah — AND THEN YOU RAN US THE FUCK OFF THE ROAD!"

"Yeah, you thought you could drive like The Intimidator!" Jed yells. "I'm the fucking Intimidator! Number 3!"

Juan Carlos starts to unbuckle his pants. "You wanna see the Intimidator!? I'll show you!"

"That's enough!" Officer Radzikowski shouts. "I've collected sufficient data to make my decision and take proper action." As the groups wait for his judgment, Julio considers making a run for it.

—

Neon signs for the New York Yankees and Labatt Blue hang in the front window of Third Base. Their blue and red glow turns the snow on the sidewalk a faint color of purple. The muffled sound of rock n' roll combined with the promise of booze draws Bob closer like a tractor beam. Shuffling his way to the front door, he pushes it open and enters the bar. There he's greeted by a warm, malty gust of air and Axl Rose screeching out, "Used to Love Her". Inside is sparsely occupied with college students sitting at the bar and playing pool. Multicolored Christmas lights twinkle around the edges of the large wall mirror behind the beer taps.

Bob and Lisa, the female bartender, recognize each other and exchange a wave. He smirks as he approaches and locks contact with her eyes. While pressing his hands against the edge of the bar, he leans in. "Lisa, it's really good to see you."

Lisa stops twirling her light brown hair and bends across the bar to hug him. She whispers in his ear, "Great to see you, Bob." After releasing her embrace, she says, "It's been forever since you've been back here. How have you been?"

"I've been good, but today was crazy — like really messed up." He shakes his head as he zooms through the last twelve hours in his mind. "Any chance you have alcoholic beverages here?"

"As a matter of fact, we do. What can I get ya?"

Bob takes out a twenty from his wallet and slams it down on the sticky bar. "I'll take four pitchers of swill, please."

Lisa giggles. "Four? Now that is a bad day! And you *still* drink the good stuff!" She shakes her head. "Do you really want Koch's Golden Anniversary?"

"Hey, when it works, why change it? That's all we ever drank here."

"Apparently it works really well if you want four pitchers!"

Bob points his thumb over his shoulder back towards the door. "There's four of us. The rest of the guys are outside finishing up some 'business.' I figured it would be nice if some drinks were waiting for them when they arrive, and so why not make it a pitcher each? Plus then we don't need to hassle with glasses. See, I'm making your life easier too."

Lisa smiles at him as she pours the cheapest beer in the place. "Bob, you always did have a unique way of approaching things."

"Hey, and guess what? Zabka is one of them. He'll be in any minute."

Glancing at the door, she responds as if her mind is taking a trip to the past, "Ah yes, Zabka. God's gift to women." She pauses and stops the flow from the tap into the full pitcher. "Or at least that's what he thinks." They laugh as Lisa places the fourth pitcher in front of him. "That'll be $12."

"And there goes my Christmas bonus!" Bob shouts. "Just like that!"

"Impressive." Lisa takes his money. "Way to share the wealth." After she leaves for the register, he lifts one of the plastic pitchers to his lips and takes a few healthy gulps. Satisfied, he places the pitcher back down. She returns and places his change on the bar.

Lisa points around at her upper lip. "You've got a little bit of foam."

Bob looks at her with a straight face and one raised eyebrow. "Lisa, did you just give me head?"

With a sly grin, she replies, "Well I didn't, the beer did." While biting her lip, she looks him straight in the eyes, and lowers her voice. "But if I did just give you head, you wouldn't be looking like that. You'd have a huge smile."

Bob's heart beats faster, and he feels his internal blood flow shift in his midsection's direction. Attempting to keep his composure and distract his thoughts, he says, "So back to Zabka. Yeah, I don't think he'll ever change. I wouldn't be surprised if he propositions you within two minutes of walking in that door."

Lisa puts her elbows on the bar and exposes ample cleavage out of her low-cut tank-top. With a slight pout she asks, "So how come it's always the jackass that hits on me and never his cute friend?"

As Axl sings about his girlfriend's complaining — which he hears even when she's six-feet under — Bob finds himself in a much better place, smiling softly at Lisa, while Jennifer's nagging voice drifts from his mind.

—

Officer Radzikowski stands between the two groups and rotates to address the Miami clan. "I'm gonna impound your limo for the night and write Julio a ticket for reckless driving. You're lucky I don't throw you all in jail, but since you're out-of-state guests — I'm going to be lenient. Consider this a warning. I wouldn't make any more slip-ups if I were you. I'm gonna need you all to stay right here until the limo is towed."

Zabka approaches the officer. "Thank you for protecting and serving." Zabka extends his hand and they shake. "We truly admire all you do."

Radzikowski pulls Zabka aside. "You guys are free to go, but first tell me where you're from?"

"We're from up in Massena," Zabka tells him. "It's at the top of New York, kinda near Montreal. Heard of it?"

"No I haven't, but Buffalo appreciates you making the journey. I assume you're going to the game on Sunday?"

"Absolutely. Can't wait for it! I graduated from UB, so I always love coming back here."

Radzikowski hands Zabka his card. "Take this, son. If you run into any more trouble, don't hesitate to give me a call." He lowers his voice. "Between you and I, I can't stand these Miami sons-of-bitches."

"Me either. Thanks again." Zabka departs with a wave and returns to the guys. "Alright boys, Third Base is just a few blocks back that way. Let's go! There are several beers with our names on 'em!"

Jed notices what looks like a homeless person dragging their only possession through the snow. He points at the person as they approach. "Hey, isn't that the girl Bob was with?"

Zabka snickers. "Yeah it is." As they walk toward each other, he waits until they're close enough to holler, "How's that whole honesty thing working out so far?"

As they pass, Jennifer stares down Zabka. "Screw you! This war isn't over. It's just beginning!"

"Well boys, it looks like we just keep making friends everywhere we go. I wonder what'll happen once we really start drinking and aren't as civilized?"

—

Jennifer meanders down West Northrup Place until she arrives at Faige's house. She cautiously lifts her bag up the icy steps to the front door and rings the bell. After a few seconds, she hears footsteps approaching on the hardwood floor inside. Jennifer wipes away her tears and tries to smile before Faige opens the door.

"Hey, *Jennifa*. Come in, it's freezin'." Faige looks concerned. "What's wit' da luggage? I tawt youz was jus' droppin' off da project, not movin' in. Youz okay?"

THE SECOND QUARTER | 103

Jennifer enters, and Faige closes the door. Before Jennifer can answer, she starts bawling. Faige puts her arm around Jennifer and says, "Oh nooo, what's wrong? Come ova here. Let's go sit down." They walk into the living room and sit on a couch that's draped by a quilt with hand-stitched cat faces. Faige pouts. "Tell me what happened."

Jennifer tries to get the words out between sniffles. "Robert — Robert's a real jerk. We had this lovely weekend getaway planned." She gestures towards her bag. "And then — and then he canceled last minute to go binge drink with his stupid friends."

"Oh-my-gawd, dat's *hawible*." Faige gives Jennifer a big hug. "Dis jus' happened?" Jennifer answers with a frail nod. Faige continues, "I knew his charm lass-night was an anomaly. I'm not gonna say I told ya so — but I told ya so. He's da wawst boyfren eva."

Jennifer pulls a tissue out of her purse and blows her nose. "We were driving by that herpes-infected bar, Third Base, when he decided he wanted to go there instead. We had a big fight and I told him I wasn't going to put up with his immaturity, so I took my bag and walked."

"Good fa youz! And I know jus' what we're gonna do. We need ta go out and get 'im outta ya mind." Faige jumps up. "And get outta OUR minds! Youz got anyting sexy ta wear in youz bag?"

"Well yeah, I have this hot little dress I was gonna wear to dinner tonight."

"Perfect! We're goin' dancin' at Network! It's a YUUUGE nightclub owned by da Buffalo quawtaback." Faige claps. "Sistas befaw mistas!!"

———

While the Third Base DJ is distracted by the girls in his booth, he forgets to queue up a new song as the one playing ends. The noise level drops to pockets of chatter until the front door slams open and hits the wall with a loud thud. Zabka, Jed, and Scott enter the bar behaving like they just defeated Mötley Crüe for the "Hooker Banging and Coke Snorting" heavyweight title belt.

Zabka thrusts his chest forward and screams, "I'm back in the BUF-FALOOOOO! I heard ya missed me!"

Jed yells at Lisa, "Hey stewardess! Line up some shots, baby! Cuz this plane's about to take off!"

"Lookout, ladies!" Scott wiggles his hips and points at his jiggling butt. "You can't handle this ass!" The girls shoot him whatever-dude looks, and he covers his mouth as though his mom is going to pop out and spank him for using such foul language.

While the crowd looks at the newcomers in disgust, Bob leans against the bar and laughs. A flash of green comes over Scott's face and his cheeks puff out like a squirrel with a mouth full of nuts. As everyone watches, he waddles a beeline to the bathroom. Like Godzilla, he rips open the door, pushes a guy exiting out of his way, and rushes to the trough. The sound that follows comes from his insides violently birthing roadie beers and four semi-liquefied Whoppers out of his mouth. People wince as it echoes through the bar.

Scott exits the bathroom and uses his shirtsleeve to wipe a chunk of burger from the corner of his mouth. He stops and looks around at the gawkers. "What!? Like no one's ever puked here before? Turn on some damn music!" Satisfied with his brief, 'Yeah, I'm a drunk fat-ass! Fuck you!!' acceptance speech, the bar patrons go about their business. As Scott rejoins the rest of the pack, AC/DC's "Have a Drink on Me" starts to play.

Bob elbows Zabka while looking at Scott and asks, "Hey, so who the hell is this guy? And why is his face torn the fuck up?"

Zabka puts his arm around Scott's shoulders. "This, my friend — this is my boss, Scott. Please treat him with the respect he deserves."

"Scooter!" Bob yells. "It's a pleasure to meet you! You sure know how to make an entrance."

"Uh, that's Scott, not Scooter."

Bob laughs. "Yeah sure, whatever you say, Scooter." He turns around and grabs one of the full pitchers. "Here you go. You look like you could use it." He hands it to Scooter with a wink. "Try not to barf this up, it's the expensive stuff!"

Scooter rubs his tummy. "Don't worry, I made room for it." He then points at his facial lacerations. "You wanna know what happened?"

"Yeah I do! Can't wait to hear this!"

"I don't mean to brag, but last night there were three of us." Scooter gives Bob a friendly nudge with his elbow. "Me and my two pussies — that's what I call my frisky girls. Well, one got jealous and next thing you know there's a full-on catfight with me in the middle. Stuff got wild!"

Bob nods his head in approval. "Daaaamn, Scooter! Way to go! I'm looking forward to observing your lady slaying skills this weekend. There's always new things to learn." Bob turns to Zabka. "You and your boss seem to have a special type of relationship."

"We don't look at it as a hierarchy type of thing," Zabka replies as he pats Scooter on the head. "It's more of a partnership where I tell Scooter what to do and what not to do."

"I wish I had that with my boss," Bob confides. "Well, not with her, but with a different boss."

Zabka grabs Bob and they move over to Jed so he can continue introductions. "And this Grizzly Adams looking son-of-a-bitch is Jed. Make sure he is well fed, has a drink in his hand at all times, and no one will get hurt."

Bob and Jed exchange a handshake. "Nice to meet you, Jed. Don't you worry about the drinks part. Third Base, and Buffalo as a whole, will take very good care of you. Plus, the bars stay open until 4 AM."

"It's *the* Buffalo, by the way." Jed slowly surveys the room and nods with an impressed look on his face. "This is gonna work out just fine. One thing is missing though — midget porn."

Bob chuckles. "When the owner comes in, I'll see what we can do to fix this oversight."

"That'd be great, thanks."

"But what if all he has is a videotape of munchkins fucking?"

Jed takes a sip of beer. "That would suffice."

Bob yells, "Lisa, could you get us —" She points back near their pitchers to four shots. Impressed with her clairvoyance, Bob smiles and changes his ask. "Could you get us an underwire bra for Scooter here? Looks like he needs a little more support." Scooter laughs sarcastically.

Zabka whispers in Bob's ear, "I'll get you Lisa's underwire bra, but you're gonna have to give me at least five minutes."

"Oh yeah?" Bob replies, "I can't wait to see what you've got. It's been a while since I've watched you go down in flames."

Bob motions to Lisa for her to come over. "Hey Lisa, you're fuckin' awesome!" He points at the shots. "You knew exactly what I was thinking. Let's get one for you too."

"Sure, I'll drink with you pussies," she says as she pours another.

Bob hollers, "Guys, get over here!" He hands out the shots as they gather. "I'd like to propose a toast." They raise their shot glasses. "I'm happy you're all here — we're gonna have one hell of a weekend! Here's to the Bills destroying the Fins!"

Zabka adds, "And all of us getting our pee-pees wet!"

The whiskey burns as it goes down their throats like gasoline. Scooter's face scrunches like a tightened sphincter, fearful of penetration. "What the hell was that?! Are you guys trying to kill me?!!"

Bob laughs at Scooter's horrified expression and wipes away a few tears. "That, my friend — that was Wild Turkey 101! You never forget the first time your cherry's popped. Unfortunately, the experience never gets better."

Jed looks curiously at his empty shot glass. "Was mine watered down?"

Scooter tells Bob, "Fuck. Please don't do that to me again. I was just starting to feel better after I vomited."

Zabka slaps Scooter on the back. "Hey! Don't ever let me hear you say that again! You're in the big leagues now — you need to step up your game. Are you a big boy, Scooter?"

Scooter tries to muster some enthusiasm. "Yes Zabka, I'm a big boy."

Zabka leans against the wall to the left of the bar and next to the DJ booth. Behind him is a crudely drawn picture of a baseball player sliding into home plate. The caption reads, "You can't go home without going to Third Base." A steady-stream of college students enter after their fake IDs are checked. With the bar around half-capacity, the guys carve out an area around Zabka as he holds court. In mid-sentence, Zabka pauses to watch a group of four giggling girls come in. The rest of the guys pick up on Zabka's distraction and turn to observe.

Zabka hits Jed in the arm. "Look at 'em. Those girls there are just what I've been talking about. Wait until they take off their jackets and expose their winter layers." The girls remove their coats and their figures are revealed. "See! It's not the jackets that are big and puffy — it's the girls that are big and puffy!"

Bob adds, "And their faces are what? Fives, maybe sixes?" The guys return yeah-that's-about-right nods. "But they think they're nines or tens. And they act like it!"

"Yeah, they're nines or tens — on a scale of a hundred! Unfortunately, though, they're about the best you'll find," Zabka says apologetically.

Scooter looks them over. "I don't think they're all that bad. Actually, a couple of them are kinda cute."

"You're just saying that cuz you're drunk and in the same weight class," Zabka counters. "The girls here don't take care of their bodies. In their world, nutrition and exercise don't exist. In Buffalo there's no competition and no natural selection. So they just don't give a damn."

"A couple of 'em have big noses too," Jed points out. "Like elephants."

"Their noses aren't that big. Actually they're more like polar bears," Bob corrects him. "They grow an extra layer of fat to survive in the cold."

Zabka nods his head. "In any other town I wouldn't even look twice at them, but here I'm pretty much forced to give them the honor of an occasional bang." He downs the remains of his pitcher. "But first I need a few more drinks to lower my standards." He spies Lisa at the other end of the bar and waves for her. "In the meantime, I might as well give the uni-corn in this joint a shot at me."

After Lisa finishes with another customer, she approaches Zabka. "I'm afraid to ask, but what can I get for you?"

"Nothing, actually." Zabka returns a soft smile. "I know you think I'm a jerk sometimes, but I wanted to share with you that I'm now a regis-tered organ donor." He pats his chest earnestly. "I have compassion."

Lisa crosses her arms. "I really hope this isn't another bullshit line."

"It's not." He squints his eyes deviously. "And I've got just the right or-gan in my pants to prove it. Ready for the best 'donation' you'll ever get?"

Lisa rolls her eyes. "Oh my god, you're such a charmer. For once, lis-ten to me closely. Nothing is *ever* going to happen between us. Got that?"

Zabka returns an exaggerated pout. "Yeah, got it." His expression morphs into a smirk. "It's cool, I like girls that play hard to get." He whirls his index finger in the air. "Barmaid, get us another round of swill." Lisa shakes her head and walks back to the taps. He turns to Scooter. "As I sus-pected, I'll have to put a little bit of effort into this one. I'll put her on simmer for now and come back later — if I'm in the mood."

"No offense," Scooter says. "But your conversation didn't sound too promising to me. Actually, I don't think that line worked at all."

Annoyed, Zabka responds, "Listen here — she put up her bitch-shield, and I didn't let it bother me. You just brush off shit like that — they like that. Also, I put in her head the image of her and I doin' the wild-thing. That has to be implanted first. It's a primal caveman fact!"

"That's all you have to do? I feel like I'm missing something."

Zabka's agitation level increases. "No, that's not *all* you have to do! And yeah, you're missing a lot because you don't understand women like I do!" He takes a drink to calm down. "No offense, I recognize that you are not as experienced as me — even though you are older and have been married — but that was just step one with her. I'll explain more later."

—

Outside Network, between red velvet ropes and a brick wall, about twenty people wait to enter the downtown club. Puffs of cigarette smoke and chilled exhalation drift upward from the crowd. With the wall mounted heat lamps broken, they huddle together, attempting to stay warm. The muted bass thumping from inside bounces the frozen mob around like a beer bottle on a subwoofer. Jennifer and Faige arrive in a cab in front of the club and exit onto the sidewalk.

"Holy fuck it's cold!" Jennifer exclaims. "And there's a line to get in!? For Christ's sake, we're wearing dresses!"

Faige glances at the door. "Fuhgeddaboudit, I can get us right in. I used ta kinda date da doorman. Follow me."

The girls walk around the crowd and receive a few nasty looks as they arrive at the front of the line. Faige approaches the aptly titled doorman — his massive size nearly matching that of the front entrance. Behind Faige, Jennifer shivers — her winter coat covers her tight black halter-top, but not her glittery silver miniskirt.

Faige adds as much sexiness as she can muster to her New York City tongue. "Hey Bruno, good ta see ya. Youz look so han'some." She waves him to come closer. "Gimme a hug."

To embrace, Bruno has to bend down almost 90 degrees to get to her level. As they hug, he whispers something in Faige's ear while looking at Jennifer. Faige releases from him and pulls back. After a pause, she leans in and whispers a response. Rising back to his fully erect stance, Bruno opens the door and ushers the girls inside.

Hanging from the thirty-foot ceiling, disco balls spin and shoot out multicolored beams of light across the dimly lit warehouse-sized club. From elevated balcony areas, the patrons relax and observe badly imitated *Club MTV* moves on the large dance floor and pickup attempts at the three surrounding bars. Faige grabs Jennifer's hand and pulls her through the mob of clubbers toward the nearest bar. After snaking through the crowd, they get close to the bar and prepare to fight for the bartender's attention.

The music is blasting, so Jennifer must shout in Faige's ear. "Wow! This is crazy! How did you manage to get us in like that?!"

"Um, I hadda do some negotiatin'! No biggie!"

"Whaddya gotta give him a handjob later or something?!" Jennifer laughs.

"Well, um... let's getta drink and have some fun!"

"Yeah! I need to blow-off major steam. Let's do something crazy — let's get shots!"

Faige gets lucky and catches the eye of the male bartender. She places their order with him, "Two cosmos *and* two stiff-dicks!"

"Now that's what I'm talkin' about!" Once their shots arrive, they shoot them back. Jennifer uses her tongue to clean the excess from her lips. "Those are tasty! What's in that? Butterscotch and Baileys?"

"Yep. I figga'd dat be a good kick-starta fa us. And dey taste much betta dan a real stiff-dick, right?"

Jennifer confirms with a nod. The girls sip their cocktails and take in the dance floor energy. Jennifer scouts the crowd and says analytically, "There sure are a lot of good looking guys out there."

"See what I mean? Tonight, ya need ta get out dere, flirt, and fuhgeddaboud Mr. Go-Fuck-Himself."

Jennifer thinks back to the summer wedding she went to with Robert. "I love dancing with Robert. He's so fun. And I seriously don't think anyone here's gonna want to dance with me."

"Would-ja stop it already! Dat's da last time I wanna hear his name tonight — and stop being so negative! Dere's plennia guys here who'd love ta dance wit' youz. Let's go!"

As Faige drags Jennifer out on the dance floor, the music transitions to a song by Salt-N-Pepa. Jennifer's a bit stiff at first, whereas Faige isn't shy about shaking her booty. The other dancers engulf them while they flow with the music. As the club grooves, the ladies get ready to participate with the chorus. On cue, they throw their hands up and shout, "Let's Talk About Sex!"

Two men approach the girls from behind, and one of them starts dancing very close to Faige. She notices and reviews his short but stocky frame. The guy hockey-checks her out-of-the-blue and sends her stumbling to the ground. He quickly runs over to help Faige up and apologize.

As Jennifer attempts to process this episode, the guy's tall friend starts dancing in front of her. While they make eye contact and exchange smiles, she notices how handsome he is. After dancing together for a minute, he leans into her ear and asks, "Can I get the name of the most beautiful woman here tonight?"

"Who me? Oh, I'm Jennifer."

He takes her hand with both of his. "I'm Jim. Pleasure to meet you."

She smiles bashfully. "You too, Jim."

"So how can a girl as pretty as you not have a boyfriend?"

She blushes. "Well um, I guess I just don't. I mean, not at the moment."

His perfect, white teeth glisten. "I guess I'm pretty lucky then. I mean, at the moment." He twirls her around, and brings her chest into his. They smile and laugh together, before he spins her back out. They continue dancing until he shouts in her ear, "How about we get a drink and go upstairs? This song got me in the mood."

"That sounds nice. We can go chat and get to know each other better."

Jim spins Jennifer 180 degrees and presses into her backside. Synchronized with the beat of the music, he rubs his pelvis against her cushy behind. Jennifer's initial discomfort quickly turns to shock. She whirls away and slaps him in the face. "You sick bastard! Put that *thing* away!"

The people around them notice the commotion and stare at Jim's midsection as he attempts to use his hands to conceal his offending appendage. Like a pinball knocked by the machine's flipper, Jennifer bounces rapidly through the crowd and over to Faige. She grabs Faige away from her dance partner, and pulls her off the dance floor.

"That was disgusting!" Jennifer exclaims. "I can't believe that just happened! What kinda place is this?!"

"What da hell's dis all about? I was havin' fun!"

Jennifer points at the dance floor. "That fuckin' jerk poked me!"

"Poked ya?"

"Yeah — with his — his *thing!*" Jennifer shakes her head. "I need shot."

"Youz sure youz wanna 'nother stiff dick?" Faige grins. "Isn't dat what jus' got youz so mad?"

Jennifer lightly slaps Faige's arm and laughs. "Yeah, perhaps you're right. I don't need another. I got that department well covered!" She replays the incident in her mind. "So what was up with that anyway?"

Faige shrugs. "It's da singles scene. Dat type-a-shit happens."

"I can't believe it." Jennifer frowns. "Alright, I'm getting us cosmos." The bartender from their first round recognizes them, and Jennifer places her order.

Faige taps Jennifer on the shoulder. "Hey, looka dis!" Faige points at the guys they met earlier, and they watch them dance over to two other girls. The guy who was dancing with Faige moves in first and, in similar fashion, hip-checks his girl to the ground. Just after that, Jim swoops in and dances with the other girl.

Jennifer's jaw drops. "Those assholes! They've gotta routine!"

The bartender returns with two cosmos. "Here you are, ladies."

Jennifer hands him some money and guzzles down her drink. "Two more, please."

Faige points-out, "But I haven't even taken a sip outta mine yet."

"Yeah. I'm not ordering for you."

—

As Lisa delivers four full pitchers of beer, Zabka shouts, "Alright boys, grab a fresh one! I want to discuss the elephant in the room."

Jed points at the four girls they were examining earlier. "Don't you mean *elephants?* Plural?"

"No, but good one." Zabka laughs. "The topic is *Robert's* fucked-up 're-lationship' with his girlfriend." His attention turns to Bob. "What the hell is going on with you?"

Bob puts his hands up and shrugs. "What can I say? It's complicated."

"Come on, man, we need more than that." Zabka puts his arm around Bob's shoulders. "You and I go way back. No woman should interfere with *our* time together."

"Honestly, I don't know what's going on with her. Ever since I toned things down, everything has been pretty good with us. Then she heard that message from you and lost her mind." As Bob continues, he counts off on his fingers. "One, she deletes the message before I can hear it. Two, she plays me perfectly so I agree to take her to Canada this week-end. And three! She comes up with this *Phase 2 shit* outta nowhere!"

"Wow!" Zabka shouts. "We need to go through each of these. Starting with the 'toned things down' crap. What the hell's that all about?"

Jed raises his hand. "May I interject? Most of what you said completely bored me, so can we just jump straight to the Phase 2 topic? That sounds like it could be good. It's gotta have something to do with anal, right? Please tell me it does."

Bob laughs. "No, I wish! It's about as far from anal sex as I can imagine — like the other side of the universe far. According to Jennifer, it's all about the next phase of our relationship and has to do with honesty, trust, and some other bullshit."

Jed winces. "Oh, for fuck-sake, that's not anything I hoped it would be." He takes a drink from his pitcher. "Shit, that reminds me I haven't called the wife since I got here." He takes another gulp as the other guys stare at him. "What?" he asks.

"So are you gonna give her a call?" Bob inquires.

"I just said, 'that reminds me.' I didn't say I was gonna call. I'm way too engrossed in this conversation."

Zabka looks at Bob. "Shall we continue? So you've *toned things down?* Seriously, what's up with that?"

"Well, there were a couple of incidents when I was drinking that Jennifer wasn't too fond of. One of them you know very well, because it was the last time you were here and the first time you met her."

"Yep, that was crazy!" Zabka acts giddy as he remembers. "She really needs to lighten up."

"Yeah, well, it put me in the doghouse," Bob complains. "Plus something occurred after that incident at her law school ball that really got me in trouble. Bottom line is this — I had to change or she was gonna leave me. After I made some changes, her nagging stopped and things were a lot easier for me."

Zabka sneers. "To summarize — you're basically saying you gave in and fundamentally changed who you are as a person to appease her?"

Bob turns pink and falters, "I, I didn't really have a choice."

"Sure you did — we always have choices. Did you ever think that you should be you? And if she doesn't accept *you*, then she's not the right girl?"

"Sometimes you've got to compromise, Zabka. That's why I'm in a relationship, and you're not."

"If I wanted to be in some kind of dysfunctional relationship — where the freedom to do what *I* want is taken away — well then, I guess I'd be like you." Zabka pauses to let it sink in. "By the way, did you ever stop and think about how this affects *me*?"

"No Zabka, I didn't!" Bob shouts back. "I can't believe you made this about you! Scratch that — I can!" Scooter and Jed nod in agreement.

"Think about it. Jennifer masterminded a scheme to put an international border between us this weekend." Zabka points at himself. "That has everything to do with me!"

"Yeah, apparently so! She must really like you a lot!"

Jed thrusts out his hands to stop them. "As an outsider, can I just say that it seems like below the surface you two are in some sort of unhealthy relationship? Zabka, seriously, how jealous of Jennifer are you? Do we need to get you both on the Jerry Springer show for DNA tests and figure out which one of you has a vagina? Maybe it's both?"

Everyone laughs, breaking the tension. After a drink from his pitcher, Bob notices something and points at the green ceiling. "Hey guys, see that white streak up there?" They look up. "That's from Halloween a few years ago."

"Oh yeah? From what?" Scooter asks.

Before Bob can explain, Zabka's head movement tells them to check out the entrance. "Look at what we have here," Zabka tells them. "Those Cubano sandwich eating mother fuckers actually have the audacity to come into our bar."

Bradford notices Zabka's crew, grabs Summer's hand, and leads the others over. "Well, this is shocking to find," Bradford says to them. "You four losers without any women, standing here, circle-jerking each other off. I never would've predicted that. So which one of you is gonna have to eat the ookie cookie?" He lets his reference to the masturbation game played by frat pledges simmer before directing his attention at Scooter. "I'm gonna put my money on dough-boy here. I bet you cum last on purpose because you can't stand the thought of missing out on dessert!"

"Oh yeah, well guess what?!" Scooter barks. "I'd be a gentleman and let your girls share it! I'm sure it's already a steady part of their diet!" Wide-eyed and glowing, Scooter fishes for Zabka's approval. After Zabka obliges with a look of praise, Scooter cups the side of his mouth with his hand and whispers in Zabka's ear, "I don't know what an ookie cookie is, but I figured a deflection might be a good come back. Anyway, a cookie does sound kinda good. Can we get some?"

Zabka resists his impulse to whack Scooter, and instead steps toward and points at Juan Carlos. "Why doesn't captain douche-taint put all of you on his shitty raft and take you back to Cuba?!"

"Well — well —," Juan Carlos stammers. He looks around the bar. "I don't need to because I already feel right at home right here! This place reminds me of the Bay of Pigs!"

Zabka's head twitches as he takes a step back. "Oh shit! Did you just insult our fuckin' women?!" Juan Carlos smiles calmly as Zabka screams, "Goddammit, nobody insults our women! Only we insult our women!!"

As Summer and Bambi scurry behind their men, they second guess for a second time their decision to join the trip. The half of the bar that wasn't already examining the flashy dressers from out-of-town now has its attention drawn by the escalating verbal sparring match.

Feeling the piercing eyes on them, Bradford interjects, "Hey, hey, let's all calm down." He pumps his palms toward the floor. "We're just here for a friendly football game, and we shouldn't let the passion we have for our teams make things get out of control. You agree?"

Zabka, Jed, and Bob all cross their arms across their chests and scowl. Scooter's position doesn't change, but after noticing his friends' stance, he imitates their pose. Bradford continues, "Come on, be realistic about the game, guys. You know our boy Cox is gonna destroy your Bills."

Zabka's blood boils as an outburst bubbles up his throat and out of his mouth, "Your BOY COCKS!!? Your itty-bitty boy cocks are gonna destroy us!? Ha ha! I don't think so!!"

Bradford, realizing how his last remark sounded, attempts to course correct, "Our boy — Cox. You know, he's our boy." He weakly thumps his chest with his fist. "Bryan Cox! Our boy Bryan Cox!"

Zabka sticks his head out. "Whatever, man. Your *boy* cocks sound *real* scary to me, so please don't bring them to the stadium. Believe me, nobody wants to see that." He feels a tap on his shoulder and turns around. Instantly, he recognizes the muscular forty-year-old and gives him a firm handshake. "Brewer, good to see you! How the hell are ya?!"

"I'm good, hippy. You guys okay?" Brewer sizes-up the out-of-towners. "We're not gonna have any of the usual trouble, are we?"

"Oh, no." Zabka grins. "We're just having a nice conversation with our friends from Miami."

"Yeah, I noticed that." Brewer steps toward the Miami group. "Welcome to my bar — I'm Brewer. I notice you've already had the pleasure of meeting a couple of our regulars." He smiles at Zabka and Bob. "I promise you not everyone here is like Zabka. Come with me, and I'll get you your first round. Sound good?"

The Miami group nod their heads yes and Bradford responds, "It's about time we're treated with respect. Normally we wouldn't lower ourselves to come into a joint like this, but we gotta wait for our replacement limo." He puts his arm around Summer as they follow Brewer and whispers in her ear, "I don't want you talking to those guys. You're mine, and they're beneath us."

"I didn't really have an interest in speaking with them," Summer replies while brushing his arm off her like it's a pesky fly. "But I can speak to whomever I want."

As they near the back end of the bar, Juan Carlos asks, "Are you taking us to the VIP section?"

Brewer chuckles and shouts back over his shoulder, "Yeah sure, it's right over here." He leads them to a spot at the bar and says to Lisa, "Can you get our Miami pals a round on me, please."

"No problem." Lisa is in awe of Bambi's beauty as she asks the group, "What are you in the mood for?"

Summer jumps forward. "We love Piña Coladas!"

Lisa looks at Summer like she just ordered a drink from another planet. "Sorry, but our blender is currently in the shop. How about we start you off with a round of Jägermeister. Welcome to Buffalo!"

———

After her interaction with Jim, Jennifer had a couple more drinks with Faige, but no other men approached her. From the balcony, she sits and watches the people below. As she studies the clubbers, she can't help but think of herself as a biologist analyzing a simple experiment in a Petri dish — mix all types of personalities, soak them in alcohol, and record the results. What happens is typically just as expected — random fornication combinations, hangovers, and the swearing to never do it again — or at least "never again" until the following weekend.

As Jennifer nurses her cosmo, she thinks about the experiment she was just in. In a sea of revelry, two conniving perverts successfully executed a plan to separate her from her ally. This enabled one of them to pounce, quickly woo her, and then sneak in an unexpected fondle. *Maybe I mistook what happened? Jim did pick me out from all the other girls. He's handsome, charming, and I guess "that" sometimes happens when a guy gets excited. Shit, I should totally take it as a compliment. Men still want me!*

Jennifer watches as Faige dances from guy to guy. *Did I royally fuck up with Robert? I have a good thing, right? I don't want to lose him — I can't deal with this scene here. I'll never find another guy, and I'll be single for the rest of my life.* While staring at the spinning disco ball, she cries, "I'm gonna be a crazy cat lady!" She drops her head. *Fuck, I hate cats.*

Faige drips with dance-floor-sweat as she climbs the stairs. She vigorously waves her hands to try to draw Jennifer's attention. She approaches and asks, "Are ya doing okay, honey?"

Jennifer stands up and almost stumbles, barely catching herself by grabbing Faige's shoulder. "I'm fine, but are we in a revolving bar? You know, one of those places that spins around?"

"Nooo, it's not. Dat's a clear sign dat it's time fa us ta go home."

Jennifer wobbles. "I don't want to rain on your parade, but yeah, that sounds like a good idea."

"Okay, but dere's jus' one ting I gotta do befaw we go. Rememba Bruno da doorman? I needa go lend 'im a hand so ta speak."

"Oh yes, I remember him." Jennifer's eyes widen and her mouth opens in shock. "I knew it! You gotta go —" She strokes an imaginary penis. "You gotta go give him a handjob!"

Faige laughs. "Yeah, kinda. Like I said, I gotta lend 'im a hand — and by hand, I mean mouth. I got *both-a* us in tonight!"

"It's kinda like jerking him off, but with your lips. Your efforts tonight are much appreciated!" Jennifer gives her a high-five. "But first, help me outside. I'll go puke and then wait for you in a cab." They begin to walk downstairs.

"This won't take long," Faige assures her. "Bruno's a quick one."

———

While Beck sings the chorus in "Loser", Zabka's booze-filled mind drifts into a potential scenario involving the two girls from Miami and getting crazy with Cheese Whiz. He looks at his friends and notices they're just quietly drinking their beers while watching everyone else.

"Alright, fuck this shit!" Zabka shouts. "Gather 'round. Here's what we're gonna do — the old divide and conquer. Since technically Scooter and I are the only guys here with our balls still in our scrotums, and not in a goddamn marriage or relationship — which, of course, I respect the sanctity of — we're gonna be the ones who take those Miami chicks away from their loser boyfriends. Then at that point, we'll have our way with them. However, we need the help of you two." He pauses to look at Bob and Jed. "I know both of you are pretty good at darts, so I want you to challenge the butt-fuck twins over there to a game. That'll give me some time to work my magic. Any questions?"

Bob thinks it over. "We didn't exactly get off on the right foot with those guys, right? So I don't think we can just go over there and suddenly be pals who want to play darts. My suggestion is first we send over a round of shots. Buffalo's version of an olive branch."

"Good thinking. Any thoughts on what we send them?" Zabka asks.

"As a matter of fact, I do. I say we get 'em Goldschläger. You know that cinnamon schnapps with the little gold flakes in it? They look like the type of rich assholes who would get off on that sort of thing."

"I agree! Know your audience!" Zabka turns to Lisa. "We want a round of Goldschläger shots for us and a round for the Crockett and Tubbs crew over there. Can you do that?"

"Sure," Lisa replies. "You guys weren't getting along too well with them earlier. You trying to patch things up?"

Zabka smirks. "Appearance is everything."

Lisa lines up the shots for both groups and they suspiciously toast each other across the bar. After downing the shots, Zabka says, "Alright guys, it's show time. Let's go over there. I'll take the lead — stick to the plan."

The group works their way through the crowd and comes up against an elephant herd wall. Bob taps one of the girls on the shoulder and says, "Sorry, can we get by?"

As the girl turns around, she hits Bob with her meaty elbow. "Excuse me? We're here on a girls' night, so you can calm down and put your dicks back in your holsters."

Zabka pokes his head in next to hers. "What do you think this is? The wild-fucking-west? My cock is locked-and-loaded, but even with that humungous target you call a forehead, I have no desire to hit it. Sorry to disappoint you." As he scoots by, he leaves her with a fuck-you smile.

When they reach the two couples from Miami, Zabka puts forth his best mea culpa demeanor. "My mother always told me to treat others like I want to be treated. So we came over to apologize for our initial behavior and to press the reset button. Can we do that?"

There's a collective hesitation before Bambi takes charge. "Yes, we can give that a try." After the two groups partially exchange awkward introductions, Jed coaxes Bradford and Juan Carlos to move over to the dartboard for a game.

Bob asks Bambi, "Did you notice the gold flakes in the shot?"

"I did!" Bambi answers with delight. "Do you know how many shots I need to take so tomorrow I can crap out a gold nugget? My mom loves gold, and it would be great to bring her back a souvenir from Buffalo."

Bob nudges Zabka and gives him a this-is-gonna-work look. "You're funny, Bambi."

"I am?" Bambi asks.

"Oh, you're serious?" Bob smiles as he follows her ample curves down to the floor. "I'm sorry, I don't know how many shots. But maybe we could have another and start counting?"

Summer undoes two blouse buttons before sticking her hand out. "Hi Bob, I'm Summer. It's nice to meet you."

Bob barely takes notice of her while they exchange a quick handshake, and refocuses on Bambi. "So tell me about your mom. I bet she's beautiful." Two stools open up at the bar right in front of them. "But first let's sit and get that shot we were talking about."

Zabka glares at Bob as he takes Bambi away. *What the hell is he doing? He's not following the damn script.* Zabka takes a breath and clears his mind of the previous erotic Cheese Whiz images. He turns to Summer and slyly says, "I'm gonna sink my teeth into you and take a bite outta crime."

Summer looks at him oddly. "What are you talking about?"

Zabka leans closer. "Well, it must be illegal to look that good."

Summer looks at him coyly. "That's so sweet of you to say. No man has ever been so kind." She gives him a sexy pout. "So, do you want to fuck me now or wait 'till later?" Zabka stammers before Summer continues with a sterner tone, "Come on, do I look like the type of girl that line would work on? Try that on Bambi or some other dimwit." Having overheard them, Bambi conveys, "please do" with a nod of her head. "Plus you've insulted all of us multiple times. I'll tell you who you can go fuck — yourself!" She turns her back to him and tries to flag down Lisa.

Zabka pulls out a twenty and holds it over Summer's head. "Come on. Let me buy you a drink or something. Give a guy a chance."

Summer ignores his money. "I can get my own drink." She twists her torso so he can see the look on her face, which says, "I want to flatten your gonads with my heel."

Scooter tugs Zabka aside and asks, "Was that another successful first step in your caveman-sex-system?"

Zabka steps away from Summer and reflects on his moves. "That last 'buy you a drink' part — I shouldn't have said that. It seemed needy. But overall I say yes, it was a success. You've got to look at the positives. Anytime a woman puts the words 'fuck' and 'me' together, it's a good sign. The rest of what she said is irrelevant. It's all a game and you gotta deflect that other shit. I'm sure-as-hell not gonna walk away and say I've been defeated, because I haven't." He looks over his shoulder at Summer while she gets her drink. "Right now she's not gonna give in to me because for some fucked-up reason she *perceives* that as losing. I just need to switch up the game to where if she can get me, she wins." He pauses to think for a second. "Actually in her case, it will probably be if she doesn't get me, she loses." He grins and continues, "A woman hates to lose, especially to another woman."

The expression on Scooter's face is one as if he was just explained the meaning of life. "Are you serious? That's how it all works?"

"Yep. That's how it works. Well, except for one more essential thing."

"Oh yeah? What's that?"

"You gotta not give a fuck." Zabka slashes his hand horizontally. "Not one single fuck."

Scooter tilts his head. "I can't give a fuck?"

"Yep, you genuinely can't care if she accepts or rejects you. Think about it. If you want her, you'll get excited and your mind will drift to a place where," Zabka mimes his description, "you're slapping that ass as you're doing her from behind." He points to his skull. "Once your head goes there you're screwed. You'll make mistakes. Conversely, if you think about her rejecting you, you'll lack confidence and be timid. That's not attractive and you're equally as fucked. Understand?"

Scooter nods his head vigorously. "From now on when it comes to me and the ladies, I don't give a fuck!"

Zabka grins like a proud teacher. "Good, remember that. Because at some point this weekend I want you to show me what you've learned." He looks at the back of the room where Jed has corralled Bradford and Juan Carlos next to the dartboard. "At least Jed is sticking to the plan. *Fucking* Bob is over there talking to Bambi — although I don't know how he's managing it."

Bob leans back and laughs. "You're actually pretty funny for an attractive woman, you know that?"

Bambi puts her lips around her cocktail straw and sucks. "And you're actually pretty attractive for a funny man, you know that?"

"You're too kind." Bob bows his head. "Hey, would you like another Goldschläger shot? You gotta keep working on that gift for mom."

Bambi scrutinizes the bottle of glittery liquor behind the bar. "I'm gonna guess there's about one-tenth of a gram of gold per bottle. So that means I need to drink about two hundred and eighty bottles to produce one ounce. Holy shit, I'm gonna be hammered!"

Astonished, he says, "Don't take this the wrong way, but wow! I didn't think you'd come up with something like that."

"Oh, um, I don't even know what I just said. I must've heard someone else say that once." She waves to Lisa. "Let's get that shot."

Meanwhile, Jed grips pretend handlebars and bounces up and down as he speaks. "So I said, 'Zabka, we should ride our snowmobiles across Lake Ontario to the Buffalo.' And he says, 'No, that's a stupid idea' or something like that. Sometimes I think he's stupid. Ya feel me? You guys ride jet skis and shit like that, right? Why didn't you ride them up here?"

"Yeah, we do have a few jet skis on our yacht," Juan Carlos answers. "But for long distances we prefer to travel on our jet."

Impressed, Jed says, "Damn, you guys got a jet? You ever been to the Buffalo before?"

"I have not, but it's everything I expected," Bradford replies. "Sorta reminds me of a frozen version of hell."

Jed shakes his head. "I gotta disagree with you on that one, Bradford. If hell is anything like the Buffalo, I vow to commit more sins — if that's even possible. This is my first time here too, and this place has everything. Beer, wings, football — it's fucking awesome!"

"That's so blue-collar — it's something I'd expect a guy like you to say." Bradford picks a hair out of his mouth. "We're different people. We're white-collar — high upper-class. We don't wear uniforms to work with our names stitched on them. We put our names on buildings." Juan Carlos snickers. "Sure, we both enjoy football, but at the game you'll be up in the nose bleeds — if you can even afford that. Meanwhile, we'll be tenth row on the 50-yard line, behind the Dolphins bench."

"That's right, section 111!" Juan Carlos brags. "Great seats — ones you could never have. Our butler really came through!"

"While you may have a *but*-ler, we have a *butt*-head and his name is Scooter." Jed sticks his nose up in the air. "I don't know where our seats are, but I'm sure they're great. So why don't you try dialing down your condescending attitude?"

"Condescending?" Bradford points confusingly back and forth to himself and Juan Carlos. "Who, us? It's not condescending if you tell it like it is. Hey, we've got problems just like you. Your lawnmower breaks down — our gardening staff all catches the flu. You run your snow mobile into a tree, our cigarette speedboat won't start. See what I mean?"

"Yeah, I see what you mean. I just wanted to play a game of darts, while you guys would rather stick chess pieces up each other's asses." Jed glares at Bradford. "I bet *you* have a fetish for playing hide the bishop! Checkmate, bitches!" Jed grabs his pitcher. "Good day. I'm out."

As Jed walks away, Bradford shouts, "It was nice talking with you! We should do this again sometime!"

Zabka notices Jed coming over and asks, "What's going on? You're supposed to be playing darts with those guys."

"Those guys are a couple of patronizing pricks," Jed steams. "All they did was put us down and the Buffalo down, and talk about their goddamn jet and 50-yard line seats. We seriously need to fuck those guys over."

Zabka puts his arm around Jed and calmly adds, "And we need to fuck their women. And oh yes, fuck them we will." Zabka pats Jed's chest. "Don't worry, we'll come up with something."

"How's your part of the plan going?" Jed asks.

"Bob is over there, cock-blocking the shit out of me," Zabka replies. They turn and find Bob sitting between Summer and Bambi at the bar.

"So who's dating who here?" Bob asks. "Bambi, you with Juan Carlos?"

"I wouldn't say we're dating, we just met at a club two days ago. He's dying to get in my pants though." Bambi laughs.

"He can have the pants — I'm dying to get in your shirt." Bob smiles and talks directly to her breasts. "I'd like to get in between those puppies, curl up in a ball, and take a nap. *Mmm, mmm!*"

Bambi giggles. "Oh, if I had a dollar every time I heard that. Actually, come to think of it, sometimes men do put dollars between them." She reaches in her bra and pulls out a twenty. "Well, look at this! I guess I got the next round!"

Summer swivels to face Bob and grabs his arm with one hand. She sighs seductively. "What about getting in my shirt *and* in my pants?"

Bob grins and shakes his head no. "I'm sorry — and don't take this the wrong way — but I just don't want to sleep with you."

Summer feels a strange tingle and finds herself getting damp. She grabs his arm with her other hand, too, and pouts. "I was kinda joking — but wait, are you sure?"

Bob withdraws his arm from her. "Yeah, I'm sure. Plus, aren't you dating Bradford?"

"Yeah — well — I guess technically."

"Well, there you go — case closed. You've got a boyfriend and, in all honesty, you're not my type. You and I — it's not gonna work."

Paralyzed, Summer's inner voice wonders, *Why is my pussy salivating? It's out of control down there!* She nibbles on her right index finger and puts her left hand on Bob's knee.

Fumes come out of Bradford's ears as he watches them. He runs over and shouts, "What the hell's going on over here?!"

"Nothing man. We're just talking," Bob replies.

"That doesn't look like nothing to me! First of all, Summer, I told you not to talk to these guys. Then you touch him like that. What in the shit is that all about?"

Summer turns away from Bradford and locks eyes with Bob. "I was gently letting him know — well, after he asked — that he can fuck me any which way he wants."

Bob and Bradford yell in unison, "What the fuck!!??"

Bradford pokes Bob in the chest. "I'll fucking kill you!"

Bob slaps his hand away. "Don't fucking touch me. I never said that!" Bob stands up so he can stare down at Bradford. "You're not even tall enough for carnival rides!"

Summer begins to laugh like she's insane. As Bob and Bradford stare at her, their angry faces are altered by bewilderment. Summer composes herself. "Holy shit that was funny. I was just screwing with you guys!"

Bradford steps away from Bob and tries to be cool. "Yeah, I knew that."

"However, your over-possessiveness has managed to dry-up my soaking wet panties." She looks at Bradford like he's pitiful. "Congratulations, you're becoming very skilled in that department." She pauses and then adds, "You're so pathetic — I don't even have the desire to queef in your face right now."

"Is that why you're acting like this? Because of your period?"

"Ugh. You are so fucking stupid." Summer shakes her head and turns her back on him.

Unable to discern if she is continuing to fuck with him or if there's a hint of truth in what she said about her dried-up panties, Bradford darts away.

Scooter, having observed this bizarre battle-of-the-sexes, drowns in a sea of confusion. He fast-forwards through the most embarrassing discussion of his life — "the birds and the bees" talk his father had with him when he was twelve. His father stripped Barbie and G.I. Joe of their clothes, except for Barbie's top. He felt exposing a doll's breasts to his son crossed the 'decency line.' After a disturbing multi-position simulation where the plastic action figures mashed their non-existent genitalia, his father wrapped up his lecture with this — "Son, if there's one thing I want you to always remember from today, it's this — bitches be crazy."

As "Gin & Juice" comes to an end, Brewer yells, "Last call!"

"Damn, it's 3:30 already," Bob gripes before calling to Brewer. "Hey, same drinking rules still apply to the old-time regulars?" Summer and Bambi eavesdrop on the conversation.

"For you Bob, of course," Brewer answers as he wipes down the bar.

"You gonna wrestle Zabka at 4:00?"

"If he wants his ass kicked again. Yeah sure, I'll wrestle that fool."

"He always thinks he can beat you." Bob laughs. "He'll never learn."

"Sorry, but your Miami friends are gonna have to leave with the others." Brewer senses an argument starting between Juan Carlos and Lisa at the other end of the bar.

Juan Carlos looks at Lisa sideways. "What do you mean my card doesn't work here? Do you *even know* what type of card this is?"

Lisa gives him his card back and puts her hands on her hips. "Don't you have another so I can close you out?"

"See this?" Juan Carlos acts like his credit card is a heavy weight in the palm of his hand. "This is a black card — very exclusive. I bet this pig sty's never seen one before."

"Like I told you, it's a little too thick so it won't slide through the slot."

Juan Carlos sneers. "You've probably never experienced that problem either." He pulls out a couple of hundred dollar bills and tosses them at her. "Keep the change and fix your machine."

Brewer turns to Bob and says, "God, what a jackass." He leans in so the Miami girls can't hear. "I'm not sorry that schmuck has to leave, but I'm sorry the girls do. However, I'm pretty sure you'll have some replacement company joining you on the dark side." Brewer glances at Lisa and then back at Bob. "I think she's gunning for you tonight."

Bob smiles and turns around to the girls. "Too bad ladies, but it looks like you're gonna miss the wrestling show."

Summer says, "Something tells me this show isn't going to end tonight." She straightens up like some something just popped into her head. "Hey! Tomorrow we'll be at the Buffalo Brewfest downtown. We have some work to do there, but why don't you guys come?"

"That sounds about our speed. If I'm not currently blacked out and I remember tomorrow, maybe we'll see ya there." Bob grins and squints at Summer. "But I'm still *not* gonna fuck you."

Lisa places two shots on the bar near Bob. "Okay girls, time to go."

Summer and Bambi's men join them as they put on their coats to depart. Like an angry little child, Bradford can't help himself but to leave a final departing shot. "Buffalo's wonderful! You guys are lucky that you live in the world's asshole!"

Zabka starts to jump forward, but Brewer grabs him by the collar before he can. Scooter puffs his chest and yells, "Oh yeah! You're wrong! Geographically speaking, that would be Antarctica! I bet you failed Social Studies!" Bradford shakes his head as a bouncer ushers them out.

Bob looks back at the shots and says to Lisa, "I take it these are for us?" Lisa comes around to the other side of the bar and stands next to him.

"They sure are." As the Nat King Cole Christmas classic plays, Lisa sings along, "Everybody knows, a turkey and some mistletoe."

Bob sniffs his shot. "Doesn't smell like mistletoe." They clink their shot glasses and raise them up. "So it must be turkey! Wild Turkey!"

"Yep, but maybe we just pretend there's mistletoe here too." Lisa gets on her tippy-toes to inch closer to Bob's height. "Here's to joining you on the dark side."

After shooting back their shots, she leans into him and almost topples over. He grabs her around the waist so she doesn't fall and tells her, "Whoa, careful there. I almost grabbed your chest-icles."

Lisa stabilizes herself and shrugs. "Woulda been just fine with me."

As though horse blinders are being strapped on Bob's head, blackness enters his peripheral vision. After he takes a sip of beer, Lisa's face gets closer and begins to blur.

The Third Quarter

As the sun peeks over the horizon, yellow fire shoots west across the icy, snow-trapped ground, and long shadows sprout from the buildings and trees. Inside an apartment, Jennifer struggles from her prone position on the couch to open her eyes into the blinding rays. *Where the hell am I?* To avoid the eye-poking light, she rolls to her side, falls, and slams onto the floor. THUD!

A voice from the next room shouts, "Youz okay?"

Is that Faige? Am I at her place? With her cheek stuck to the hardwood floor, Jennifer yells back, "Yeah, I'm okay. I just fell off your couch."

Faige shuffles into the living room wearing jumbo kitten slippers and flannel PJs. "Why'd youz do dat?"

Still in her evening dress, Jennifer picks herself up from the ground. "I didn't know where I was."

Faige curls up in a big accent chair. "Youz feel as lousy as me?"

Jennifer sits on the couch with her head between her hands. "I haven't drank like that in a while. Please don't ever let me do that again."

"Welcome back ta single life. Invest in a bottle-a vitamin B-complex. It helps — a lil'."

Jennifer slowly lifts her head. "Faige, I'm not single. Robert and I just had a bad fight — we'll work it out."

"Yeah, maybe, but is dat sumptin youz really wanna put effawt into? Youz know youz don't need a man, right? Fa now, I'm perfectly happy witout one. Mo freedom, less headaches." Faige chuckles. "Well, maybe not less headaches, but a different kinda headache. Doze cosmos was killa!"

"Ain't that the truth? I had like four of them or something."

"Actually, we had seven each. Youz musta stopped countin' early."

"Oh sweet Jesus," Jennifer moans. "Anyway, back to Robert. Yes, I want to work things out with him. Especially after this."

"But what about youz and I?" Faige alternates between pointing at Jennifer and herself. "We made a pretty damn good team lass-night. Not ta be cliché, but dere's plennia fish in da sea. Youz gotta tro da bad ones back, so youz can catch a good one."

Jennifer replies forcefully, "He's *not* a bad one, he just needs guidance." *Why does she want me to leave him so badly?*

"Sawree, but as ya friend, I gotta be honest wit' youz. I've been watchin' youz in dis relationship, and ta me youz seem like an owna of a disobedient dawg." Faige puts her hands in front of her chin like paws and sticks her tongue out like a puppy. "You put a leash on 'im and tried ta train 'im. And when he shits on da carpet, youz scold 'im."

"Yeah, but that's what it's like to have a boyfriend. Let's face it, in general, men are pretty stupid — they need direction from us. It's up to us to mold and shape them into what we want."

Faige nods her head. "But Robert won't follow along."

"Was he resistant at first? Yes. But I expected that. It took time, but I got him to fall in line. Now he's just temporarily off-track. I'll get him back." Jennifer holds up two fingers for emphasis. "There are two keys to success in getting what you want with your man. The first is to be persistent. You will eventually wear him down. Use words like *compromise* and *give-n-take* to guide his behavior. Whatever you do, don't make anything seem like it's a threat to his freedom. Instead make it be —" She uses air-quotes. "For the good of the relationship."

Faige looks like she's taking mental notes. "By bein' persistent, youz mean nag 'im, right?"

"No, not at all. Be cool and patient *while* you're being persistent. That way you're not nagging. Make sense?"

"I guess. Okay, what's da second key?"

"The second key is to know what your man's carrot is. This can be used to lead him where you want and punish him when he disobeys. It's basically your negotiating tool."

Faige processes this information. "Okay, so I tink I've got da second key figga'd out. A man's carrot is basically his dick, right?"

Jennifer laughs. "Yeah, and that's our leverage, because a guy wants us to do all sorts of things to please it." She takes a moment to think. "Actually, if his carrot isn't his penis, then you're with a guy who doesn't realize he's gay and so it's time to move on anyway."

Faige chuckles. "Yep, dat makes complete sense. Tell me mo about da two keys. What youz done and how it's worked."

"Okay, I'll tell you about William. He was the last guy I dated seriously back in Orange County." Images of sun and surf flip through Jennifer's mind. "Actually, I could tell you about Mathew too — both of them were similar to Robert and had a little too much fun at times. Anyway, I'll just stick with William. So a few months into our relationship he told me he was going to Vegas for his friend Chuck's birthday. I told him to be a good boy while he was there and that when he got home I would 'rock his world,' if you get my drift. No matter how much he wanted it, I wouldn't have sex with him the week prior. I was *persistent* on saying *no*. What I was doing was guiding his mind so he'd only think about me while he was away. I was strengthening our bond."

Faige gasps — her mouth agape.

"I know, right? You're impressed," Jennifer says proudly. "When William got back that Sunday evening, I told him to come to my place so I could see him, but he said he was too exhausted. I then said that I would *compromise* and go over to see him. He was initially resistant, but eventually gave-in once I showed up. Here's the weird part — that night he was very standoffish, and even though I tried, we didn't have sex."

Faige's tone expresses concern. "He didn't wanna have sex?"

"Yeah." Jennifer shrugs. "He was man-struating."

"Man-struating? Like menstruating? What are youz talkin' about?"

"It's when a guy gets moody and doesn't want to do it. When I have my period, I don't want to have sex. It's gross."

Faige sheepishly comments, "I actually kinda like ta do it den."

"Well, it's not for me. Anyway, obviously what brought on William's time-of-the-month was his little trip without me. So I concluded that the problem needed to be dealt with head-on. From that point forward I did what was necessary to help him understand that we needed to put our relationship first over any of these meaningless guys trips of his."

Faige begins to speak, but Jennifer proceeds over her. "Sure, there was some tension in the beginning, but he learned to not even ask about going away. Here's the crappy thing, though. Once I got our relationship to where it needed to be, William became dull. He'd sit around the apartment and play video games all day. He was like a zombie, and we hardly talked. Our sex-life became nonexistent too." Jennifer emphasizes her next points with her palms. "So on the one hand I had him trained, but on the other hand I was losing interest. Anyway, we lasted another few weeks before I broke up with him."

"Can I speak now?" Jennifer nods for Faige to go on. "I'm impressed. Ya way of handlin' men is pafection. Flawless."

"You really think so?"

"No. Are youz off ya rocker?" Faige shakes her head. "I did my best ta bite my tongue, but dere's so much ta tawk about, I'm not sure where ta begin. I guess first I'll ask about da no-sex episode. Assumin' William's like all da guys I know — which means down-ta-bone 24-7 — didn't youz find it strange dat afta ova a week witout sex, he comes back from Vegas and isn't interested?"

"Not really, he just kept telling me he was too tired. I chalk it up as a man-period excuse." Jennifer fidgets in her seat as Faige's question sinks in further. "What are you trying to say? That William fucked around on me in Vegas?"

"Well, awviously I don't know — I'm jus' reviewin' da facts. Youz wit'held sex from 'im before he goes ta Vegas, of all places, and den he doesn't jump all ova youz when he gets home? Dats biz-a."

Jennifer stares into space. *Fuck! Did William cheat on me? I teased Robert's carrot and withheld sex from him too. What did he and that asshole Zabka do last night? Go slut-banging?!* She leaps up from the couch. "I gotta go. I need to see Robert now!"

"No, dere's mo we needa tawk about!" Faige gets up, grabs Jennifer by the shoulders, and looks her in the eyes. "Did youz tell me da whole troot about what happened wit' Robert lass-night?"

Jennifer turns her head away. "I told you, I need to go!"

—

In the Grand Suite of the Hyatt Regency, an empty bottle of Dom Pérignon lays on the beige carpet at the foot of a king size bed. Beneath a fluffy white comforter, a wall of pillows and a mink coat separates two sprawling bodies. Movement softly bubbles on the left side and creeps its way beneath the wall, forcing the middle of the barrier upward. Sensing the breach, the body on the right side wiggles away to the edge of the bed.

"Keep your paws away from me," Bambi squeaks. "I told you, you can't have your way with me — not yet."

"But you're so pretty — so sexy," Juan Carlos whines.

"Why is everything always about my looks? Why don't you compliment me on my smarts or my sense of humor? I know I'm funny because everyone is always laughing at me."

"You're all those things, baby. You're like the perfect woman."

"Well, I appreciate it. That reminds me of the time I was at the mall and this guy was chatting me up. Mid-conversation he pointed and said,

'See this naked mannequin? That's the *perfect woman.* You're practically her, except you're deficient in one way.' And I said, 'I don't get it. We both have great figures, but I can talk.' And he replied, 'Exactly,' and grabbed the mannequin and ran out the door."

"I'm sure there's some deep meaning there, but let's get back to us. You can't deny that we have intense chemistry."

Bambi rolls towards the wall and presses it down so she can look at him. "Yes, I know," she sighs. "There's nothing more I'd like to do right now than ride you like a bucking bronco until you scream for your mommy, but we just met a few days ago. I need to know more about you first. Like, I want to know more about your business with Bradford."

Juan Carlos's morning wood has swelled into a morning sequoia. "What do you want me to tell you?"

"Like, how do your magic fat dick pills work? What's the cream do?"

"It's real complicated bio-chemistry type stuff. There's chambers and tissue and blood flow. I think it will be over your head."

Bambi pouts. "Well, why don't you put it in my head? I have a fetish for that sort of thing." She crawls her hand like a tarantula down his chest above the covers. "Maybe this little guy can tell me?" She stops near his navel, pokes up her middle-finger like it's the creature's head, and moves it back and forth.

Juan Carlos squirms. "Let's just say that these pills *enhance* a man's confidence."

Bambi smiles. "And how's your confidence doing right now?"

"My confidence is strong." He grimaces. "Painfully strong at the moment. No need for pills here."

"But do these pills actually increase a man's size?" Bambi's tarantula crawls a step south. "I want the truth. And if you lie to me —" The tarantula crawls backwards two steps. "Sadly, we'll never play rodeo games together." She bats her eyelashes. "Think hard before you answer, because I *really* like to play rodeo — and I brought my reverse cowgirl boots."

As Juan Carlos's head spins, he recalls what Bradford beat into his skull on the day they started their business. While never anticipating a scenario like this, he lets out a big exhale, and brushes away Bradford's guidance. "Okay, forget what I said about the bio-chemistry stuff, here's how it works. If a man believes his penis is getting bigger, then it is. When a man gets bigger, his confidence grows. So ultimately a mind-penis thing happens. It's symbiotic."

"This is fascinating." Bambi puts down her elbow and rests her chin in her palm. "But I'm still confused. Are you saying the pills make a guy's Johnson bigger or not?"

Juan Carlos instinctively looks around the empty room before answering, "You can't repeat this to anyone, okay?" Bambi nods. "Mentally, the pills do — at least at first. Men stare at their dicks and think it's working. Physically, it's not doing anything. But then there's the cream, which does have some temporary physical effects."

"*Hmmm*, all very interesting. I want to know more about that too."

"I'm sure you do, but it works like this. I told you something —" He reaches for her hand. "Now it's time for you to —" She pulls her hand away.

"I'm saving *that* for after the game tomorrow." Bambi pushes her hair back behind her ear. "It will be our grand finale."

Juan Carlos groans. "Fine, let's talk about this afternoon's promotional event and what I need you to do."

"I'm all ears," Bambi tells him.

"You need to be all T&A at the Brewfest. I want you to flirt with the guys, ya know, make 'em think you're into them. Help them realize they need a product like ours, and then get them to purchase at least a 90-day supply. You think you can manipulate guys like that?"

Bambi smiles slyly. "Yeah, I think I can pull something like that off."

"Great."

"Should we get out of bed and get going? Mom always told me, 'the early worm catches the bird.'"

Juan Carlos squeezes his eyes shut and exhales forcefully. "We're the bird, not the worm. You never want to be the worm." He puts his head into a pillow to muffle his scream.

—

As Bob staggers around the corner into the living room, the snoring gets louder. Wearing just his boxer shorts, he stops to scratch his crotch and survey the carnage surrounding him. Zabka is sleeping under a comforter on the stained fuchsia couch that Bob found on the curb. Jed, the main snoring offender, is fully clothed and laying on his side in the middle of the room. His arms hug, and his head perches on a makeshift pillow of crushed beer cans. In the corner, next to the Christmas tree, is a rat's nest of clothes, blankets, and couch-cushions. Buried in there, he assumes, is Scooter.

As Bob makes his way to the heap-of-garbage, he wonders what might to jump out. He cautiously picks-up the couch-cushion at the peak and uncovers Scooter's unconscious, torn-up face. Bob squats, puts his mouth next to his friend's drool-encrusted ear, and very kindly screeches, "Wake up sleeping beauty!!"

Startled, Scooter juts upward and nearly headbutts Bob. Unable to open his eyes from exhaustion and borderline alcohol poisoning, Scooter begs, "Can I please get some aspirin? I need water and aspirin, badly."

"Sure, no problem." Bob walks to the kitchen.

Zabka adds, "Scooter, this is dangerously close to pussy-like behavior."

Bob returns with two aspirin and a drink. Scooter, barley conscious, pops the pills in his mouth and, with a shaky hand, tips the glass back to swallow them down. Immediately, his eyes explode open — he tosses the glass, and it lands squarely on Jed's nuts. Scooter grabs himself by the neck and unleashes a gurgling yell, "What the FUUUCK!!? That's not water! My throat's on fire!"

"I'm sorry, did you say you wanted water?" Bob mockingly asks. "I guess I misheard you. I thought you said vodka."

"Good one!" Zabka flops his arm in Scooter's direction. "Congrats, Scooter! You've officially entered full-on pussy-territory!"

Jed grabs the glass that's resting on his nads, sits up, and gulps down the booze that survived the flight. "Thanks for the morning pick-me-up. So what's on our agenda today?"

Zabka answers to the ceiling, "Well there's a lot we can do in the Buffalo. We can go to Niagara Falls. We can go to Toronto. The options are limitless."

"He's mostly right, but actually there is something else we can do." Bob tells them, "We can go to the Buffalo Brewfest!"

"I like the sound of that!" Jed shouts.

Zabka jumps onboard. "Fuck yeah, Bob! Great idea!"

Scooter groans, "*Fuuuuuck*," and pulls a couch cushion over his face.

Bob shares, "Yeah, I heard about it on the radio, but totally forgot until Summer reminded me. Should be a good time."

Jed reflects on the previous night. "Is she one of those Miami whores?"

"Yeah, that's her."

"Does that mean the rest of them are gonna be there?" Jed asks. "I bet it does. I don't need some jackasses telling me about how their goddamn butler got them seats behind the Dolphins bench. I hate those fucktards!"

"Speaking of seats," Zabka says. "Scooter, where are ours? Please tell me right in front of the butt-plug bunch."

Scooter hunches-over. His hand fumbles around until it finds his glasses. He puts them on, and says like he's in Confession, "Guys, I need to tell you something."

"Oh, fuck." Zabka whines, "I don't like the sound of this."

"Please don't kill me." Scooter wrings his hands together. "I — I thought I could just buy seats at the box-office at the game. I don't have tickets right now, but I swear I'll find us some. I promise!"

Zabka blasts off the couch. "Son-of-a-cunt, Scooter! Are you fucking kidding me?!"

Jed yells, "The network was down, Scooter! The damn network was down! And now this!" He uses one arm to scoop and fling crushed beer cans across the room. "You're horrible at smoothing things over!"

Bob moves into the middle of the living room and presses his hands in the direction of Zabka and Jed. "Guys, you need to calm *the fuck* down! We'll figure this out!" He pauses to give the grumblers time to relax.

Jed looks up at Bob who's standing next to where he's sitting. "Fine. Not to switch topics, but shouldn't we talk about last night's affairs? You know, debrief?"

"Actually, that's a good idea based on our current dilemma," Bob replies. "Those Miami cock suckers might be the answer to our problems. We should debrief."

Jed nods. "I'm glad you agree." He then quickly pulls Bob's boxer shorts down to his ankles. Everyone laughs hysterically and throws empty beer cans at Bob's junk while he scrambles to pull up his shorts.

"Alright, assholes!" Bob shouts with a red face. "Enough fucking around! We need to talk through our situation. This is serious."

Jed clears tears from his eyes. "You're right. Sorry, I couldn't resist."

"Save that sneaky, fucked-up shit for our enemies," Bob commands. "You're looking at our predicament the wrong way. Every problem presents an opportunity, right? In this case, we've got two problems. The first problem is obvious — we don't have any tickets. What's our second problem?" He looks at each of them and receives blank stares in return. "Christ! Come on guys, we were just gonna talk about it. Our second problem are those pricks from Miami. We hate those fuckers, right?"

Jed nods. "Personally, I wouldn't mind taking a steaming dump on Bradford's face."

"Yep, that sounds a touch like hate to me. So let's extract their tickets!" Bob plucks them symbolically from the air. "Which obviously fucks them over. We like that, right?" Everyone agrees. "And it solves our ticket problem — two problems, two opportunities, ONE solution!"

Zabka thumps his chest twice. "I like it, but we need a game-plan. This is a battle we can't lose. Last night Bob, you went off fuckin' script. We all gotta stick with what we come up with here."

"We'll come up with a plan, but sometimes in the heat of battle — when shit is blowing up all around you — you have to use instinct, improvise, and adapt. Just realize that might happen again, and no matter what, we must focus on our goal and fight to achieve it!" Bob pounds his fist into his palm. "Let the goal guide your decisions and ultimately lead us to victory!"

"So where do we start?" Jed asks.

"We start with intelligence," Zabka replies. "What do we know about these mother-fuckers?"

"Exactly." Bob applauds. "Let's first review what we know about their group. They're rich, from Miami, and they're Dolphin fans. Summer mentioned they have some work to do at the Brewfest — I'm not sure what. Anything else?"

Scooter adds, "Yeah, they've got itty-bitty boy cocks."

"That's right!" Bob shouts as he paces the room. "That's a key piece of data we can't forget. Okay, so let's talk about each one of them individually. Let's dig into their personalities. What can we exploit to our advantage?"

"Obviously, Bambi is a bimbo," Zabka remarks. "So we could probably convince her to do just about anything we want."

Bob shakes his head. "Maybe she's a bimbo at first glance, but after talking with her one-on-one, I think she's brighter than she wants everyone to believe. She's up to something for sure." He taps his chin. "Also she just met the others — hardly knows them. I think there might be a way she could help us, but I can't quite put my finger on it."

"Oh yeah? Well I can put my finger *in it*," Zabka replies. "In her juicy vagina."

"Really, Zabka?" Bob claps his hands chop-chop. "Next there's Summer — she's like a banana that looks tasty, but when you peel it back, you find it covered with bruises. Anyway, not to brag, but she's pretty into me. I think we can use her to get Bradford riled up — she's the stick that we poke him with. He's the type who'll get hotheaded, make mistakes, and play right into our hands."

Zabka sticks his chest out. "Good analysis, but sorry, Bob — Summer's into me. I can handle her."

"I apologize, Zabka, because I know you have a fragile ego, but did she tell you she wants to fuck you?" Bob asks.

"Well, not exactly in those words. Let's just say it was conveyed." Zabka smirks before noticing Bob's devilish grin. "Wait, no way she said that to you."

"Yeah she did, so let *me* handle her. Lastly, there's Juan Carlos. The guy is obviously a sucker for brainless floozies and seems to be more of a direction taker. Knowing all this, what's our plan?"

As the guys ponder the question, Scooter knocks himself in the head with the insides of his wrists. Jed confesses, "Guys, for some reason my brain isn't functioning at peak performance this morning. Honestly, I've got nothing."

"I'll get something to help." Bob goes into the kitchen and returns with a cold can of Genny. "Here Jed, drink this. It's not the breakfast of champions — it's the breakfast of second place! You're in Buffalo."

Jed opens the beer and chugs it in about five seconds. "Damn! I feel some clarity coming on already."

"Okay, tell me what you think about this," Bob requests. "You three geniuses prod the Siamese jack-off twins until they can't help but spill where they're keeping their tickets. They're the type to talk and brag, so figure it out. I'll then manipulate Summer into taking me to wherever they are — I imagine they're located in one of their rooms — and I'll snatch the tickets." Bob puts his hands out. "Sound like a solid plan?"

"Works for me." Scooter raises his fist. "Fuck those guys."

"Don't screw this up, Bob," Zabka orders. "And when you need me to take over, just tap me in."

"The plan is legit," Jed says. "Now how about a plan to eat? You know if it's Taco Tuesday anywhere? I could really use a burrito."

"I'm not sure how to respond to that since it's Saturday, but rest assured, we'll get you some food. Gotta feed the troops!" Bob claps his hands. "Let's get ready! This is gonna be fun!"

Jed sniffs his armpit. "I suppose I should shower. It's been a few days."

"I'll speak for everyone here." Zabka waves his hand in front of his nose. "We'd really appreciate that."

"Sure, but let me jump in the shower first," Bob says. "I feel like I should run over to Jennifer's and talk before we get moving."

"Whoa, whoa, whoa, *Robert*," Zabka barks. "We don't have time for your relationship nonsense to interfere with *our* nonsense. Plus, what the hell were you doing with Lisa last night? She's one of my girls."

"What? What do you mean? What did I do?"

"Ah, fuck — who cares? We've got bigger problems to deal with. Remember what you said about focus? No distractions — this is civil war! And again, the North will prevail!"

———

After a painful taxi ride from Faige's apartment to her place in North Tonawanda, Jennifer takes a hot shower and hopes the remaining alcohol will sweat out of her system. She does her best to make herself presentable before running downstairs to grab a cab to Robert's place. She jumps in the backseat and they depart. *Why didn't he leave me a message last night? He always calls first when we have a fight.*

As they pull into the apartment complex parking lot, Jennifer spots Robert's car parked next to hers. After paying the driver, she marches up to his apartment and takes a deep breath. She places her ear on his front door and hears only silence on the other side. *Maybe they're still asleep?* She knocks and waits anxiously. *Maybe his friends stayed elsewhere?*

After no one answers, Jennifer unlocks the door with the key Robert gave her. Borderline terrified of what she'll discover, she creeps into the living room. Minus an orgy, the wreckage she finds matches her worst fears. *Did a pack of raccoons get loose in here? And good lord, what is that smell?! Pepperoni and beer farts?* Between two distinct sleeping mounds — one on the couch and one in a corner — is an ocean of garbage composed of empty beer cans, a half eaten bags of chips, and an XXL pair of tighty-whities with "Sex Panther" written in block letters on the waistband.

The kitchen table also looks like it contains an assortment of waste. During her inspection, Jennifer finds four white t-shirts identically modified with spray-paint. She picks up something that resembles a large, square, blueberry lollypop made by a second grader in art class — a one-foot-by-one-foot piece of Styrofoam duct taped to a two-foot plastic rod. *There are four of these things too. What the hell are these bozos planning?* Before leaving the kitchen, she glances at the answering machine. *No messages from any whores. Check.*

Jennifer enters Robert's bedroom. *Everything looks normal so far.* She walks over to his bed, peels back the covers, and feels the sheets. *It's cold. Did he come back here last night? Usually the electric blanket leaves some lingering warmth for a while. Fuck, I can't tell.* She scans the room again before deciding to leave. On the way out, she looks into the small wastebasket next to his desk and notices two scraps of paper. *Hold on, I emptied that yesterday morning. He's been home.*

She grabs the papers from the basket and looks at the first. *A Mighty Taco receipt. Not surprising.* She throws it back in the basket and unwrinkles the next. It's a note adorned with a smudge of red lipstick reads, "Lisa 555-6969 call me." Jennifer howls, "Who the hell is this Lisa bitch!? That slut banging slut is gonna pay!" She crumples up the evidence and stuffs it in her pocket.

Fuming to the point where she's looking for shit to break, Jennifer pauses. *Calm down before you do something you may regret.* She strolls into the living room pretending like she hasn't a care in the world. "Naw, fuck that! Somebody's gonna get cut!" She kicks the pile of empty beer cans and sends them flying into the kitchen.

Wait, her number was in the trash. She slipped him her number, he didn't want to be rude, and then he threw it out because he wasn't interested. Jennifer dances into the kitchen to pick up her mess. After cleaning for a few seconds she stops and straightens up. *No, he threw it away after he banged her and was done with her!* She rants, "I bet there's a used condom in the trash!" She chucks the cans back on the floor and runs into the bathroom.

As Jennifer rips through the trash, all she finds are dirty tissues and an empty beer. *No condoms anywhere. I'm totally over-reacting.* She looks in the mirror and gives herself a thumbs-up. *See, I'm not crazy.* As she's about to skip out of the bathroom, the toilet says to her, "That asshole flushed the evidence!" She hurries into the kitchen and combs through drawers. After finding a book of matches, she considers what to burn first. *No, no, don't do that.*

With her heart racing, Jennifer returns to his bedroom, sits down at his desk, and begins to cry. *Stop it. You'll get through this.* She grabs a tissue and wipes away her tears. After a few sniffles, she opens the drawer, pulls out a pen & paper, and begins to write, "Dear Robert —"

———

As the white Bronco races south on Niagara Falls Boulevard, Bob remarks from the backseat, "I really like your O.J. mobile, Jed."

"Thanks. Hopefully, dozens of cops won't soon be following us."

"With us, there's always a chance," Zabka adds. "But no need to worry — we're in fine hands. Jed is our Al Cowlings."

Scooter attaches snap-on sunglasses to his prescription glasses. He then pulls out a small bottle and uses it to spray his wrists and neck.

Zabka's nose curls up and he turns around in his navigator seat. "What the hell is that smell?"

"That my friends, is pussy catnip." Scooter smiles from ear to ear. "The hot girl at the counter told me this would make me irresistible."

"Those girls are paid to tell you that." Zabka rolls down his window. "Jesus! It smells like flowery air freshener trying to mask a turd."

"Whatever. Dudes, check this out." Scooter flips his sunglass lenses up and down. "Pretty cool, right? I can wear these inside and outside."

Zabka shifts his attention to Bob. "Can you take care of this problem before we are out in public at the Brewfest?"

Bob laughs. "Yeah, I'll handle it."

Scooter tells them, "You guys just don't understand how to be hip. Anyway, how are we getting there? Can we take the subway?"

"Subway?" Zabka asks. "Are you still drunk? There's no subway in the Buffalo. I would know — I lived here for four years."

"Sure there is. I read about it in my encyclopedia. It was finished in '86. Tell 'em, Bob."

"Surprisingly, he's correct," Bob confirms. "I know we went to college here, but I just recently found out about it. Funny enough, it basically starts at UB near Third Base and follows Main Street to downtown."

"The tunnel to nowhere," Zabka adds.

"Pretty much, because most of downtown dies in the evening," Bob says. "But you can hit the Allentown and Chippewa bars, or go to the Aud for a concert or Sabres game. I guess it could come in handy for that, although I've never taken it."

"Well, it serves us no purpose today, we need to get to the Connecticut Street Armory," Zabka tells them.

Bob shares, "It could get us close, but then we'd have to take a cab."

"I'm driving us," Jed says emphatically.

"Although I would love to ride on a subway for the first time," Scooter says. "I would much rather swing by Millionaires' Row and see all the mansions. Can we do that? It's a few blocks on Delaware Avenue."

"First a subway and now mansions?" Zabka scratches his head. "There's a whole other Buffalo world I didn't even know existed — like a real city or something. Yeah, we can drive by that on the way."

"Super cool!" Scooter replies. "You probably didn't know this either, but when the 1900's began, Buffalo had the most millionaires per capita of any city in America. Back then, trade, grain milling, and steel production were huge here. All thanks to Lake Erie and the Erie Canal. Buffalo was the 'Gateway to the West'."

Jed puts up his index finger. "Scooter, one question. Is any of the information gonna get us Bills tickets?"

"Well, um, probably not," Scooter answers.

"That's what I thought. So how about we keep the jibber-jabber shit to a minimum today, okay?"

"Scooter, pay no mind to Jed," Bob says. "I like that you appreciate coming here. You're cool in my book." Scooter returns a look of thanks. "Go on and tell 'em what you want to do today. What you told me earlier."

"You mean about squishing the fish?" Scooter asks.

"Yes, but that's not how you say it. Say it like you mean it!"

"Squish the fish!" Scooter screams. "I wanna squish some fishes, bitches! Squish some today! All day!"

"Squish the...!" Zabka pauses. "What? Some today? All day?"

"I'd really like to squish some fish today, wouldn't you?" Scooter asks.

"The game is tomorrow. What are you talking about?"

Scooter's brow furrows. "You can only squish the fish on game day? That doesn't make sense."

"Wait a sec," Bob cuts in. "What do you think 'squish the fish' means?"

"It means squish the fish, ya know? Get laid. Pound some pussy. Why else would you guys be screaming it all the time?" Everyone laughs at Scooter, but instead of falling into his usual embarrassed silence, he punches back. "I don't understand why that's so funny. A woman's fishy odor comes from the fact that we evolved from the sea — it's simple biology. Why else would they call fishnet stockings, *fishnet* stockings? *Hmmm?* In this context, 'squish the fish' makes complete sense." He shakes his head. "You guys are a bunch of dingbats."

Bob pats Scooter on the shoulder. "That's right, screw these morons — they probably failed biology. I like where your head's at, but in this case 'squish the fish' is actually in reference to the Miami Dolphins. Get it?"

"Not really." Scooter shakes his head. "A dolphin's not a fish."

"Yeah, but try not to be so literal. The words rhyme, so just go with it. But I admit, I do like your interpretation better."

"Hey, Scooter," Zabka says. "After all your reading up on the Buffalo, all you know about the Bills is what I told you yesterday, isn't it?"

"Not really," Scooter answers. "Of course I know about O.J. Simpson and the 'Trial of the Century'."

Zabka grabs his Bills cap from beneath his seat and puts it on. "Hang on. Is that how you see the Bills? As cold-blooded murders?"

Scooter shakes his head. "I never said that. Plus O.J. was acquitted, so technically there's no linkage between the two."

"Oh there's a linkage there alright, but I call it something else," Bob begins. "I call it Buffalo's dominos of disaster, and I believe they will continue to fall. You know O.J.'s 'dream team' lawyer Robert Kardashian?"

"Yeah, what about him?" Zabka asks.

Bob answers, "I watched that guy and have a weird feeling he'll have a hand in producing something mindless and awful. Who knows? Maybe he already has?"

"Sure Bob, that makes a ton of sense," Zabka mocks. "How about we stick with something relevant, like football, and educate Scooter?"

"By all means, Zabka. Go for it."

"Thanks for your permission, Bob. So the Bills have an outstanding team made up of superstars. Guys like our quarterback Jim Kelly, who runs the K-Gun no-huddle offense and disintegrates opposing defenses. There's also Andre Reed, Kelly's go-to wide receiver. Unfortunately he's been injured most of this season, but let's hope he plays tomorrow. And then there's Thurman Thomas, our All-Pro running back. The guy is a beast! Those guys are the core of our offense." Zabka gets more animated. "And we can't forget about Bruce Smith, our killer defensive end! We spoke about him yesterday. He's responsible for what, Jed?!"

"The dome that Bruce built!!" Jed shouts. "The BRUUUUUCE DOME!!!"

"Correct! Tomorrow's game is critical, not only because it's the fucking Dolphins, but because *when* we win, we're in the playoffs! And we need to be in the playoffs to get back to the Super Bowl and finally win the goddamn thing! This is the year we do it!"

"So the Bills have never won the Super Bowl?" Scooter asks.

"No! They made it four years in a row and lost each time!" Zabka screams as he tears his hair out. "From the '90 season through the '93 season! Bob and I were going to college here at the time." He shakes his head. "Talk about getting repeatedly kicked in the balls. Fuck!"

"Yeah, it was painful," Bob adds. "But that's the past! I'm looking at the future, and it seems pretty bright! Anyone want to join me in tasting over a hundred craft beers?!"

The Bronco erupts, "Hell yeah!!!"

———

Inside the Hyatt Regency's top-floor Huron Suite, Summer is in her white silk pajamas and doing stomach crunches on the carpet. During each upward movement, she looks through the corner windows to panoramic views of Lake Erie and the Peace Bridge. A sheet of ice breaks free and slowly drifts away from shore across the choppy, navy blue water. Eighteen-wheeler trucks sit at a near standstill on the bridge, waiting to cross into Fort Erie, Canada.

Bradford gets out of bed wearing only Burberry pattern PJ bottoms and walks over toward Summer. He gets down near her and begins doing pushups. His toned pecs, arms, and back muscles flex as he exercise-humps the ground. Summer rolls onto her stomach and in unison they double-team the floor. After fifty reps, they stop and sit.

Bradford meekly asks, "So what the heck happened last night?"

"From what I can remember, we got close to blackout drunk."

"No, I mean why were you messing with me last night?"

Summer cocks her head and mockingly asks, "What ever do you mean?"

"I mean you were flirting with that nobody Buffalo guy, Bob." Bradford scratches his arm. "And trying to get under my skin."

"*Pfff.* Looks like it worked."

"Yeah, it fucking did. Don't do that," he pleads.

"You know what?" She turns to him with burning eyes. "You need to stop being such a pussy. A real man would just fuck me right now."

Bradford leans away from her. "He'd what?"

"God, what the hell is wrong with you? You're pathetic."

"Nothing's wrong with me!" His face ignites. "If I see those guys again, I swear I'm gonna tear their dicks off and fuck 'em in the ass with 'em!"

"Why?" Summer laughs. "Is that what gets you off these days?"

"You know what? No more of this shit. Just do your job today." Bradford stands up. "And make sure Bambi flirts and says all the right things."

"That's a tall order," Summer scoffs. "Why don't you ask me to teach her the alphabet too? Or how to multiply?"

"Just do it." Bradford looks down at her. "Or you'll find yourself hitchhiking back to Miami."

"What's that I see in your pajamas? It looks like your balls are starting to grow back." Summer claps slowly. Bradford grabs his PJs where his junk is, and shakes it at her. Knuckles rap twice on their door, and freeze him with his hold. She asks him, "Who's that?"

"Um, I don't know. Go take a shower, and I'll take care of it."

Summer taps her foot. "I'd like to see who it is first." The knock repeats. "Fine, I'll get it then." She jumps up and jogs to the door. She opens it to find a chipper male member of the hotel staff with a bouquet of red roses. "Good morning, Mrs. Threadgold. I believe these are for you."

Summer shakes her head. "First of all, I am *not* Mrs. Threadgold. Second, is this a joke? This isn't fucking funny."

"I'm sorry." He scrambles to look at his delivery sheet. "I must have the wrong room or something?"

Summer puts her arms up on the sides of the doorway. "You got the Threadgold room correct. Let's ask the asshole behind me to explain."

Bradford pops his head under her arm and through the doorway. "Hey, um, hi. Can you do me a favor and deliver those to Juan Carlos's room just down the hall there? Um, that's where they're supposed to go."

"By all means, sir." The staff member nods and leaves quickly.

Summer slams the door shut. "What the fuck was that all about?"

Bradford puts out his arms and shrugs. "Just a misunderstanding. I'm trying to play match maker."

Summer crosses her arms. "You remember what Lorena Bobbitt did?"

Her question petrifies Bradford. "Uh, yeah, I remember."

"Well, if you ever try to give me flowers again, there will be a reenactment." Summer grits her teeth and slices her hand at his midsection. "Understand?"

Bradford gulps. "Um, yes."

——

A crowd swarms outside the Connecticut Street Armory, a castle-like building with square and round towers, constructed of reddish-yellow sandstone. Bob spots the ticket line and leads the guys in that direction. He notices Summer and Bambi floating around and talking with various guys. Each of the girls has a red plastic bag filled with some sort of knick-knacks. Their mink coats leave their legs exposed from their knees down to their high heels. Any female flesh in the dead of winter will attract plenty of male attention, but their toned calves make them prime targets. Some of the men scurry away after initial conversation, while others are escorted over to a table where Bradford and Juan Carlos sit.

"Hey guys, check it out." Bob points. "The Miami chicks."

"What are they doing?" Zabka asks. "They're up to something."

"Only one way to find out. Let's go talk to them."

As the guys make their way through the crowd, a disheveled, old woman stalks them like they are her prey. She's wearing Elvis sunglasses with one lens popped out, a torn Sabres jersey, and a bright yellow leggings with several suspicious looking stains.

Jed says to the others, "*What-in-the-fuck* is coming our way?"

Bob tries to move the group in a different direction to avoid contact. "I don't know, but I have a bad feeling she's aiming for us."

The woman jumps in their path and crashes down in her purple moon boots, forcing them to stop. She extends her arms in the crucifixion pose and proclaims, "I'm married to Jesus and pregnant with two hundred of Michael Jackson's babies!" Scooter's eyeballs almost pop out of his head and he slaps his forehead. As she continues to rant, her breath, which smells like it's from a chain-smoking horse, pulverizes their noses. "I'm running for mayor, and I need you to vote for me! I'm running on the alien ticket!!"

The guys quickly shuffle around her and Zabka responds, "Absolutely. You've got my vote!" He turns his head to Jed. "Hey, why didn't you tell me your grandmother was gonna be here?"

Jed replies, "Because if I did, I know you'd try to bang her. My grandma's way too good for you!"

Bob laughs. "Just another day in downtown the Buffalo, boys."

As they near the girls, they overhear a guy say to Bambi, "You've got to be fuckin' kidding. I don't need that," before he leaves in disgust.

Bob ignores Summer on purpose. "Hey, Bambi, what's going on?"

Summer waves at him. "Hi Bob! I'm here too! We've got free tickets to the Brewfest. You want some?"

Zabka grills her, "Of course we do, but what's the catch? We saw a few guys that didn't seem too pleased after speaking with you."

Bambi locks her arms around Zabka's arm. "Those guys were jerks. They don't care about making a woman happy." The corners of her mouth turn down. "You're not one of *those* types of guys are you?"

Zabka rips his arm away from her. "Believe me, I know how to make a woman *veeery* happy. Just call your mom, she'll tell ya."

Bambi frowns. "No, unfortunately I can't. My mom told me to stop calling her when guys say stuff like that." She recomposes herself. "I'm being serious here. Do you really know how to make a woman happy? Or is that just what she fools you into believing?"

"Okay, what the *fuck* is this all about?" Beyond irritated, Zabka crosses his arms. "You're some new strain of dumb, aren't you?" Summer and the rest of the guys watch with amusement from the sidelines, wondering who'll be the last one standing in this verbal brawl.

"Hey! I may not be a genius like Frankenstein!" Bambi shouts. "But I know what I like and you sure as hell don't have it."

"Like Frankenstein?!?" Zabka howls. "I assume you meant Einstein, but then again, you might not!" Zabka takes a step back, scans Bambi's body, and scratches his chin. "So I'll admit it. You're a hot piece of ass. However, I sense I'm gonna have a problem fucking your brains out, because somebody else's already beat me to it!!"

The guys roar and Jed slaps Zabka on the back. "Good one! Nailed it!!" Summer tries to hold in a chuckle, but does a poor job.

"Shut up!" Bambi yells. "I've been getting my brains fucked out for years, and I'm *still* gonna keep getting my brains fucked out! But not from guys like you! You don't care about satisfying a woman, because you've got a little tiny prick." She holds up her pinky. "And you won't do anything about it! What do ya got to say to that, Mr. Under-Equipped!?"

"Oh, shit!!" Bob howls. "Sounds like you two have hooked up in the past!" The rest of them laugh so much, it draws the crowd's attention.

"This is fucking bullshit!" Zabka shakes his head at the group. "Believe me, she doesn't know what she's talking about!"

"Sure I do! I've given enough filthy bar bathroom blowjobs to recognize a guy who over-compensates with an egotistical attitude!" Bambi gives Zabka a body scan. "I bet you drive a sports car. Maybe a Viper? A Corvette?" The inference strikes her. "No! A *used* Corvette! There's no way you could even come close to affording a Ferrari."

"Holy shit!!" Jed yells. "She does fucking know you!"

Scooter laughs so hard that he cries and makes high pitch sounds. After his face turns purple, a few bystanders wonder if he's having a seizure. Zabka clucks and quakes like a chicken trapped by a wolf in a hen house. While the others are distracted, Bambi winks at Bob.

With mock sympathy, Bambi tells Zabka, "All I wanted to do was help you out." She changes into her best game show host impression. "By introducing you to supernatural horse schlong pills and cream! Brought to you by Huge Member!" She pulls out a sample box from her bag and tosses it to him. It bounces off his chest and falls into the slush at his feet.

Still bent over from laughing, Scooter falls silent as he recognizes the box and picks it up. Summer tells him, "You're welcome to keep that. You should come sign up for a 90-day supply with auto-renewal and we'll give you a free ticket to the Brewfest. That's a win-win!"

Scooter's inability to speak makes Summer more aggressive. "Take my hand, I'll walk you over there. I can tell you're a real '90s-type of guy. The kind that brings satisfaction to all his ladies by giving her *more* of what she desires. *And* the kind that seizes an opportunity for free beer!"

Jed says to Bob, "While these two deal with their dick issues, you want to go drink some beer? My mouth is as dry as a desert, and through those doors is an oasis. Let's go."

"I agree, but we should also be good friends and revive these two out of their comas with some liquid hops. You grab Scooter. I'll grab Zabka."

"Sure, like Dionne Warwick said, that's what friends are for."

Summer fumes as Bob and Bambi exchange lingering smiles. Bob breaks his invisible connection with Bambi and says, "Ladies, I know these guys are super grateful for your generous offer, but I get the feeling they're gonna pass." Scooter grunts in agreement.

As the four guys go to buy tickets, Bob slaps Zabka on the back of the head. "Dude, I've never seen you speechless before." Zabka looks over at Bob like a stunned boxer. "And I've also never liked you more than I do right now." Bob takes a breath through his nose that he seems to really enjoy. "There's a refreshing *lack* of cockiness in the air."

—

Collapsed across her couch like a rag doll, Jennifer rests her head on a throw pillow. A steaming cup of herbal tea sits on the coffee table, untouched since she poured it. Wrapped in silence, the thumping in her skull is amplified. A sharp tap-tap on the door startles her into a brief epileptic seizure. She pushes her hair back and yaps, "I'm not home."

A voice on the other side yells, "*Jennifa*, it's me! Faige! Lemme in."

Jennifer groans so loud that Faige hears her. "Okay, okay. Hang on a sec." She struggles to get on her feet and walks like a zombie to the door. After removing the bolt lock, she lumbers back toward the couch.

Faige huffs as she opens the door. "Jesus. Thanks fa da help."

"Sorry," Jennifer replies over her shoulder. "My hangover, and the Robert situation has put me in a horrible state."

They move into the living room and sit down. Faige looks concerned. "I wan' youz ta know dat I'm ya friend, and da whole Robert ting is why I'm here."

Jennifer picks up her head, revealing her bloodshot eyes. "You are?"

"Yeah, and I really don't know how ta say dis, so I'll jus' say it." Faige takes a deep breath. "Youz got some sorta destructive pattern wit' men dat I don't fully undastan, and dat *youz* definitely don't undastan. I tink it's hurtin' ya relationships, and I wanna try da help. I don't wan' youz repeatin' da same mistakes."

Jennifer pulls a crumpled piece of paper out of her jeans pocket and tosses it to Faige.

Faige opens it and reads it. "What da hell's dis? Who's Lisa?"

"Great question," Jennifer cries. "I found it at Robert's this morning."

"Oh, nooo. What happened?"

"Nobody was home, and the place was a pigsty." Jennifer points at Lisa's number. "And *that* was in his trash."

Faige tilts her head and shrugs. "So maybe it's nothin'?"

Jennifer's face contorts into an are-you-fucking-kidding-me expression. "Oh, come on. That's something."

"Yeah, probably. Maybe. Maybe not. So whaddya gonna do?"

As Jennifer speaks, she uses her hands to show her intended action. "Well, the first thing that came to mind is to slice off his saggy nut sack. No more ball tickling for that cheating son-of-a-bitch."

Faige laughs like a mini-devil before an odd sense of reason washes over her. "Put da castration plan on hold until youz have proof."

Jennifer ponders her suggestion. "Fine. Once I feel better, I'll go down to Third Base and investigate. I'm sure those guys spent the whole night there, because that's what those drunk idiots do."

"Sounds like a good plan. Gatha mo intel befo' jumpin' ta conclusions. But if tings don't add up, I'll provide da hedge clippers." Faige clips her fingers like scissors. "Snip, snip."

Jennifer gives her a weak high-five. "I appreciate your support, but I honestly hope it doesn't come down to that."

"Okay, next orda a business," Faige says like she's running a meeting. "I wanna know what really happened wit' Robert yesterday. Did he honestly blow off youz weekend getaway fa his friends at da lass-minute? Dat sounds strange, even fa 'im. And I could tell dat youz wa hidin' sumptin from me dis mornin'."

Jennifer slouches into the couch and crosses her arms. "I don't know what you're talking about."

Faige's stare burns a hole in the bridge of Jennifer's nose. "Do youz wan' me ta help youz or not? Dis is serious — be trootful wit' me."

Like a child caught eating a contraband cookie, Jennifer won't open her mouth for fear of exposing evidence. After a moment, she gives in and exhales. "Did he blow off our *planned* weekend together for his friends at the last minute? The answer is a definitive yes."

Faige hasn't broken her stare. *"Buuuut—"*

Jennifer holds her breath until her face starts turning red. "Alright, I may have left out a few *minor* details. What I did, though, I did for a good reason." Faige grins like an investigator when the suspect is about to spill the beans. "So here it is. The whole truth and nothing but the truth, so help me god. Robert's douchebag college friend, Zabka, left a drunk message for 'Bob' — I hate that nickname — on his answering machine late Thursday night. I heard it, but Robert didn't. Zabka said, 'we' — whoever the fuck 'we' are — 'are coming for the Bills game and to party our faces off.' Robert doesn't need to hang out with bad influences like that, so I took matters into my own hands. I deleted the message and made plans for us to go to Niagara on the Lake. What's so wrong with that?"

Faige teeters between wanting to slap Jennifer or give her a girl-power hug. "A lot, but I'll stick ta da main ting. Youz got caught."

Jennifer mockingly replies, "Ha ha."

"But seriously, youz can't manipulate like dat. Youz always eventually gonna get caught, and ya man's gonna be pissed."

"Yeah, well, I sure found that out the hard way." Jennifer shakes her crestfallen head. "But there's more you should know. Maybe this will help you understand why I did what I did. Zabka came into town over the summer and that was the first time we met. He and Robert went out together that night and an incident occurred — like, some crazy shit. I didn't tell you because I was so embarrassed."

Faige rubs her hands together and moves to the edge of her chair. "So da plot tickens in dis week's episode of da *Robert Shit-Show*. Continue."

Jennifer picks up her tea. "Give me a second."

—

Inside the Brew Festival, the Great Court is lined with two levels of cherry wood arches and illuminated by a vaulted sky light. Flags from different countries hang above the tasting tables along the edges of the room. A swarm of craft beer enthusiasts walk crooked lines through the crowd across the golden oak floor. A dank warmth from the crowd and malty beverages permeates the space.

A despondent Zabka enters the room with the rest of the crew and mumbles to himself, "I'm gonna kill her — I'm gonna kill the rest of them too — I'm gonna kill her."

"Here's an idea," Bob suggests. "How about you do what Metallica would do and —"

Zabka slowly lifts his head. "Kill 'em all?"

"Correct!"

"Kill 'em all," Zabka repeats. Then, as if an adrenaline needle stabs into his heart, he screams to the ceiling, "I'm gonna kill 'em all!! Kill 'em all, I say!!"

"It's about time you got back to normal." Bob points to a tasting table. "How about we go grab a beer at Ellicottville Brewing Company?"

"Sounds good to me," Scooter agrees. "Is that the same Ellicottville that's called the Aspen of the East?"

Bob laughs. "Yeah, that's the same Ellicottville. Nice place, decent skiing, but it's no Aspen."

The guys make their way to the table, itching to hand over their tasting glasses for some samples. The group in front of them leaves and the silver bearded server asks, "What can I get you, boys?"

"I like beer," Jed answers. "I'll have one of those."

The server chuckles. "It's all beer here. You want me to pick which type I think you'd all like?"

"Works for me," Jed replies as the rest of the guys nod in agreement.

"Okay, let's start with you." The server pours a glass for Jed. "You look like a good ol' boy who enjoys fast cars and, no offense, toothless women." Jed confirms with a thumbs-up. "So I'm gonna have you sample our Lager. It's like Budweiser, only it tastes good."

Jed takes a healthy guzzle. "Excellent choice for my first beer of the afternoon." He talks to his glass, "Beer, don't deny me your fine taste for so long ever again."

"It's been what? A whole two hours?" Bob asks.

"Yeah, and that's two hours too long."

The server addresses Bob, "For you, how about our Blonde Ale? You look like the type that enjoys a blonde every now and then."

"Goddamn, you're like some sort of beer psychic." Bob accepts the beer and toasts to the sky. "May you leave a better taste in my mouth than my current blonde." He relishes a sip.

Zabka offers his empty glass. "Try me next, I'm thirsty."

The server takes it from him. "Sure, I can do that. You seem a little bitter about something and in need of a kick in the ass. I think our Double IPA with its extra alcohol content will be perfect for you."

Zabka grabs the full beer and watches tiny bubbles float to the top of the light brown liquid. "I ain't fucking bitter!" He chugs the contents and dries his mouth with his sleeve. "That was *goooood*!"

The server returns a smile. "I'm happy to hear that. And now, last but not least —" He turns to Scooter. "You need a beverage." White foam tops the black beer he hands over. "It's probably obvious why, but I selected our Stout for you. Enjoy."

Scooter grimaces. "I'm sure you're saying that because all my African ladies like cream on top." Scooter puts the beverage to his lips and tilts the bottom up. Foam dribbles out the sides of his mouth as he gulps. After several forced swallows, his head jolts forward and he expels a room-shaking belch. The white froth that covers his mouth and chin makes him look like a rabid bulldog. He burps out, "*Thaaaat's goooooooood.*"

"Nice, Scooter." Bob asks the server, "Can you top off our glasses?"

"Sure. Gotta love how a tasting is a full glass of beer, right guys?"

Jed hands his glass over. "Love it." The others place their glasses on the table for the same service.

They move away from the table and Bob turns to face his merry band of beer drinkers. "Zabka and Scooter, we need to discuss what happened outside with the Miami girls and that stupid product they're promoting. Who wants to go first?" The targets of his question physically react like they were asked an embarrassing question in high school health class and have nowhere to hide. Bob focuses on Zabka. "Why don't you go?"

Zabka squirms for a second. "I don't think this needs to be a topic for discussion."

"And why not?" Bob asks. "Last night you dug into my Jennifer shit, so now we dig into your shit. It seems like Bambi touched a nerve. Anything you care to share with us?"

Zabka puffs out his chest. "That bitch don't know me! She gets lucky guessing my car, and then she thinks she knows ME! Saying shit about my cock!" Zabka scans the room on his tippy-toes. "Next time I see her, my dick's gonna knock her uvula around like a punching bag! And have a *loooong* conversation with the back of her throat!"

"Holy shit! You have a magical talking penis?!" Jed shouts. "Mine can only spit!"

"Yeah, it's special!" Zabka snaps back.

"Alright, alright, Zabka," Bob says. "You gotta keep your rage under control until we need it." Scooter tries to drift backwards into the crowd, but Bob catches him. "Hey, you're not going anywhere! It's your turn!"

"Oh, I wasn't going anywhere," Scooter answers timidly. "I just thought someone called my name from back there." He points and wiggles his finger at the other side of the room behind him.

"Nope, I'm pretty sure no one over there knows you. Anyway, go ahead. Explain."

"It's um, kinda, um embarrassing," Scooter fumbles through his words like he does with parts of the female anatomy. "I mean, not for me, but for this friend I got, ya know?"

Bob's eyeballs pivot to Zabka's, and with a half smile he says, "I see. Please continue."

"To get to the point, my friend tried the Huge Member pills." Scooter kicks the floor. "And has been less than enthused with the results."

"Does that make you mad?" Bob asks. "I mean, mad for your friend?"

"It does, but I try to control my temper."

"Well, put your temper on the back-burner. Oh, and tell your friend that those pills don't work."

Scooter looks surprised. "What do you mean they don't work?"

"It's just like I said, they don't work. Everybody knows it's all bullshit." As Scooter's face transforms into a ripe tomato that's about to burst, Bob grabs him by the shoulders. "It's okay, no need to have a heart attack. Can you calm down?" Scooter nods as his face slowly deflates and returns to its normal watermelon pink color.

Jed blurts out, "Here's an idea — how about we talk about something other than Scooter's wang? Like, anything."

Happy to change the subject, Scooter raises a finger. "I do. Bob, what was it like to live with Zabka in college?"

"Yeah, did you wanna kick his ass every day or just every other day?" Jed asks.

"I thought you didn't want to talk about dicks, but then you bring up Zabka?" Bob laughs. "There was no need for me to scuff my pretty knuckles. There were plenty of guys — and girls — who took care of that."

Zabka adds, "So there may have been a few incidents, but whatever. Hey, it's not like you were a dream to live with. In fact, I think Jimmy the Italian once described living with you as, 'a nightmare he couldn't wake up from.' Coming home drunk at 4 AM and blasting Van Halen's 'Fools' didn't win you any friends. Actually, I take that back. I loved the shit out of it!"

"Hey, I loved it too! We were crazy back then!" Bob goes into story telling mode. "So Zabka brings this girl home from the Base and is doing her from behind." Zabka reinacts the sex movements as Bob paints the picture. "From my room I heard her yell, 'Wait! Wait! Stop!' I guess hot wings, cheap beer, and Zabka's pounding is some sorta magic combo, because it set off a toxic-liquid anal-eruption!"

"Oh, damn!" Jed yells. "She sharted on you!"

Zabka laughs. "Yeah, pretty much. At first I thought she just farted, but then I saw I was pumping her shit-sauce from one hole into the other. It all happened so fast that when I caught a whiff, I blew chunks on her back!"

"Zabka *literally* fucked the shit outta her!"

"And into her, I might add." Scooter gags and covers his eyes. "I wish my mind could un-see that! I can practically smell it too!"

Zabka continues, "She was so embarrassed that she tried to run out of my room but instead ran into the protruding closet wall next to the door, which briefly stunned her. I laughed my ass off! Once she recovered she opened the door and, you won't believe this, ran into our stoned house-mate Satan in the hall. He had no clue what was going on — other than some naked chick was sprinting out of my room with barf and diarrhea oozing down her body! The chick raced downstairs and out of the house without her clothes! Talk about a walk of shame. She's damn lucky it wasn't the middle of winter!"

"Wow!" Jed shouts. "I wish I went to college with you guys. That sounds like a fun house!"

"Oh, we could tell stories for days," Bob boasts. "But I see we need to refill our glasses."

"Hey! I see a fine microbrew over there." Jed points at a table. "Let's go try something from the Genesee Brewing Company. It sounds amazing!"

"Oh man, that shit gives me the shits," Scooter cries.

"Yep, there's a reason the cream ale is called a Genny Screamer," Jed tells him. "It's well known for its laxative qualities. Let's go have a few. You do realize the human body is an amazing thing, and over time you'll build up a tolerance. It's Biology 101." Scooter looks at him with a frightened, non-believing look. Jed adds, "Or in your case, maybe not."

"Hold on, we've had plenty of that 'amazing beer' already," Bob says. "I see another brewery that looks interesting. Follow me." The four of them snake their way around other groups until they reach the Zoo Brew Co. table. Bob and Zabka decide to sample the Flatulent Fox, while Jed and Scooter taste the Erect Eagle.

Zabka scopes out the room like an elephant seal that's in heat, yet cunning like a fox. "Guys, this is how I'm reading things. There's about five hundred people here and around thirty percent are chicks. That brings the mating-pool down to a hundred and fifty. And as we all know, only the top ten percent of that are semi-attractive, and thus worth our valuable time. So that leaves us with fifteen lucky ladies."

Bob comments, "Yeah, fifteen lucky ladies who'll bitch-slap the shit outta you, Zabka. Lucky them!"

"Hey, not everyone bats a thousand. You gotta take a few big swings to hit one out of the park. But today is not *all* about me — it's also about Scooter. Sure, I could get him laid, but what he really needs is Zabka boot camp. I believe the saying goes something like this — 'Give a man a fish, and you feed him for a day. Teach a man to fish, and he eats pussy for life.' Did I get that right?"

Jed nods. "That's exactly the way I've always heard it."

"So Scooter, are you ready?" Zabka asks.

Scooter licks his lips and lifts a clenched fist. "I'm ready! Ready to squish the fish!"

—

With people shuffling inside to the Brewfest, Bambi and Summer decide to take a break and stroll over to Bradford and Juan Carlos. A red and black "Huge Member" banner drapes over the front of their table. A crisp breeze unravels one of the strings tying down the banner and blows a corner upward. Bradford squats to fix it, as Juan Carlos holds down the paperwork.

"Hey, so we ran into those guys from last night," Summer says.

"Who?" Bradford asks. "Those buffoons that got our limo towed?"

"Yeah, and Bambi did a good job putting the one with curly hair in his place," Summer tells them. "It was impressive — for her."

Juan Carlos praises Bambi, "Nice work."

"It was easy," Bambi replies. "I know how to read men." She bends her leg back to where her heel almost touches her butt and blows Juan Carlos a kiss.

"The pudgy one though — you know the one that looks like he face-fucked a cheese grater?" Summer asks. "He acted really weird when he was checking out the sample box."

"He was probably in shock by the concept of it all," Bradford answers. "Some men can't comprehend that a product this revolutionary exists."

"I'm not sure why. Science is amazing," Juan Carlos states. "If breast implants work for women, then an all-natural supplement can work for men." He extends his forearm and fist. "And turn their Johnson into a powerful weapon like this!" Bambi gasps.

"Hey, Bradford. You need to up your dosage!" Summer remarks.

He shakes his head. "Ha, ha, very funny."

"Speaking of funny," Bambi interjects. "There were a lot of guys that got pissed-off when I introduced the product to them."

"How's that funny?" Bradford asks. "This is our damn business."

"I thought you didn't like these Buffalo people and so you came here to insult their dicks to their faces. That seems pretty funny to me."

"Hold on," Bradford tells Bambi. "As much as I look down on these people, we came here to spread the word about our product. Unfortunately, what we sell is not socially acceptable." He pounds his fist on the table. "We're the company to change that!"

"Hear, hear!" Juan Carlos shouts. "Okay, enough talk. Ladies, get back out there and sell. We're underperforming on our sales projections."

"We're doing the best we can," Summer tells him.

"Well, work harder. We'll stay outside another half-hour to catch the late comers before we go in."

Bambi shivers and whines, "But it's cold out here."

Juan Carlos folds his arms. "You're just gonna need to suck it up."

Bambi nibbles on her pinky. "I thought we'd save that for later." Satisfied with his open-mouth expression, she saunters into the crowd.

—

Jennifer takes a couple of sips of hot tea before placing it back on a porcelain saucer. "So like I was saying, Zabka came here to visit Robert this summer. We all met up for drinks at Ruby Tuesday — you know the one in the Boulevard Mall?" Faige nods. "Anyway, from the moment I met him, I could tell he was trouble. And I could tell he didn't like me — well, maybe not necessarily me, but the concept of me."

"Whaddya mean?" Faige asks.

"What I mean is, I felt like he didn't want Robert to have a girlfriend. Like I was invading his turf or something."

"Does dis Zabka characta have a crush on Robert or sumptin?"

"Damn good question. I don't know. But what I do know is when they get together — their stupidity has no boundaries. Zero! Yesterday I was trying to contain Robert."

"Oh, now I see. Ta keep 'im in da 'boyfriend yard,' youz put up invisible boundaries and acted like a dawg's shock colla." Having uncovered Jennifer's mad genius side, Faige strokes her chin. "Witout youz, what happens? He runs away and gets sprayed by a skunk?"

"Exactly. Or pees in a neighbor's flower garden, or worse — humps an underage pug."

"So what da heck happened on dat fateful summa night? Youz obviously failed ta lock 'im down."

"I sure did," Jennifer shamefully admits. "So after we had drinks, they said they were going downtown, and so I just went home. The next morning at around 9:00 AM, the phone rang." Jennifer picks up an imaginary phone. "Hello? What?! You're in fucking jail?!"

"No fuckin' way?"

"Yeah, way!" Jennifer's anger bubbles as she relives it. "The next day, after I calmed down, he gave me the full story. Apparently they drank in some bar until 4:00 AM and *then* went to a college house party to play beer pong with Bacardi 151. They got kicked out, get this, for humming the 'Chicken Dance' and, at the clap, clap, clap, clap part, they took cheap dinner plates and smash, smash, smash, smashed them on the kitchen floor. They clucked and stomped on the plate shards until they turned into dust! Those idiots were pretending they were at a Greek Wedding!"

Flabbergasted, Faige says, "Wow, youz right! Doz two are idiots!"

"But wait, there's more. I haven't even gotten to the jail part yet!"

Faige pretends like she's eating popcorn. "I can't wait."

"Those two started walking aimlessly and stopped to take a leak." Jennifer pretends like she's whipping a man's genitals out of her pants. "They chose the nearest wall and, as fate would have it, they not only picked a church, but whizzed on it as nuns were exiting onto the street."

"Oh, shit! Great timin'!" Faige snickers.

"Those knuckleheads heard something, turned toward the sound while peeing, and basically exposed themselves to these women of faith. And here's the icing on the cake — guess who was driving by at that exact moment?"

"I'm gonna go out on a limb and guess a cop?"

"Ding, ding, ding! So they were arrested for open container, public lewdness, disorderly conduct, and vandalism."

"Daaaamn!"

"Yep, and I refused to go pick them up," Jennifer says proudly. "To be honest, I was surprised he had the balls to ask me for a ride. I was actually even more surprised he told me everything that happened."

Faige ponders Jennifer's last sentence. "It sounds like Robert doesn't hide anyting from youz. Is dat true?"

Jennifer reviews her past with him. "Yes, that is true."

"So I can't believe I'm gonna say dis — even dough he did fuck up, he's an honest guy, and dat's a very important quality ta have in a man."

With a mixture of anger and sadness, Jennifer blurts, "Yeah, but I don't want him to fuck up — like ever. Don't you get it?"

"I do, but hear me out. Don't youz tink havin' a convasation wit' Robert about ya concerns, and seein' where his head's at, woulda been a betta way ta go? Dat way youz could've used dis weekend as a test. If he blew it, den you'd know he's not da right guy fa youz."

Jennifer laments, "But if he did screw up, that'd really suck."

"As much as we wanna, or sometimes feel we need ta, we can't lock guys down. If youz do, resentment will jus' boil unda da surface." Faige puts her hand on Jennifer's leg. "Guys need ta adjus on dere own. If dey don't, dere eitha gonna wanna breakout of da loony bin youz put dem in, or dere gonna behave like sedated mental patients. Youz seen dis behav-ya befaw."

"Yeah, I realize I have with William and Mathew. So what do I do?"

"First off, I get where youz comin' from. Youz care fa Robert and wan' him ta be da one. I also agree dat youz were justified in bein' concerned. So here's what I'd do. Figga out what happened wit' Lisa, and if he crossed da line, dump his ass. If nothin' happened, den find out what he's doin' dis weekend and assess if youz can live wit' it."

"All this logic is hurting my head worse than my hangover," Jennifer whines. "I'm not used to this."

"Well, get used ta it, girlfriend. Lastly, youz deceived 'im, so youz need ta make up fa it. Youz need ta do sumptin bold."

"And how exactly do I go about doing that?"

"Look at how youz been behavin' and try sumptin different. Change is good. If youz keep doin' da same ting ova-an-ova in ya relationships, youz continue ta get da same results. My advice is take a step back — tink about Robert and who *he* is."

Jennifer contemplates the guidance. "I guess I could try."

"Oh, and one mo ting."

Jennifer's facial tick silently screams, "There's more?!"

Faige squints at Jennifer. "Youz a big girl. Youz can handle it."

—

Zabka asks Scooter, "Remember that 'bite outta crime' line I taught you last night?"

"Yeah, kinda." Scooter squeezes his eyes shut and pokes his forehead twice. "I was a wee bit drunk."

"To refresh your memory, I'm gonna use it again. Then you can try. Cool?"

"Yep, sounds good."

"Alright, not that I need to, but I'm gonna take a little batting practice first. Warm up with an easy pitch." Zabka scans the room and points at an average looking girl with unkempt, brown, shoulder-length hair. "Batter up!"

"Hang on a second," Bob cuts in. "How about I give it a go and use the same line?"

"You? We wanna show him how to hit, not whiff."

"Hey, I may be a little rusty, but I can do this."

"Well then, by all means." Zabka ushers Bob forward with his hands.

"I'll take the same target. I saw you eyeing the messy-haired girl there." Bob points. "Is that her?"

"Yep, she should be easy. Go for it."

Bob walks behind the girl and taps her on the shoulder. She turns and says with a huge smile, "Hey Bob! Long time no see! How are you?" She jumps forward and gives him a hug.

Utterly confused and unable to hide it, Bob stumbles. "Oh hey, I'm good — girl. How are you?"

She puts her hand on her hips. "You don't remember me, do you?"

"I'm sorry, but it's really light in here, so maybe you look different then when we met? Or — is that a new mole on your forehead? Actually, I know what it is — you changed the color of your eyes."

"You're fucking with me, right?" She gives him a hard punch in the chest and points at herself. "It's Tammi. I did change my hair though — it was long and blonde when we met. Remember that Buff State house party? We had a few beers, danced, and had *a lot* of fun after."

"This sounds familiar, but I'm sorry, you're gonna have to be more specific." Bob grabs one of her hands and with a sly look proceeds, "This will help me narrow things down. Who's place did we go back to? And are you a screamer?"

Tammi balances on her toes to stare at him at eye level. She grabs the back of his neck and places her mouth against his ear. "So you *do* remember. That night I screamed so loud, your friends threw sneakers and beer bottles at the bedroom door." She exhales into his ear. "Wanna repeat?"

Terrifying memories race through Bob's mind. "Well damn, I have a super busy schedule today." He looks down at his watch. "But if I'm drunk, horny, and bored at around 4 AM, can I call you to come over?"

"You're such a romantic," Tammi gushes. "That sounds perfect."

"Okay, cool." Bob rushes to leave. "Maybe I'll see ya later."

"Wait!" she yells at his back. "You still have my number?!" He hustles without turning to rejoin his friends.

Zabka punches Bob's arm. "Way to go, stud! Looks like it went well."

"Hold up. You know that girl." Scooter accuses Bob. "That's cheating. I was expecting to learn from you."

Stunned from his chance encounter, Bob replies, "I can't believe that just happened. Of all the girls in the world."

"Tell us. Who is she?"

"I had forgotten about her — or maybe blocked her out of my mind is more accurate," Bob admits. "But then she reminded me of the night we met." He shakes his head. "That was a nasty curveball running into her."

"How's that a nasty curveball?" Jed asks. "It looks like you just let a softball pitch go by to me."

"Okay, so how do I say this? That chick is certifiable. I can't believe I didn't recognize her — not one bit. Zabka, you remember Tammi? She changed her hair, but that's her."

Zabka laughs as he squints at her face. "Oh shit! Of course I remember her. She's the crazy, tramp-stamp screamer." He slaps Jed and Scooter. "I told you guys about her on our drive yesterday. That was some classic head-case drama!"

Bob takes a deep breath. "Did he tell you she's bipolar? Most-likely, triple-polar? Truth be told — all women are at least mildly bipolar. But that one —" He glances back in Tammi's direction to make sure she can't overhear. "She's off the fuckin' chart! So bad, that I heard three psychiatrists quit on her. And those are people who've been professionally trained to handle the craziest nut-jobs!"

"Naw, I didn't tell 'em all that," Zabka casually replies. "I told 'em this." As loud as he can, he screams like a woman getting her leg sawed off.

Horrified, Bob jumps and clasps his hand over Zabka's mouth. "You fucking jackass! If she hears you, who knows what disturbing itch it will scratch. Frankly, I don't care to be around for that!"

Zabka rips Bob's hand away so he can let out a sidesplitting roar. "Relax man, what's the worst that could happen?"

"Fuck you, you know! You know how she gets!"

Zabka wipes tears of laughter from his eyes. "That I do, my friend."

"You guys better warn me if you see her coming this way," Bob nervously tells them. "She could burst outta nowhere like a rabid dog."

"I got your back." Jed presses two fingers on an imaginary earpiece like he's in the Secret Service. "Crazy chick is safely outside the biting zone."

"Thanks, buddy."

Commotion near the front entrance draws their attention. As they look to see what's going on, they overhear a guy on their left say, "Hey, check it out. They let the hookers inside."

Zabka peers above the crowd. "I see 'em. There's Bambi and Summer, and behind them are the two dick twats. It's game time."

Bob huddles the group. "Let's think, guys. If we run up to them, it'll seem suspicious. They'll eventually come to us. I guarantee it."

"Yep, you're right," Zabka agrees. "Let's get back to our previous nonsense. Alright Scooter, fuck it — let's try this again. I was thinking there's no better way to learn than by just getting out there. Time for papa bird to push baby bird outta the nest. Pick a girl and go for it. Remember, this is a warm up, so don't be a fool and go for your dream girl or anything."

Scooter briefly examines the room until fixating upon a small group of Mexican girls. "You see those girls over there?"

"Who? The chiquitas?" Bob asks.

"Yep. Those girls make me wet."

Zabka is taken aback. "What? Did you actually just say they 'make you wet'?!"

"Yeah, ethnic women make me wet," Scooter replies. "You got a thing against ethnic girls?"

The rest of the guys crack-up before Bob quiets them down and jumps in. "No, that's not it. Scooter, can I give you a quick biology lesson? Girls get wet when they get sexually excited. Guys don't." Bob then gives Zabka a look that says, "I can't believe we're having this conversation."

Zabka crunches his neck with his shoulders.

"Let me stop you right there," Scooter says. "When I see a hot chick my balls start to sweat, and I get wet. Are you telling me that doesn't happen to you guys?"

"Not really, buddy," Bob replies. "But how about you keep the whole 'I get wet' thing to yourself? Cool?"

Scooter thinks for a second and raises his eyebrows. "What if instead I said, 'I get moist'?"

Zabka shakes his head. "Let's refocus. Scooter, pick a girl and tell her, 'I'm gonna sink my teeth into you and take a bite outta crime.' After she asks you what you mean, say, 'Well, it must be illegal to look that good.' Confuse then compliment — simple as that. Women are crazy and like that sorta shit cuz it messes with their brain. For whatever reason, they need a mind-fuck first before they'll want to have sex with you. Think of it as foreplay. Confuse. Compliment. Got it?"

"Yep, I got it. Easy as pie. And I like pie." Scooter's attention gets caught. "Here comes that girl I like. She's hot!" His eyes follow her.

Zabka grabs Scooter's arm. "No, don't try anything with her yet. You need to practice first."

"Yeah, but she's coming right at us," Scooter pleads. "This is my chance, and I'm going for it." He takes a big gulp of his beer and flips down his clip-on shades. "I'm going in."

Zabka considers holding him back again but decides against it. "Don't fly too close to the sun! Good luck!"

Scooter steps in front of a very attractive Mexican girl as she's about to pass and says, "Excuse me, miss."

She stops before running him over and with a strong accent asks, "Yeah, what up?"

Scooter blurts out, "I'm gonna bite you because you're illegal and that's a crime." The guys cringe while eavesdropping.

She pokes her chest into him. "What da fuck, you talkin' 'bout?! Me and my posse will cut you! We ain't no illegals!"

Scooter sputters, but tries again to lay on the Buffalo charm. "I mean, I mean you look so good I wanna sink my teeth into you."

Jed leans into Zabka and asks, "Should we save him?"

"Nope, he wanted this. Let 'em burn, let 'em learn."

The Mexican girl yells, "Man, you outta yo' mind with this shit!" She scrutinizes him from toe to head. "The way yo' damn face looks, you done this before! You get off on women attacking you, you sick fuck?!"

"No, no." Scooter backs up with his hands out and shaking. "Confuse and compliment."

"Confuse? Yeah, you're confusing as fuck!" she shouts. "I don't want no more words! Ya hear me?!"

"Yes. Yes, ma'am."

She juts her forehead at him. "What-in-the-hell did I just tell you?!"

"You said no more words," Scooter cries.

"How stupid is you?!" she asks. He attempts respond. "I said shut the fuck up! That means don't say nothing. Now get the hell out of my way!" He steps aside, and she and her crew storm past. Scooter mopes back as the guys clap slowly.

Bob yells, "Way to crush it, buddy! That's the quickest I've ever seen someone adiós a group of girls." He salutes Scooter. "So I gotta ask. Are you still wet?" Everyone laughs, even Scooter a little.

Jed adds, "The way you butchered that line was beyond impressive!"

Zabka comments, "I'm surprised you didn't ask them for Chiclets." He puts his arm around Scooter's shoulders. "So, in the future, are you going to listen to me?"

Scooter drops his head. "Yeah, I will. I promise."

"You gave a fuck, didn't you? You cared and got nervous."

"Yeah." Scooter nods his head like a boy waiting for his punishment.

Zabka messes up Scooter's hair with his hand and talks to him like he's a puppy, "Good boy. Now let's get you a special treat. I hear they serve beer here."

The guys walk to the closest microbrew table for a refill. "Hey, I gotta go drain the python," Zabka announces. "I'll be right back. Don't move."

"Sure, no problem," Bob says.

Scooter inquires, "Hey Bob, can I ask you about what's going on with your girlfriend?"

"Yeah, I guess. What do you want to know?"

Scooter places a finger on his cheek scar. "Last night you said, your relationship is better after the changes you made —"

Bob stops him. "Correction — the *compromises* I've made, not changes."

"Semantics, whatever. So after you made these *compromises*, are you happier?"

"That's a tough question to answer. I hate nagging and fighting, and so I'm glad that pretty much stopped — well, until this recent event, which wasn't my fault. Although she'll claim that my past antics caused her to do what she did." Bob twirls his finger. "Classic spin move. They must teach that in law school."

Jed interjects, "Actually they teach it at *women* school."

Bob replies, "Good point. I think you're right."

"Hey, what about that hot bartender girl from last night?" Jed asks. "Why don't you just be bang-soul-mates with her? She likes you."

"Who? Lisa?" Bob replies. "Oh, that was nothing."

"Didn't look like nothing to me," Jed refutes.

Bob's recollection of the details of the previous evening is blackout fuzzy at best. "What were you asking me again, Scooter?"

"Since you've made these compromises, have you been happier?"

Bob digests the inquiry. "To be honest, last night and today with you guys has been way more fun than I've had with her in quite a while — minus the occasional blowjob, of course."

Scooter thinks about how awesome an "occasional blowjob" would be, before shaking away the thought. "So you haven't been happier?"

"It's complicated. Yes and no." Bob shrugs. "What I do know is right now I kinda feel like I escaped prison. It feels fuckin' good, ya know?"

"I can relate," Jed confides.

Bob turns to Jed and asks, "So your wife keeps her thumb on you?"

"No, I was just pretending to relate with you," Jed confesses. "She's a bigger lush than me — if that's possible. I do whatever the hell I want."

Scooter sips his beer. "I can't really relate to the prison thing, but what I can say is that I never get to do this sort of stuff. I'm having an blast."

Bob beams. "I'm glad to hear that, Scooter."

Scooter tells them, "Even though my head and body feel beat up, my soul feels alive." He gives Bob and Jed high-fives. "It's a great feeling!"

Bob shares, "Buffalo has that effect on people. Hey, I also have a few questions for you guys since you've both been married, but I can save them for later. We don't need to talk about relationships all day and overanalyze everything. We're not chicks, right?"

"*Definitely* not," Jed says. "Although, I'm not so sure about Scooter."

Bob scans the room. "When's Zabka coming back?" He points to a microbrew table near the front. "I wouldn't mind heading there to try a few." As he continues to look for Zabka, he's blindsided. "Holy shit."

"What is it?" Jed asks.

"Zabka's gonna flip when I tell him who's here," Bob replies.

"Who? Tell us," Scooter demands.

"You see that redhead over there?" After Jed and Scooter acknowledge they've spotted her, Bob's mouth transforms into a big cheesy grin. "That, my friends. That's mutha fuckin' Hurricane Hillary. That's who."

—

Jennifer wrings her hands as she looks across the coffee table at Faige.

"*Jennifa*, I swear dis is da last ting I'm gonna say, but it's important. Youz ready?"

"Not really." Jennifer sighs. "I know you're just being a good friend, but I have a feeling this is gonna sting."

"I'm not gonna sugah-coat it. But first I need ta know if youz wit'eld sex from Robert priah ta leavin' fa da weekend?"

"I did," Jennifer replies nonchalantly. "And I teased him something fierce. I didn't want him to back out — but that obviously didn't work."

"Oy vey." Faige presses her palm against her cheek. "Don't take dis da wrong way — have youz considered goin' to a terapist?"

"You're kidding, right?"

"Maybe." Faige shrugs. "*Anyyyway*, youz need ta stop doin' dat. Like, stop all ya twisted ways. Youz even hit on da key ting dis mornin' — men are stupid." She urges Jennifer, "So, insteada manipulatin' dem, youz jus' need ta communicate betta — spell it out fa dem, wud-fa-wud. Dere simple minds don't get stuff dats obvious ta us."

"Spell it out for them? Word-for-word? I suppose I can work on that."

"Back to youz wit'oldin' sex. I know youz plan didn't fo-see Robert bein' wit' his friend dis weekend, but youz don't give a guy a hawd-on, and den not give 'im a propa release — specially when he's gonna be away from youz and boozin'. Does dat sound like a good combo ta youz?"

Jennifer pouts. "Well no, now that you put it that way."

"A guy who's recently had great sex wit' his girlfrien's less likely ta stray and fall into a compromisin' position, right?"

Jennifer's mind replays the previous times she's pulled the same stunt. As correlations between her behavior and her relationships going south become clear, she begins to sweat. She pats her brow with a napkin. "I gotta go fix things with Robert, like now."

Faige advises, "Yeah, but first youz need ta go tawk ta Lisa and see if dere was any funny business. If she says sumptin happened, get details — proof — so he can't weasel outta it! But fa youz sake, I hope dere's no smokin' gun."

"I hope not too." Jennifer bounces from the couch and gives Faige a hug. "Thanks for all your help. I'm gonna go get my man back."

—

Bob spots Zabka strutting back from the bathroom and waves him to hurry. When Zabka rejoins the group, Bob says excitedly, "You're not gonna believe this! Guess who's here?!"

"I don't know. Horse-face from *Melrose Place?*" Zabka replies.

"No, much better! Hurri-fuckin'-cane Hillary!"

"You better not be shitting me! That's fuckin' awesome!" Zabka exclaims like his lottery ticket just hit. "So where is that ho-bag?"

Bob surveys the other side of the room. "She was just over there near that tasting table. I don't see her now, but we should head that way."

"Are you guys gonna tell us why she's called Hurricane Hillary or what?" Scooter demands. "That's a rather interesting name."

"It's quite simple," Bob replies. "When she drinks, she gets super wet and is ready to blow." Zabka nods in approval of the description.

Jed's eyes light up. "You can relate to the 'gets super wet' part can't ya, Scooter?"

Scooter rubs his hands together. "Oh yeah I can. She sounds fun!"

"She is fun, but in more of a we-might-die-skydiving type of fun," Zabka tells them. "And like a hurricane, she's dangerous. I've seen her hit Category 5 and hurl pieces of furniture at people. Believe me, it's best to evacuate the area when bat-shit crazy is spinning at you!"

"This is true," Bob says. "I've witnessed it as well."

Zabka starts moving. "Yeah, let's walk over there." The guys follow his lead. "She still owes me half a blowjob."

"Sorry, but half a blowjob? What's that?" Jed asks.

Zabka explains, "Last time we hooked up, I was so drunk when she was giving me head, I couldn't finish. Thus, she owes me the second half of the BJ. Ya know, to finish the job."

Jed double-taps his head. "That's some solid logic there. I gotta start keeping tabs on insightful knowledge like that."

They shuffle through the dense crowd, enveloped in a kaleidoscope of chaos and nebulous chatter. Carousers carom off one another, spilling more ale on their already damp, spotted clothing. When they reach their destination, Zabka feels a tap on his shoulder. He turns around, and like a slow-motion video through an opaque tidal wave of beer, he sees Hurricane Hillary's fiery face in a burst of orange. With no time for evasive maneuvers, the liquid sheet slaps him in the face, leaving him drenched. She screams, "Take that you fucking asshole!"

Having witnessed the incident from fifteen feet away, a security guard rushes through the surrounding people to prevent escalation. Upon reaching them, he finds Hurricane Hillary with her legs wrapped around Zabka's waist, fully engaged in a violent make-out session. The security guard shakes his head and leaves.

With her arms around his neck, Hillary leans back. "Why didn't you call me back, you prick?"

Confused, Zabka asks, "When, after graduation? Did you call me?"

"Of course I called you. I was horny, honey," Hillary says sweetly.

"After graduation, I moved to Massena." Hillary's eyes move independently in different directions, leading him to wonder if one or both is searching for a sharp object. "Look, I swear I never got the message."

"Where the hell is Massena? It sounds made up."

"Top of New York near Canada — but whatever, I'm here now."

"I don't know where that is, but what I do know —" Her hands squeeze his skull as she dry humps him. "Is we're gonna go bone RIGHT NOW!"

Stunned, Zabka asks, "We are? Where? In the bathroom?"

"No, you dimwit. In my ass!" Hillary whacks his chest. "Out back behind a dumpster. Stick your pecker in the snow first, and get it ice cold."

"Good lord, I have so many questions." Zabka wavers. "What's up with my dick having to be cold? Why in the ass?"

"I'm a born again virgin, that's why!" She looks down at her groin. "My cooter had been taking such a beating that it was starting to look like raw hamburger meat. That's when I decided to rejuvenate myself."

Zabka looks at her cross-eyed. "Um, okay. And the cold dick thing? Will this even physically work?"

"After being revirginized, I started experimenting and found out that push-up popsicles really do the trick for me." She puts her middle and index fingers together and jabs toward her butt. "And yes, it'll work. If I'm outta lube, you can always use nature's lube — spit."

Zabka shakes his head, "But we've never done any of this sort of stuff."

"Well, I have, and I love it!" Hillary punches the air above her. "I wanna feel like Bumble the Abominable Snowman is banging me in the pooper."

"Hold on. You wanna roll play where I pretend I'm the white, hairy monster from Rudolph — the one with goofy eyes and jagged teeth?"

"Yeah, and you're nailing me from behind. It's fucking Christmas time, don't sound so confused." Hillary's eyes bulge and spin like Bumble's do in her claymation fuck-fantasy. "You got a problem satisfying one of my childhood hormonal urges?"

"Do I have a choice?" Zabka asks, already knowing the answer.

"No, you don't." Hillary's stare pierces his pupils. "Time to go, *bitch!*" She climbs down and pulls him by the belt toward the rear exit.

Zabka yells over his shoulder to the guys, "I'll be back in a bit! I gotta job to do!"

Jed's raised eyebrows and expression conveys, "Damn, they move quick." He says to Bob, "I see what you mean about her. She's crazy."

"Yeah, and she gets around, like *a lot.*"

"How much is a lot?"

Bob taps his chin for a moment. "Let's put it this way — she's had north of fifty dicks in her. And those are the ones I know about."

Scooter is shocked, yet intrigued. "How do you know?"

"A couple of fraternities had their way with her — or maybe it's the other way around? Anyway, I heard all about it at the Base one night."

Jed says to Bob, "I bet you're one of those fifty-plus dicks. This means you and Zabka are Eskimo brothers, right?"

"What's that?" Scooter inquires. "You've shared the same igloo?"

Jed thinks about his answer for a second. "If igloo is an Eskimo euphemism for vagina, then yes. When two guys have banged the same girl, they share the same bang-lineage and thus become Eskimo brothers. So are you guys, Bob?"

"With her? Surprisingly, we're not. But I bet there's a handful of guys here today that are." As Bob looks around the Great Court, he almost expects to see animated arrows pop up and point out each one

Standing a few feet away with her back to Bob is a familiar looking blonde. *Oh shit, is that Jennifer?* After she turns, he's relieved to see that it's not her. *Good. I don't wanna deal with one of her confrontations today.*

The girl's similarity to Jennifer, and the fact that she's randomly singing a song to her friends, brings him back to the karaoke bar where they first met. The two of them killed it as they sang the Grease duet, "Summer Loving". After receiving a huge applause, they walked offstage arm and arm, and went in the corner to dance to the next song.

In the middle of laughing and spinning Jennifer around, Bob pulled her in close and said, "I've been told I'm a good kisser."

Jennifer replied, "I'll be the judge of that," and kissed him passionately. The rest, as they say, is history.

Slightly intoxicated and fully drifted into this memory, Bob doesn't notice the Jennifer look-a-like approaching him until she's in his face. He snaps out of it as she says, "Ya know, gawking with a giddy smile is no way to attract a lady."

Bob smirks. "I beg to differ. It seems to have worked just perfectly."

"Very funny." She smiles and puts her hand out to shake. "I'm Jenny."

"No way. It's nice to meet you. I'm Bob."

"Why no way?"

"Oh, it's just you remind me of my girl —" Bob pauses uncomfortably. "You remind me of my girlfriend. We had a bad fight, and we're kinda on a break. Oddly enough, her name is Jennifer."

"Well, I like her name, and she sounds pretty." Jenny grabs his bicep flirtatiously. "Do you need a fill-in girlfriend for today?"

Before Bob can answer, Summer grabs his other arm from behind and swings around to box out Jenny. "Hi honey, have you missed me?"

"Excuse me, but who are you? You can't be Jennifer." Jenny looks at Bob. "You implied she's a blonde like me. Unless you're full of shit."

"Who am I?" Summer asks. "Who the fuck are you, and who the fuck is Jennifer?!"

"Alright, everyone calm down." Bob pushes the two girls away from each other. "Jenny, this is Summer, we met last night. Jennifer isn't here, she's blonde. Summer, Jennifer is my girlfriend. We had a big argument, and we're figuring things out."

As Jed and Scooter watch things unfold like a dirty movie, they wish they had a tub of buttery popcorn. Between sips of beer, their private discussion revolves around whether or not Bob can pull off a threesome.

With jealousy and horniness at elevated levels, Summer asks, "You have a girlfriend? You conveniently left that out last night, didn't you?"

"To be honest, I was trying to forget her at that time," Bob replies. Out of the corner of his eye he notices Zabka's head bobbing up and down as he skips through the crowd. Upon arrival, Zabka comes up to the three of them without saying a word and pretends he's at the plate in a baseball game. He takes a big swing and then trots around them counterclockwise while holding up his arms. The girls look at him like he's crazy, while Bob laughs having gotten the joke.

"What the hell is he doing?" Scooter asks.

"He must've hit Hurricane Hillary out of the park," Jed answers. "Because he's rounding the bases."

After Zabka 'touches them all', Bob slaps his butt like a baseball manager. "Way to go!" Zabka continues around two more times.

"Who is this guy?" Jenny asks. "He's out of his mind."

"I'm Zabka, and I just got LAAAAAAAID!!!"

"Nice work, but why three trips around?" Bob asks.

"Cuz I did her in the backdoor," Zabka proudly announces. "So to me, that's like a three run homer. Ya know — for hittin' the three hole."

"Kinda makes sense," Bob replies. "So what would a grand slam be?"

Zabka thinks for a second. "I guess hittin' all four holes at one at bat."

"Four holes? There's three. What's the magical fourth?"

"Ah, you forgot about the often underutilized, but lots of fun —" Zabka presses his pecks together. "Slip and slide between 'em, titty fuck!"

"Okay, I've had enough of these shenanigans." Jenny storms off.

"Who was that bitch?" Zabka asks without really caring. "Anyway, what's up, Summer? You want of piece of this too? I'll carve out some time for you."

"What an untempting offer." She rolls her eyes. "I'm gonna pass."

"No big deal. You're pretty low on my 'girls to bang' list anyway. You're like charity work. You know, pro-bono type stuff that I'll get around to if I have time. Occasionally I try to give back to the community. Yeah, that's right — I'm a real giver."

Although intrigued by his new attitude, Summer still asks him in a bitchy way, "Can you just leave?"

"Yeah, whatever. I need a beer." Zabka rejoins his Massena buddies.

Summer sizes-up Bob before poking one of his pecs. "It's bullshit. You don't have a girlfriend." She squeezes the two mountains surrounding her silicone valley. "These are pretty nice, aren't they?"

"I'm gonna be honest with you — completely honest. Besides the fact that you have a slightly crooked tooth —" Bob brushes his fingers through her black hair. "You're also just not my type. I'm sorry."

Summer inspects the alignment of her teeth with a slide of her tongue. "Okay, then I'm gonna be honest with you too. If I took you back to my hotel room right now, I'd have my way with you."

Bob hides his excitement with an eye roll. *Tickets time! Close her!* He squints at Summer as he prepares to hook her mouth and reel her in with low-self-esteem bait. "I want you to listen closely to what I'm about to say. My bang list *never has,* and *never will,* have your name on it."

Summer grabs his hand and holds it tightly like she'll never let go. "We'll see about that!" As Bob is yanked toward the exit, he throws a thumbs-up high above his head so the guys can't miss it.

—

Standing in her bra and jeans, Jennifer opens the bottom drawer of her dresser and shuffles through her sweater collection. *I need to show this Lisa whore why Robert will never leave me.* She pulls out a hot red sweater with a plunging neckline, slips into it, and mentally reviews her game plan. *Go down to Third Base, find her, and politely ask, "Why the fuck does my boyfriend have your number?"* The muscles around her mouth twitch. *We'll keep this whole thing very civil.*

As Jennifer walks to the hallway closet to fetch her coat, a wave of depression hits her and she stops just shy of reaching the door. *What if he did do something with her? Do I kill him or her — or both of them?* She shivers thinking about it and opens the closet.

While putting on her warmest winter coat and gloves, she looks up at the bright hallway light. "God, please let everything turn out okay." After making her plea, the light flickers and she flinches. *What does that mean?* She shrugs and exits her apartment.

—

As Summer and Bob are cutting through the drunken mass for the exit, Bambi catches them. "And where exactly are you two going? We still have work to do, Summer."

"I'm going to do some one-on-one work at the Hyatt — it's none of your concern."

Scooter stumbles forcefully into Bambi and nearly knocks her out of her stilettos. She yells, "What the fuck, dude!"

Scooter juts his finger in Bambi's face. "I gotta bone to pick with you!"

"A bone?" Bambi looks around. "What bone?"

"I'm talking about your pills! They're bullshit!"

"No, they're not." Bambi counters, "They're made of all natural ingredients, not bullshit! That's just gross."

"Let me translate for you. What I'm saying is — They! Don't! Work! For fuck's sake! It's impossible to have a conversation with you. It'd be easier to talk to a four-year-old from one of the Koreas!"

"Come on, Scooter, lay off," Bob tells him. "No need to be insulting. You say a lot of stupid shit too."

Bambi grins like Bob just threw a shoe at a heckling comedian and hit him squarely in the face. "Thank you. I appreciate a gentlemen."

Summer steps in and grabs Scooter. "Let me see if I can help. Have you been using the cream?"

"What cream? There's cream?"

"Yeah, there's cream." Summer pulls out a sample and hands it to him. "You need to apply it each night before you go to bed. It'll tingle, but that just means it's working. You'll see immediate improvements in your girth. It's the combination of the pills and the cream that will get you the best results."

"Really?!" Scooter asks, excited at possibilities.

"Yes, really. But one thing you should know — and it's clearly written on the tube — *do not* apply the cream and then have intercourse."

Bob laughs and gives Scooter a friendly punch. "Not that he really has to worry about the intercourse part, but why?"

"Her reaction will be less than pleasurable." Summer raises an eyebrow. "How do I put this? It would be like taking a handful of fire ants and injecting them into her coochie." The men cringe in response.

Scooter points at his manhood. "And I'm supposed to put *that* on my ding-a-ling?!"

"Wow!" Bob yells. "In comparison, that *almost* makes Bryan Cox's gonorrhea Christmas present for Buffalo seem like a better option!"

Summer tells Scooter, "It'll tingle on the outside, which means it's working, but no matter what you do, keep it away from your pee hole. If you get it in there, it'll feel like a pissed-off hornet is stinging its way down your urethra to your testicles." Scooter winces. "Oh, and one other thing. Have you been taking the pills rectally?"

"What? No. Of course not." Scooter leans away from her. "I'm supposed to do that?"

"No, I'm just fucking with you." Summer snickers. "Gotcha!"

"Oh, funny. Kinda. I just want to do it right so I can get a girlfriend."

Bob notices Bradford in the distance coming their way and grabs Summer. He says to her, "Don't look now, but here comes your douchebag boyfriend — and I mean that in the most respectful way."

She rolls her eyes. "Oh, great."

"What are you guys up to tonight?"

"Someplace outside of Buffalo, but I don't remember where. I'll find out and let you know. We'll pick things up again later."

Bob smiles mischievously. "Sounds perfect."

Summer turns to Bradford as he arrives, and before any words can come out of his mouth, she gives him the finger. "Yeah, I know. Back to work." Bradford scowls at Bob as he escorts the girls away.

Bob returns a friendly wave and a fuck-you grin. "Hey Bradford! Why don't you invent something that's useful?! Like a pill I can use to get rock-hard after drinking all day! But make that shit actually work!"

Summer looks back over her shoulder, smiles at Bob, and points to herself. Bob chuckles. *Oh, so she's the cure for that problem.*

Scooter puts his hand on Bob's shoulder to keep his balance. "But aren't you like twenty-four or something? You have that problem?"

Bob shrugs. "Hey, I like to drink a lot and occasionally there's issues."

Scooter puts his face within millimeters of Bob's cheek. "I tried to cock block that cock blocker, Bambi." As he speaks, spittle sprays into Bob's ear. "I tried so you and Summer could leave together. I failed you."

"You know what?" Bob says like a father talking to his son after he strikes out swinging. "You sensed the situation, and you gave it your best shot. No one can fault you for that."

"Thanks, I appreciate it." As they return to Zabka and Jed, Scooter slips and almost falls down. Bob puts his arm around Scooter's shoulders and ushers him safely. "One more thing, Bob. When you were talking to Summer, Bambi asked for my contact info and told me something —"

"What the hell happened?!" Zabka shouts. "You get the tickets?"

Bob frowns and shakes his head. "Guys, I thought I had a good chance of that if I got back to her hotel. We were headed in that direction, but shit didn't work out."

"Dammit-to-fuck!" Zabka yells.

Scooter sways and nervously taps his foot on the ground. "Guys, I'm feeling a wee bit intoxicated. Can we eat something today?"

Zabka holds up his beer. "What the hell do you think this is?!"

Bob raises his glass. "Yeah, like my buddy Big Al says, beer is food!"

"Come on guys, I'm flippin' serious," Scooter begs.

"And so are we," Zabka replies.

"No, come on." Scooter squirms. "I'm not gonna make it much longer if I don't eat something."

Bob asks, "Are you telling me those chips you found in my pantry weren't sufficient? Why you gotta make me feel like a terrible host? I'm really hurt."

"Bob, I dug up a pop-tart one year past its expiration date and found it to be quite delectable," Jed remarks. "So thank you for that."

"You're welcome, Jed. Okay, so here's what we're gonna do. Scooter, since you love Buffalo history and food, after they kick us out of here, I'm gonna take us to a famous place nearby to eat. You good with that?"

"Sounds great!" Scooter replies. "I bet I even know where we're going!"

Bob says, "Zabka's been before, but let's keep it a surprise for Jed."

"All I care about is that there's beer there. There is, right?" Jed asks.

"Of course," Bob replies. "Would I ever steer you wrong?"

"I don't think you would. So far so good!"

Zabka moans. "Hey, if you're thinking where I think you're thinking, I say we go elsewhere."

"No way! We're going!" Scooter commands. "I want the original!"

Something catches Jed's eye at the back of the room and he points in that direction. "Hey guys, you see that curtain over there? There seems to be some movement behind it."

"Oh yeah, with all the beer and pussy here, I didn't really take notice of it before. Is that a stage?" Zabka asks.

"I think you're right," Bob answers. "It'd be cool if a band comes on!"

"Maybe it'll be a midget band!" Jed shouts. "Ya know, a band full of midgets and dwarfs and shit. That'd be awesome!"

"Good lord! You and your midget fixation!" Zabka yells. "Is there a psychological name for what you have?!"

"Yeah! He's a midgophile!" Bob slaps his thigh.

Zabka laughs. "G! O! Good One!"

Jed puts on imaginary professor spectacles and swipes his hand like he's flipping through a book. "If there's a condition named after it, then that means I'm not alone. So you two can go fuck yourselves."

"Seriously guys, let's figure out what's going on," Scooter urges.

Zabka scours the room for someone who looks like they're working the event, but to no avail. So he decides to question the next person walking by. He stops an unattractive girl with a cow nose ring and black eyeliner. "Hey, you know if there's a band coming on?"

The girl's friends, who look nearly identical to her, wait behind as she answers, "Yeah, I think they're coming on soon. It better be Pearl Jam."

"Alright, thanks."

As Zabka is turning away, she says, "Hey, while you're here, can you take a picture of us?" She hands him her camera and the girls line up. The group strikes an indifferent pose, but before Zabka can snap a photo, she tells him, "Make us look good." Zabka takes the camera away from his eye, thinks about her command for an instant, and hands it back to her. Confused, she asks, "What are you doing?"

"You told me to make you look good. But I ain't no miracle man." The girls give Zabka the finger, and he spins around to the group. "Alright guys, good news. There's gonna be a band performing!"

The house lights flicker and attract everyone's attention like moths. A man wearing a Jim Kelly number 12 jersey walks onto the stage with a microphone in his hand. When he reaches the center, he stops to address the crowd. "Hi everyone. Thank you for coming out to the annual Buffalo Brewfest! We sure hope you're having a good time!" The inebriated mob shouts out their appreciation. "Great! All of us working the event are having a good time too! And it's about to get better. For our grand finale, it's my pleasure to welcome to the stage — presented to you by Huge Member — our very own Queen cover band, Queen City!!"

As the MC hurries off the stage, there's a mixture of applause and boos from the audience. The purple curtains remain closed while the a-cappella beginning of "Fat Bottomed Girls" vibrates from the stage speakers. As the guitar and drums kick in, the curtains part and reveal a four-woman band dressed in black leather. The lead singer's vocals could pass for Freddy Mercury with a tongue swollen from excessive cunnilingus — a condition she's experienced far more often than him. She'd be his spitting image if she lost a hundred pounds and had a slightly thicker mustache. Her horse-teeth however, are a perfect replica.

The rest of the band looks like a pudgy version of the Hells Angels. As they rock-out, the crowd gets into the music and starts pulsating. People

186 | SQUISH THE FISH

playing air guitar and air drums perform in sync with the group. Flailing arms send several beers flying through the air. Just as the song is about to finish its closing notes, all of the power goes out — leaving the room filled with loud jeers and in near darkness. The only sources of light are illuminated green exit signs at the fringes of the room.

The guys look at each other. "What the fuck?"

"You guys alright?" Bob asks.

"Yeah, couldn't be better," Jed answers. "I just got a fresh beer."

Scooter says, "I can't believe this."

"Can't believe what? That a disaster like this would happen in the Buffalo?" Zabka scoffs. "Get used to it."

"No." Scooter's mind is floating. "I can't believe that the Brewfest blacked out before I did."

Bob looks at the glow-in-the-dark hands on his watch. "Let's go, guys. This thing is almost over anyway, and the fat lady *literally* just sang. Plus I think I saw Tammi creeping around, and I wanna slip out before we have another encounter."

Zabka tells him, "You realize dogs have a great sense of smell?"

"Yes, I do — hey, are you saying she's ugly?"

"Well, I ain't sayin' she's pretty."

"Whatever. Let's get outta here."

Jed stops them. "Hold on. What about getting the tickets? Besides getting shit-faced, did you do anything to get us closer to our *other* objective?"

Scooter answers, "I got some info that might be valuable."

Before they can discuss further, a person in the shadows moves closer, and Bob's eyes widen. "Shit, I sense Tammi. Follow me."

———

Jennifer slams her car door shut in front of Third Base. *Am I crazy? What if I'm wrong, and Lisa tells Bob about this?* She pauses on the sidewalk and looks through the window into the sparsely populated bar. *It could be worse, I could be right.* She slowly inhales the frigid air as she scans for a potential Lisa.

Jennifer pulls open the door and makes her way to an empty bar seat. She eyes the bartender talking to a fraternity brother. *That better not be Lisa. She might be as pretty as me, and Robert would like her rack.*

Lisa spots Jennifer and finishes her conversation. She walks over and puts down a cocktail napkin. "Hi, what are you having?"

"I'm not quite sure yet," Jennifer replies. "You have any tasty recommendations? Just not a cosmo." She rubs her temple. "I had too many of those last night."

Lisa grins. "How about a Long Island Iced Tea? It will serve you well."

"Sure, if you say so, I'll go for it." Jennifer taps her nails on the bar as Lisa scoops ice into a highball glass. "I'm Jennifer by the way."

"Nice to meet you." After pouring a healthy amount of tequila, Lisa accepts Jennifer's handshake. *Why's she squeezing so hard?* After they release, Lisa tilts her head and examines Jennifer. "You're not a regular?"

Jennifer glances at the girls playing pool while answering, "No, I'm not. I just felt like grabbing a drink." She turns back to face Lisa. "I'm sorry, I didn't catch your name earlier."

Lisa simultaneously pours vodka and rum into the liquor concoction. "My name's Lisa." Jennifer's eyes erupt and trigger a red flag. Lisa pauses and speculates, *What's going on with this girl? She's up to something.*

——

Jed's Bronco plows through snow as he speeds east on North Street. The street light at Delaware Avenue turns red, forcing Jed to slam on the breaks, sliding them to a stop.

"Nice driving, Jed," Zabka shouts over "Man in the Box" on the radio.

"I aim to please, gentlemen."

Scooter reviews the night sky and spots a building to the south. "Hey guys, look on top of the roof of that tall building down there. There's a couple of miniature Statues of Liberty on it."

Jed squints. "That's fucking weird. We're seeing double already?"

"Actually you're not," Bob says. "But I don't know why they're there."

"I do," Scooter tells them. "Liberty Bank put them there while constructing the building. One statue faces east toward the rail lines and the other faces west towards the lake. It represents Buffalo's strategic location on the Great Lakes."

The light turns green and Jed drives through the intersection. "We're almost to our watering hole," Zabka informs the passengers. "Park once you get across Main Street."

"There it is." Bob points at a dark red brick building. "That's where wings were invented. It's a Buffalo shrine of sorts."

After parking, they get out and cross the slush-covered street. Scooter eyes the sign above the entrance and reads it aloud, "Frank & Teresa's Anchor Bar. Home of The Original Buffalo Chicken Wings. Established in 1935." He puts up his arms like he's indicating a field goal is good. "This is fucking awesome! I love Buffalo wings!"

"We all do." Bob playfully slaps Scooter on the back. "But you don't call them Buffalo wings in Buffalo. It's just wings. Got it?"

"It's *the* Buffalo by the way," Scooter advises Bob like he's the smartest kid in class. "But sure, I got it." Bob half smiles and shakes his head.

"Scooter, I'm surprised that after all the exhaustive research you've done, you didn't know how to refer to wings here," Zabka comments.

"I know a lot, but there's still stuff I'm learning that's not in books. Keep teaching me. I want my PhD in *the* Buffalo."

As they open the front door, a gust of warm air mixed with the scent of spicy wings fills their nostrils. Instantly they begin drooling like teenage boys hoping to catch a glimpse of a young woman's panties as she bends over in her schoolgirl skirt. Zabka crouches behind the guys and nervously scans the restaurant and bar. They queue up behind ten others in line to the hostess.

Scooter removes his glasses and wipes off condensation with the bottom of his shirt. "Guys, it's packed in here. How about I go get us a pitcher while you wait here?"

"Now that's a brilliant idea!" Zabka says. "Way to take control, boss."

License plates from every state cover the walls. As Scooter walks to the bar, he notices a blue California plate with "BF BILLS" stamped in yellow lettering and a white New York plate that reads "SKYWAY 1" in blue. The rectangular bar in the center of the room is accessible from any side. Scooter makes his way around until he spots a gap between the people sitting at the bar. After squeezing his way in, he attempts to get the bartender's attention by waving his arms like he's in a swarm of mosquitoes. A double tap on his shoulder freezes his arms, and he turns around.

A cute brunette with golden highlights says to him, "It's okay, you can relax. I know the bartender and will help get you a drink." She does a quick double-sniff. "And damn, I gotta say, you smell good."

"Oh, thanks. It's my cologne." A bead of sweat hangs from the tip of his nose. "Help with drinks would be great. I actually need to get a round for me and my friends back there."

"We can do that too. I'm Hope. What's your name?"

He wipes away the perspiration with the back of his hand. "I'm Scooter — I mean Scott."

Hope holds out her hand, and he takes it. While they shake, she doesn't break eye contact. "Well, Scooter or Scott, or any other adorable names you may have, it's a pleasure to meet you."

Scooter releases his grip, but she does not. "Yeah, cool to meet you too, Hope."

"Thanks." She lets go of his limp hand. "Are you, um, here for wings?"

"Yeah, I am actually, but I need to get beer first or my friends will go through withdrawals within ten minutes. But speaking of wings, are they hot here?"

"Yes." Hope bites her lower lip. "But not nearly as hot as *you* are."

"Oh, you noticed that?" Scooter turns to flag down the bartender. "I'm sorry, but I'm burning up in here. Can you help me get his attention?"

Hope hides her frown. "Um, sure." She crumples up a cocktail napkin and hits the bartender fifteen feet away.

The bartender turns angrily at first, but grins after she chuckles. He walks over to her and says, "Hey Hope, whaddya need?"

"Sam, it's actually this fine gentleman here who needs drinks." She grabs Scooter's arm. "I'll let him order."

"Thanks. Can I get a pitcher of Genesee and four glasses? My three buddies are waiting anxiously."

"Don't you mean five glasses?" Sam asks. "Or a drink for Hope too?"

"No, I'm good with four glasses." Scooter looks down at Hope's glass. "She's not quite finished with her beer yet."

Hope gulps down the rest of her drink and nudges Scooter with her elbow. Scooter doesn't react and stares with anticipation at the taps. Sam shrugs at Hope and begins to pour.

Scooter turns to Hope. "Thanks again. I know how thirsty those guys can get, and if I don't get them their beer soon, they may start drinking every discarded drink they find."

She grimaces. "That's disgusting."

"I was just kidding — kinda."

"Oh, okay." Hope squints at him playfully. "I think your glasses are really cute, but do you mind if I ask what happened to your face?"

"Oh, this?" Scooter rubs his scratched cheek. "It's a long story."

"Did you go down on a porcupine or something?" She chuckles.

Scooter shakes as he giggles like a girl. "Not quite, but that's funny."

"I was gonna say, if you did, it's okay." Hope slowly caresses her inner thighs with her hands and in a sultry tone discloses, "Cuz I like a man who doesn't mind, ya know, when it's a little prickly down there."

Puzzled, he responds, "That's good to know — I guess?"

Sam plunks the pitcher and glasses on the bar. "Here ya go. That'll be eight bucks."

Scooter hands him a ten and winks. "Keep the change." After picking up his order, he says to Hope, "Later, gator," and walks away. Aghast, she smells her armpits and tests her breath.

When Scooter reaches the guys, who have moved to a corner of the room, Zabka snatches an empty glass and says, "What took you so long?"

"Sorry about that. Some girl at the bar was yapping my ear off."

"Yeah, right." Zabka puts out his glass to be filled. "How large is she? Gotta be pushing at least two-fifty."

"Actually, no." As Scooter points at her, they all turn to look. "She's that brunette over there. I guess she's kinda decent looking." He shrugs. "I wasn't paying much attention." He grins as he holds the pitcher up toward the ceiling. "Gotta keep the eyes on the prize."

"Good work. We needed this," Bob says as Scooter distributes beer. "They said it's gonna be about twenty minutes until they seat us."

Zabka stares with bewilderment at Hope. "That girl over there was yapping your ear off? For Buffalo standards, she's hot. Why the hell would she do that?"

"No clue." Scooter rewinds the conversation in his mind. "However, she did hint that her lady part area might be prickly."

"What?!" Zabka exclaims. "Meaning she recently shaved her bush and actually put some effort into vaginal maintenance?!" Zabka throws his hands up and jettisons half his beer, which lands on Jed's head. "This is incredible! There actually exists a Buffalo girl that doesn't require a machete to properly go down on her!"

Unfazed, Jed licks the beer as it drips down his face. "You're right, that is incredible."

The attention of a retired couple standing next to them is uncomfortably drawn to their loud conversation. The woman's wrinkled face pokes out of her wool coat and exudes the offense she feels. It's not difficult to imagine her making the same face at church during silent prayer if someone butt-tooted the first few notes of "Stairway to Heaven".

Feeling the couple's intrusiveness invade their space, Zabka turns to them with a smug smile. "Would you like to join our conversation?" The woman quivers and shrinks into her husband's arms as he shakes his head no. "Are you sure? Because it seems like you do."

The words tremble out from the woman's mouth, "We don't appreciate all your talk about a lady's *baby-giver*." She makes the sign of the cross.

"You mean her vagina? Well, I sincerely apolo-*jizz*." Zabka makes the prayer sign. "But if you don't appreciate what we've been talking about so far, you're really *not* gonna enjoy the next subject." He turns to Jed. "Tell them why you buy bananas for your wife."

Scooter and Bob can't hide their awkwardness and silently beg Jed not to. Jed looks at his remaining beer. "After I finish this, I'll tell the story." As he begins to chug the contents of his glass, the couple scurries away.

Relieved, Bob says, "Thanks for doing that, Jed."

"Doing what? I just wanted to finish my beer so I could drink the rest of the pitcher. Fill me up, Scooter." As Scooter follows orders, Jed begins, "So the banana thing. Yeah, I always have bananas on-hand for when Brandy's girlfriends come over. I encourage the girls to eat 'em by telling them potassium is a great hangover cure."

"And why do you want them to eat bananas?" Scooter asks.

"I like to watch the girls. I fantasize that the banana is my cock when they slide it in their pie-holes." Jed holds up an imaginary version of the phallic fruit and thrusts it in his mouth. "One of her friends — Jeannine I think it is — well, she has overly active salivary glands, and so her banana always gets a bunch of slobber all over it. So much that some drips down her chin."

"Man, you're sick." Bob shakes his head. "You're like some kind of perverted puppet master!"

"Hey, I've been married for four years. I'm bored. I needed some way to spice things up — even if it is watching them from the other side of the couch and whacking off. Fuck it."

"Oh man, that's taking it to the next-level!" Bob shouts. "Have you ever been caught?"

"Not yet, but I'm kinda hoping one of these times they do. Maybe some kinky shit will happen?" Jed smirks. "Like I said, I'm fucking bored."

"Damn. I mean you haven't really been married for that long. You haven't even hit that seven-year itch I hear about."

"Bob, I hit the seven-year itch entering year two," Jed confides.

"I guess long term relationships are tough. For me, I'm trying to figure out if Jennifer and I will make it to one year together."

"How does she make you feel?" Jed inquires like he cares.

"Sometimes she's awesome and I feel lucky to have found her. Other times she's manipulative and I want to rip her head off — not literally rip her head off like O.J., but you know what I mean."

"Yeah sure, but what I meant by feel is, how does she make your genitals feel?"

Bob laughs. "Oh, that. The sex is amazing — if we have it. In fact, I'm getting turned-on just thinking about it."

"As I expected. But here's the thing — that all fades away."

"It does?"

"Yeah, let me explain." Jed points and moves his finger in a figure-eight motion at the bar. "Imagine there's a hot chick over there."

Bob looks. "What hot chick?"

"I said *imagine*. Okay, so see the hot chick over there?"

"The imaginary one? Yeah, I see her."

"Some guy's sick of fucking her," Jed states as if it's a concrete fact.

"What the heck does that mean? If Scooter had a hot chick, I guarantee he wouldn't be sick of fucking her. Real or imaginary."

"Oh, but he would — at some point." Jed's body seems to elevate like he's stepped up on a soapbox. "What I'm saying is, no matter how hot the girl, eventually she's not gonna get your rocks off like she used to. The timing is different for each of us. At first your eyes will wander a little. And then they'll wander a lot. This will go on for a while until the temptation is just too much, and you hit that point — the point where your dick yearns to stray. Where it yearns for some strange."

Scooter gobbles up the conversation like a large pizza. "Guys, I have the solution." He smiles proudly. "My ex-wife and I came up with it."

"So you're telling me a divorcee with two cats holds some magic solution?" Zabka asks with a laugh. "The solution to what? A man's snake has the god given right to roam free!" He shrugs his shoulders. "I don't see a problem that needs solving."

Scooter tells them, "In the case of marriage, the rules are kinda different, but we found a loophole."

"You *found* a loophole or *came up with* one?" Zabka asks. "There's a difference. Oh never mind, just go ahead. I can't wait to hear this."

"So we were talking one day — my wife and I — and she thought it would be good for our relationship if were proactive and put a plan in place to handle temptation. Anyway, we decided to have an open relationship — with a couple of ground rules, of course."

"And by *we* decided, you mean *she*, right?"

"Well, she proposed the idea, and I later agreed to it after the rules were laid down."

"Okay, I'm curious. What are these rules?" Bob asks.

Scooter holds up four fingers. "There's this many of them. First, you have to get approval from the other person before you can proceed. Second, upon approval, the other person has the option to watch. Third, if there is disapproval, no grudges can be held. And lastly, fourth, you can only have sex with the person once."

Bob ponders the regulations. "So this is interesting. You're attempting to limit this to purely a sexual desire thing, while giving some level of control to your mate and not allowing a connection to be made with the person you're doing the nasty with."

"That's pretty much it," Scooter agrees. "It's a sexual outlet that takes cheating out of the equation and helps keep the relationship intact."

"Alright, so the next obvious question is, how'd it work out? What was the final score so to speak?" Bob chuckles.

"Um, well." Scooter looks down and shuffles his feet. "It didn't quite work out the way I hoped, because the game ended early when she left me. I didn't really have a chance for an at bat."

"That sucks," Bob consoles him. "So what was the score?"

Scooter gulps before answering, "It ended up 2-0 in her favor."

"Two bangs to nothing!" Zabka shouts while jumping up and down. "Are you fucking kidding me?! How is that a good solution?! Sounds like it was a great solution for her though!"

With the bar's attention drawn by Zabka's outburst, Bob pulls him down from a mid-air leap. "Zabka, you need to chill the fuck out. You get way too excited sometimes. Have you forgotten that you need to keep a low profile here?" He waits for Zabka's breathing to slow down. "Guys, enough talk about deep-throating bananas and disturbing open relationships. We need to refocus on our most pressing mission."

Jed raises his glass. "Drinking beer!"

"No, you idiot! We need tickets to the game! Remember that clusterfuck we're in?!"

"Shit, you're right!" Zabka exclaims. "Scooter, how about you come up with something that's a solution to that problem *and* that gets us laid!"

"Jesus, that's asking a lot. You want me, a guy who's only been with one woman in a biblical sense, to pull off that laid thing too?"

The hostess cautiously approaches them like they're a pack of wild monkeys drunk on stolen tourists' daiquiris. "Your table is ready."

"Thank you," Bob replies. "Sorry about the commotion, we're just excited for your wings."

"Understood. We've seen that before." She leads them into the dining area and shows them to their table. "Your waitress will be right with you." As they sit, she asks, "Are you aware it's trivia night?"

Delighted, Scooter reconfirms, "Did you say trivia?"

"Be careful using the T-word," Zabka tells the hostess. "It gets him excited. In fact, there's a good chance he just wet himself like a little puppy."

"He does claim to get wet down there," Bob informs her. "But I advise you not to ask why, because it has nothing to do with him peeing himself. Anyway, tell us about this trivia contest."

After managing to overlook the bulk of what she just heard, she tells them, "Tonight's theme is Buffalo history."

"This is right up your alley, Scooter!" Bob yells.

Scooter does a little happy jig. "Perfect! I wanna play!"

"What's the prize?" Bob asks. "A dozen wings? A snow shovel?"

She answers, "No, and I'm not sure how ownership pulled this off, but first prize is four tickets to tomorrow's Bills game."

"You're shitting me?!" Zabka shouts.

"Holy fuck!" Jed exclaims.

"This is awesome!" Scooter circles his finger at the other tables. "These bitches ain't seen nothin' like me when it comes to the Buffalo history!"

"Unbelievable!" Bob roars. "We've got a shot, boys! Our prayers have been answered! Hallelujah!"

———

After Lisa confirmed that she was actually Lisa, Jennifer felt a blow to her stomach and hunched over.

Lisa snaps her fingers. "Are you alright?"

Jennifer stammers, "Uh, your name reminded me of someone."

Lisa decides that it's time to probe. "Of all the places you could've gone, why'd you come here for a drink?"

"Yeah, so, my friend Robert likes to come here sometimes," Jennifer replies. "I thought I might run into him. You know him?"

"Robert? Let me think." Lisa pushes the Long Island Iced Tea over to Jennifer. "I don't think I know a Robert. That'll be five dollars." As Lisa waits for payment, she ponders, *Could she be talking about Bob?*

"I thought there might be a chance you'd know him because he graduated from UB and used to go here all the time." Jennifer sucks down half her drink through her straw. "You work Fridays? Like last night?"

"As a matter of fact I do, and yes, I did." Lisa wipes the bar with a towel. "Hey, what's up with all these questions?"

"I'm just curious," Jennifer replies sternly. "I like to know where Robert hangs out and who he's with."

The expression on Lisa's face reveals that she's put the pieces together. She leans towards Jennifer with an evil smile and whispers, "By any chance do you mean Bob? We had a nice time last night."

Jennifer tips backward on her stool and barely grabs the bar in time to prevent herself from tumbling off. Images of Robert and Lisa competing in a Kama Sutra decathlon rush through her mind. She manages to pull herself upward and back into reality. Looking like she's about to scramble over the bar at Lisa, Jennifer screams, "Robert, Bob, whatever the hell we wanna call him! He's my man! Stay the fuck away!"

"But didn't you just say he's your friend?" Lisa replies calmly. "Which would make sense, because last night he didn't look like he was any woman's man. As far as I could tell, he can do whatever he wants." She raises her eyebrows. "Like doing me."

Lisa's snide comment unleashes Jennifer's worst fears. Huffing and with her face red with rage, Jennifer jumps off her stool and tips it over. Her inner voice shrieks, *I'm gonna kill this bitch!*

———

From a neighboring table, Hope shouts, "Hey Scooter, come here for a second!" Scooter points to himself as if to ask, "Who, me?"

She waves him over. "Yeah, get over here." The guys look puzzled.

"Gentlemen, I'll be right back." Scooter walks over to Hope and her two girlfriends. "What's up?"

"I just wanted to say hi again," Hope replies. "You gonna play trivia?"

"Hell yeah, we are. For once in my life I feel confident. I think we can win this — well, really we have to. We need those tickets, or I'm fucked."

"Why would you be fucked?"

Scooter stares at a black gum spot on the brown tile floor. "I was put in charge of getting tickets, and basically I dropped the ball. Stupid me thought I'd just buy them tomorrow. I didn't understand the situation."

"Well now you have another problem." Hope grins wickedly. "You have to go up against *me* in trivia."

"Even though nothing ever seems to go my way, I'm gonna be a tough opponent when it comes to Buffalo history." He smiles and gives her a couple of mock boxing jabs.

Hope laughs. "Okay, Tyson. Good luck!"

"I won't need luck. You will." He points and sweeps his finger across the three girls. "I'm gonna eat you for dinner!"

"Don't make a threat like that unless you mean it!" Hope raises her beer to cheers. "Ladies, sounds like we found ourselves a *vag*-etarian!"

Scooter laughs uncomfortably having not gotten the joke and uses his fist to toast their beer mugs. "Best of luck to you."

Scooter returns to his table and sits down. Zabka says to him, "I can't believe I'm gonna say this, but I think that girl likes you."

"Naw, she's just being nice. We were just talking trivia."

"Whatever, dude. She totally just eye-banged you!" Zabka pounds Scooter's fat back. "You're gonna get laid!"

"Yeah, right." Scooter blushes. "Hey, where's our beer?"

"On its way," Bob replies. "I already ordered for us. Four pitchers of Blue, fifty hot wings, and fifty suicidal wings."

"What's Blue?" Scooter asks.

"Christ!" Zabka shouts. "How are we gonna win this trivia contest if you don't even know what Blue is?!"

Bob informs Scooter, "Blue is Labatt Blue. That's what we call it here and in Ontario."

"Hey, there's a lot of shit I know, that you guys don't know," Scooter notifies them. "During trivia, you cover the lingo and I'll cover the tough questions. Capisci?"

"Oh, some attitude. I like it!" Zabka yells. "Guys, we're gonna win this!" He slides a pad and pencil over to Scooter. "Go at it, my man. It looks like we're gonna start."

In the back corner of the dining area, a man sits at a table in front of a microphone. "Welcome everyone! Tonight is a very special night. We don't usually have trivia, but in celebration of the Bills and you as loyal customers, we are tonight. There will be prizes for first and second place. Second place will be a hundred dollar Anchor Bar gift certificate, and first place will be four tickets to tomorrow's game!" The room erupts with hoots and applause. "Each question will have multiple parts. Each part answered correctly gets you one point. You'll have five minutes to answer each question. Write down the answers on a piece of paper, along with your team name, and bring it up here before time expires. Everybody ready?!" The contestants give an enthusiastic green light.

Bob tells the table, "Guys, we need a good team name."

"What's a vagetarian?" Scooter asks. "Is that a good name? Hope used that term and seemed to like it a lot."

"Damn, that's good! It's like a vegetarian — except instead of vegetables, it's vag. It's what you call someone who only eats pussy."

"I love it!" Jed licks his lips. "No further discussion needed, my fellow vagetarians!"

The trivia MC announces, "I'm going to ask the questions in reverse chronological order. So that means I'll start with the most recent, and then go back in history."

High on alcohol and adrenaline, Scooter shouts, "We know! Just ask the damn question!"

"Sounds like you're ready, so here we go. The first question has three parts. Timothy McVeigh was recently indicted for the Oklahoma City bombing. Which Western New York town was he born in? Which local company did he work for? And what was his job at that local company? The timer starts now."

"Oh, fuck," Scooter cries. "That's too recent and not in any of my books." Sweat begins to bead on his forehead. "We're doomed already. I'm sorry, guys."

"Look at the bright side. At least we have a cool team name," Jed says.

"Shut up, Jed!" Zabka shouts. "This is serious. Think." He looks across at Bob who is grinning quietly. "Why the hell are you smiling like that?"

Bob ducks down and tells the group, "You guys are not gonna believe this, but I know all three answers." He looks around as the others duck in closer and he whispers, "I used to work with that *mother fucker* McVeigh."

"Holy shit. No way?" Scooter says.

"Yep. Now put this down," Bob demands. Scooter writes "The Vagetarians" on the top of the page and anxiously awaits the answers. "Timothy McVeigh was born north of here in Lockport. It also happens to be home to Reid's, a place Zabka and I love — but that's a side note. He worked where I work, at Techspan, as, of all things, a security guard."

Scooter finishes his scribbling. "Got it. Take a look."

Bob reviews the paper. "All good. Bring it up."

As Scooter walks by Hope's table, he taunts her with his answers paper and a finger jab. She responds in kind by sticking out her tongue. He hands the answers to the MC and returns to his table. When he arrives, the waitress is setting down four pitchers of beer.

Bob says, "This is the brain boosting power we need to win this!" The four of them pour their pitchers down their gullets with both hands.

The MC's voice reverberates through the speakers, "Time's up — and here are the answers." The crowd falls silent and nervously waits. "Timothy McVeigh was born in Lockport. He worked for Techspan. And he was a security guard." While the guys yell and fist-pump to celebrate, they are surrounded by a mixture of groans and cheers.

"Way to go, Bob!" Scooter shouts. "Now it's my turn to shine!"

The MC begins, "The next question is about the Blizzard of '77." The guys look at Scooter and he gives them a thumbs-up. "There are two parts. The first part is — how many inches of snow fell? Your answer must be within 5 inches. The second part is — to what degree in Fahrenheit did the wind chill drop to at its lowest? Your answer must be within 5 degrees. Your five minutes begins now."

Scooter presses his fingers against the sides of his temple and closes his eyes. "Okay, okay, I know this. I was reading about this yesterday just after we went to Burger King." The guys fidget while he tries to get to the answer by talking to himself. "Oh, that's right. So I just got to where they were talking about the blizzard, and I farted pretty badly."

"Jesus Christ, Scooter!" Zabka yells. "Yeah, it stunk so fucking bad we had to pull over and evacuate the vehicle! But that horrific moment is not gonna help us answer this damn question!"

Scooter's eyes open like he just had a revelation. "100 inches of snow and minus 70 degrees wind chill. That's the answer."

"Nice!" Bob shouts. "Write it down and get it up to that guy."

While delivering the answers, Scooter does the chubby-white-guy version of the moonwalk. The MC shakes his head like he just witnessed someone slipping backwards while trying to climb an icy incline.

Scooter arrives back at his table and is pleased to find two large piles of steaming wings. "This is awesome! I'm drooling!"

With a half-eaten wing dripping with blue cheese in his hand, Bob orders him, "Dig in! You deserve it!"

As he munches on a wing, Zabka adds, "He deserves it if he got those last questions right."

"Relax guys, we did." Scooter looks at the two piles and asks, "Which is hot, and which is suicide?"

Bob notices Zabka's shit-eating grin and immediately yells, "Don't fuck with him now! We need a functional Scooter!" He points to the proper mound of wings as he speaks. "That one's hot, and that one's suicidal. I advise you to go with the hot. They're tasty, but won't kill ya."

"Thanks. I appreciate that, Bob." Scooter looks seriously at Zabka and says, "And you need to remember that I can still fire your ass." Zabka freezes mid-chew, and his face turns to stone. Scooter gives him a stare down for a few more seconds before laughing hysterically. "I got you, man! I soooo got you!!"

"Come on, I knew you were fucking with me." Zabka uses his teeth to pull the rest of the meat off his wing, and he chews as he speaks. "You need someone to get work done around that plant."

Scooter looks at their food. "Is there any ranch? I just see blue cheese."

Zabka drops the bare chicken bone. "I'll pretend you never said that!"

The MC's voice breaks through the chatter, "Alright everybody, I'm gonna give you the answers to the last question and then tell you who the leaders are." He waits for the room to quiet before continuing. "During the Blizzard of '77, 100 inches of snow fell and the wind chill hit minus 69 degrees." Some whining blends with a smattering of applause.

"That wind chill is wrong!" Scooter shouts. "It was minus 70 degrees!"

"Who cares?!" Zabka cries. "You still got it right!"

The MC says, "So at this stage we only have two teams that have gotten every question correct so far. Right behind them are several teams that have missed just one. The first team to have answered every question correctly is The Vagetarians!" The room bursts into a sea of boos as the guys congratulate themselves and give the finger to everyone else.

The MC scans his scorecard. "So far there seems to be a — ahem, theme for the teams on top. The second team to answer each question correctly is The Vertical Beef on Wecks!"

Scooter leans in. "What the heck does that mean?"

"Beef on Weck is a Buffalo-style roast beef sandwich," Bob replies. "And I'm gonna go out on a limb and say it's also a vagina euphemism."

The guys review the room looking for the team they are tied with. When they land on Hope's table, they find her pointing back at them and saying, "We're gonna take you down."

Scooter silently mouths over to her, "Bring it."

Hope's eyes flirt back at him. "Oh, I will." Her team looks in the guys' direction and wag their tongues between Vs made by their fingers.

Without breaking eye contact with Hope, Scooter asks over his shoulder, "Are they pretending to lick pussy?"

Zabka continues watching the girls without blinking. "Yes, that's exactly what they're doing. Funny — I'm really starting to like 'em."

"Good, then this is fair game." Scooter pretends to jerk-off and throw imaginary ejaculate at Hope. She juts her head to the left and closes her eyes as his invisible cum smacks her in the face. She wiggles her fingers in front of her head and moves them down like it's dripping all over her.

In shock, Zabka says, "That was really fucked-up. But not as fucked-up as the fact that she actually likes you."

As she blows Scooter a kiss, he feels like he's floating in another world. His smile broadens and overtakes his face. Zabka gives him a stiff whack on the back of his head and brings him back to earth. "Ouch!" Scooter wails. "What the hell did you do that for?"

"I figured it out!" Zabka exclaims. "She's playing you."

"What?" Scooter rapidly shakes his head. "No, she's not."

"It's the only thing that makes sense," Zabka explains. "That cute, conniving, little bitch will do anything to win and is trying to take out her competition — namely us! She's distracting you!" Scooter pouts like he did when his mom would deny him pudding because he didn't eat his vegetables. "Cheer up. All's fair in love and Bills tickets trivia. Now put your pecker away and get your focus back in the game."

—

During their standoff, Jennifer and Lisa's estrogen levels spike. If a bar weren't separating them, they'd be tangled on the floor in a savage catfight. The bar crowd carries on with their business except for a chunky guy in a tight red Bills t-shirt at the far end of the bar. If he had the proper winter cap and a white beard, he'd be mistaken for Santa. With his hand in the air, he cries out, "Hey! Can I get a beer!?" Lisa's fierce glare doesn't stray from Jennifer as she slowly lifts up her arm and delivers him the finger instead of his requested drink. Bewildered, the guy shouts back, "Okay, I guess I'll just wait 'till you're done with that."

Lisa puts her arm down. "What are you gonna do, Jennifer? Just stare me down for the rest of the night?"

Jennifer's heart pounds rapidly as she leans across the bar at Lisa. "Robert is my boyfriend! You had no right to give him your number!"

"Funny. Because *Bob* never mentioned he had a girlfriend."

"That bastard!" Jennifer cries. "We've been dating six months!"

"Believe me, I don't go after taken men — even Bob," Lisa insufficiently assures her. "But if he was fair game, we'd have a problem."

"I'll ignore that last part for now." Jennifer picks up her stool and sits back down. "I'm glad you now understand he's mine."

"Yeah, I guess. And I'm glad that you now understand that he didn't mention you. What I don't understand is why you felt the need to come down here and find me? What did *he* say about the whole thing?"

"Well, it's kinda like this." Jennifer discloses, "We got in a bad fight last night, so I really haven't spoken with him yet."

"Okay, so that partly explains things. I could sense that something was on his mind, but not really troubling him. Hey, if you haven't talked with him, how do you know he got my number?"

"I went over to his place this morning to speak with him and he wasn't there." Jennifer shrugs. "So I took the opportunity to look around a little bit and happened to come across it."

"That's interesting." Lisa cleans a beer mug. "You want to know the whole story? Woman to woman?"

Jennifer responds anxiously, "Of course."

Lisa looks at her with mock sympathy. "And no matter what, you want the truth?"

Jennifer gulps. "Um, yes. Tell me."

—

Jed takes a long draw from his pitcher before setting it back down on the table. "This feast is fantastic!" He uses a soiled napkin to sloppily wipe beer and wing sauce from his beard.

Scooter tosses a bone he's picked clean into a growing pile. "We should hear the answers to the last question pretty soon don't you think?"

"Yeah," Bob replies. He dips a celery stick in blue cheese and glances at the MC. "Looks like he's getting ready."

The MC takes the microphone. "Okay everyone, here are the answers to the last question. The chemical waste dump in Niagara Falls, NY that caused a significant number of health problems and birth defects was called Love Canal." The crowd responds with a golf clap. "Yeah, that was the easy part. The last two were a little more difficult. The company that sold the land was the Hooker Chemical Company, and the buyer of the land was the Niagara Falls School Board."

The guys hoot with joy as Zabka pounds his chest like a baboon. Scooter looks across the room at Hope to feel out how her team faired. To his disappointment, she looks back at him with matched confidence.

Scooter addresses the table, "Guys, I think we're neck and neck with the vertical vaginas. We need to bring it to the goal line here."

"I got you," Bob tells Scooter. "Anything you need, I'm here."

The MC reviews his score sheet. "I just tallied the scores and there are only a handful of teams with a shot at winning, and the top two are tied. To add to the drama, I'm not gonna read out the leaderboard before our final question. Listen carefully, there are four parts."

Scooter, Bob, and Zabka lean toward the MC and intensify their focus. Jed cleans out his ear with his finger and paints it red with wing sauce.

The MC clears his throat. "Here we go. Which president was shot in Buffalo? What year was he shot? What event was the president here for? And lastly, who shot him? Your five-minutes starts now."

"I got a quick question," Jed says. "Don't get me wrong, I love it here, but of all the places in the world, why would a president come here?"

"That's actually a question we need to answer," Scooter replies.

"Is there an abundance of toothless hookers?" Jed wonders. "Presidents can be pretty perverted — look at Slick Willy!"

"Be quiet!" Bob yells in a panic. "We need to be thinking!"

As they huddle over the table, Scooter whispers, "President McKinley was shot here in 1901. That I know. The guy who shot him was some Polish guy — his last name is a goddamn jumble of consonants. The president was here for some World's Fair, but it had some other name. I read about this yesterday." He slaps his head. "Fucking beer buzz."

"Oh, oh. I think I know the name of the fair," Bob says quietly. "Scooter, you figure out the shooter's name."

"Alright, shit," Scooter replies. "Let me replay when I was reading. We were approaching the tollbooth. These two assholes," he uses his thumbs to point at Zabka and Jed, "were talking about a weirdly named expressway at the same time I was reading his crazy name."

"Oh yeah, we were talking about the Scajaquada," Zabka exclaims.

"Dammit, that doesn't help!" Scooter puts his elbows on the table, his head in his hands, and closes his eyes. "Silence. Let me think."

Bob exclaims, "I know, it was the Pan-American Exposition!" Regretting his enthusiasm, he crosses his fingers that he wasn't overheard.

The MC updates the contestants, "One minute to go!"

"Take the pencil and here's the paper with the other answers on it." Bob hands them over to Scooter. "Just get lost in it. It'll come to you."

Scooter feels like he's falling into a bottomless hole. All sound fades away as he spins into the pages of the encyclopedia in his mind.

———

Lisa tosses her mug-drying towel on the bar and places her hands on her hips. "So, Bob was a bit flirtatious last night. I'll admit I started it, but he had no problem following up. After thinking it through — not to be harsh — I get the feeling he has one foot out the door."

"I see." Jennifer's blood smolders. "And were any lines crossed?"

"Not as far as I remember. I was a little tipsy though. But we didn't sleep together if that's what you're asking? I don't just put-out like that."

"Thank god." Jennifer sighs with relief. "So how did he get your number? Did he ask for it?"

"Not exactly, but women's intuition told me he wanted it. He was probably too shy to ask."

"Okay, I think I've heard enough." Jennifer gets up to leave.

"If you don't mind, would you do me a favor?" Lisa smirks. "When things don't work out between you two, please remind Bob to call me?"

Jennifer returns a smug look. "Sorry, there's something I forgot to share with you." She shows Lisa the paper that led her here, and drops it on the floor. "Your number — it was in his trash, crumpled up into a tiny little ball." Jennifer turns her back and saunters towards the exit. As she leaves, she gives Lisa a parting gesture with a wag of her middle-finger over her head.

—

With time running out, Scooter claws through a stream of words in his mind, desperately searching for the name of the President's shooter. While in his trance, an inebriated neurotransmitter careens across a synapse and triggers a chain reaction. *My ex-wife has a Polish cousin with the same last name!* His eyes burst open. "I know it! I fucking know it!"

"Write it down and go!" Bob screams.

Scooter scribbles down the name and springs out of his chair. His first step sends him to the ground as he slips in a puddle of beer. From his stomach, he stretches and holds the paper up. Without hesitation, Bob grabs it and sprints it to the MC just before time expires. On his way back he picks Scooter off the ground. "We did it, buddy. Great team work!"

"That was awesome! I think we got this. Our only threat is Hope's vag-crew." They sit down and wait for the final results to be announced.

Jed takes a drumstick, puts it entirely in his mouth, and uses his teeth to strip the meat from the bone as he pulls it back out. After a sip of beer, he asks the table, "Have you guys ever wondered why god hates Buffalo?"

Bob chuckles. "What do you mean? God doesn't hate Buffalo."

"Sure he does." Jed inhales another wing and talks as he chews. "Did you listen to those trivia questions?" He ticks them off with his wing sauce covered fingers. "The Oklahoma City bomber, the Blizzard of '77, Love Canal, *and* a president was shot and killed here. Seriously, what the fuck?" As the guys evaluate his argument, he sucks the sauce clean from his paws. "Even if you disagree with my use of the word *hate*, you have to admit there's at least a serious grudge."

"He does make a valid point," Scooter agrees. "Add in O.J. Simpson and the Bills' Super Bowl nightmares, and the case is even stronger."

Bob nods his head. "I guess I never really thought about it, but no matter what, I love Buffalo. The people are awesome, and it's just a really fun place. Even if the Almighty is out to get us."

Zabka laughs. "I agree with you, Buffalo is a great town." He looks at Jed and Scooter. "But let me ask you two. Are you guys having fun so far?"

"I'm having a hell of a good time!" Jed raises his empty pitcher in the air. "But I need more beer!"

"I'm literally having the best weekend of my life," Scooter confides. "If we just win these tickets, I don't know how things could get any better."

A screech from microphone feedback draws the crowd's attention to the MC. "Attention, everyone. I'm going to read the answers to the final question and then I'm going to present the first and second place prizes." The room hushes. "The president that was shot in Buffalo was President McKinley and the year was 1901." The guys celebrate internally, nervously waiting for the answers to the tougher questions. Scooter nibbles on his thumb and Bob squeezes the table. The MC continues, "The president was here for the Pan-American Exposition." The guys high-five Bob as they chalk-up another right answer.

Scooter looks at Hope and they exchange nervous grins. The guys can hardly breathe as the MC proceeds, "The last question was the most difficult, not only to answer, but to spell. The person that shot McKinley was a former steel worker and an anarchist. He was of Polish descent and his name was —" The MC coughs and takes a sip of his water. "Sorry, about that. His name was Leon Czolgosz."

As the MC spells Czolgosz, groans trickle from most of the tables. Unable to exhale, Bob, Jed, and Zabka stare at Scooter's paused, blank face, waiting for his reaction. Then, like someone pressed his play button, Scooter's arms shoot up and he yells, "Vagetarians!" The rest of the guys jump out of their seats, scream with elation, and slap Scooter on the back.

"Please settle down," the MC tells them. "It is my pleasure to introduce the owner of this fine restaurant. Frank, take it away." As an older gentleman comes in from the bar and grabs the microphone, a feeling of horror overcomes Zabka. He shrinks into his chair and covers his face.

Frank addresses the room, "Thank you everyone for coming out tonight. I hope you had fun and enjoyed your dinner." He waits for the clapping to stop before continuing. "I wanted to personally hand out the prizes to the winners. So, without further ado." He picks up the paper with the winners' names on it. "The second place prize of a $100 gift certificate to the Anchor Bar goes to — The Vertical Beef on Wecks!"

All of the guys jump out of their seats again, except for Zabka who shrinks lower, still shielding his face. Bob and Jed mockingly clap for the second place team as Hope walks by to go accept their prize. When she returns, Scooter skips over and shakes her hand. "Nice contest."

She places a hand on his scarred cheek and sweetly tells him, "I hope you won." She leaves him with a cute smile.

"Alright, and the big winner of the evening — the winner of four tickets to tomorrow's sold out game is." Scooter paces anxiously as Frank squints at the paper. "Am I reading this correctly? This is unbelievable. This team — on top of having very unique dietary restrictions — got every question correct. Anyway, the winner is — The Vagetarians!"

Bob and Jed explode out of their seats, jolting the table in the process, and knock over a half-full pitcher of beer. Scooter kneels on the ground with his fists in the air like he's Rocky and just knocked out Clubber Lang. Zabka's body shakes as he pounds the table and his id screams, *Fuck yeah!!!* Jed and Bob grab Scooter under his armpits and lift him up. They then push him to go claim their prize.

With tears in his eyes, Scooter accepts Frank's handshake and gives him a bear hug. "Thank you so much. You saved us."

"My pleasure, you earned it." Frank hands Scooter an envelope containing the tickets. "I'd like to take a photo with you and your team to put up on the wall. This might just turn into a tradition each year before the Miami game." As Frank and Scooter approach the table, Zabka's fight or flight instinct takes over and he dashes to escape.

"Hey, come back!" Frank shouts. "We're gonna take a picture!"

Bob quickly gets in front of Frank and says, "I'm sorry, he's camera shy. Let's just take the photo with us. He didn't really add much value to the team anyway."

As Frank squints at Zabka's backside, his blond mullet triggers a flashback. In-between heartbeats, Frank's facial expression changes from curiosity to distress to anger. He yells, "Hey, you! Get back here!" Zabka suspends for a split-second in mid-stride before reconsidering and continuing toward the exit. Frank rips the tickets from Scooter's hand and holds them up. "Stop, or you're not getting the tickets!" The restaurant quietly watches the action like an audience dropped into the middle of a captivating play.

———

Dressed in their finest suits, Bradford and Juan Carlos sit alone in the dimly lit bar of their hotel. A Sinatra serenade about a dame dances off the walls as they nurse dirty martinis. Bradford tries not to crack a smile as he asks, "So, how are things going with Bambi?"

Juan Carlos uses the olive on the end of a cocktail pick to stir his drink. "If you're wondering if we've slept together yet, the answer is regrettably, no. Not even a handjob. And she keeps teasing me with all this crazy sex-talk. It's literally driving me insane."

"I'm kinda surprised. She seems like every other girl you hook up with. And it usually takes, what? Thirty minutes for her panties to drop?"

Juan Carlos grins like a rock star surrounded by groupies. "That may be a slight exaggeration. But for a few of them, you're not far off."

Bradford takes a swig of his martini. "I assume you try to keep the conversation to a minimum? Or at the most, talk about shiny objects?"

"Yeah, we mostly talk about nonsense, but this morning was weird." Juan Carlos thinks back to when they were in bed. "She was very interested in our business and asked questions about how our product works."

Bradford chokes on his drink and then responds, "That's strange. What did you tell her? Our standard marketing response, I hope?"

"Um, yeah." Juan Carlos reviews the colorful liquor bottles behind the bar. "Of course I did."

"You better have." Bradford looks over his shoulder. "Even though our stuff doesn't do shit, it makes us a lot of money. I swear, sometimes guys can be just as dumb as girls."

"This is true. Anyway, what's going on with Summer? Things seem a little off between you two."

"Oh, everything is fine — mostly. She's just trying to make me jealous. She wants attention or something. Who knows?"

Juan Carlos notices their girls in the bar mirror. As they approach in their cocktail dresses and mink coats, he whispers to Bradford, "Speaking of the little devils. Here they come."

Bambi taps Juan Carlos on the shoulder and covers her eyes as he turns around. "Guess who!?"

Juan Carlos's eyelids shut as he shakes his hanging head. "Gee, I don't know. Who is it?"

Bambi puts her hands on her hips. "Stop being a goofball. My voice should've given it away. It's me — Bambi."

"Oh, wow. I can't believe I didn't catch that. Anyway, we're just getting ready to roll out of here. Julio's gonna bring the car around soon."

"What's on the agenda tonight, boys?" Summer asks.

Juan Carlos smirks and nods to Bradford who says, "Ladies, we're going somewhere special to take in some much needed culture — Canadian style."

Bambi jumps up and down. "Is that like the new doggy style?"

Bradford laughs. "Not exactly. We're going to the Canadian ballet!"

"I guess I'll try anything once," Summer says. "We don't have to work this thing, right?"

"Maybe a little — we'll see. But this time we were thinking about going with a subtler approach."

"Here's a thought," Bambi says energetically. "What if you guys promote things? You know, tell guys how your things used to be tiny, and now you're huge. Stuff like that?" She pauses while the men awkwardly look at each other. "You two look like deer caught in headlights — which, coming from a girl named Bambi, is kinda funny if you think about it."

Juan Carlos stammers, "Um, I'm not quite sold on that way of approaching things."

"Why not?" Bambi asks. "Okay, remember when the beautiful bouquet of roses came this morning?" Juan Carlos nods, as Summer gives Bradford the evil-eye. Bambi looks at both of the Huge Member owners and continues, "Your pills blossom your penis — that's the new rose. It's what every girl wants. Promote and tell your story!"

Summer adds, "That actually makes a lot of sense."

"But, um, Bradford said we're taking a subtle approach," Juan Carlos rebuts. "For tonight's venue, we should stick with that."

"Yeah, you're right," Summer concedes. "Full-on promoting at the ballet is way too aggressive for an uptight crowd. As much as I actually love your idea, Bambi, let's keep it in our hip pocket for another time."

In Bradford's peripheral vision, he notices Julio standing to their side. As Bradford turns, Julio outstretches his arm and directs them. "Your limo is ready and waiting outside."

—

Frank's threat to take back the Bills tickets from the trivia contest winners stops Zabka in his tracks. His body slumps until he musters the courage to stand tall and turn around. As he walks back, one look into Frank's eyes tells him he's screwed.

Frank violently pokes at Zabka as his rampage begins. "It *is* you! You've got a hefty set of balls to show your ugly face in here again!"

Zabka raises up his hands like he's being held at gunpoint. "Listen, I told you then and I'll tell you again — it was a mistake. A slight miscalculation is all." As Frank's forehead turns a darker shade of scarlet, Zabka slows his delivery. "Honestly — if you think about it — I think you should've forgiven me by now." Zabka forces half a grin. "We good?"

Frank nearly comes out of his shoes as he screams, "You little punk-ass bastard! You punched my wife in the face and broke her nose!" The restaurant gasps. "You think I'm just gonna forgive that! So, no! We are *not* good!"

"Come on!" Zabka pleads. "That happened over two years ago — you remember what happened, right?" He turns to deliver his case to the diners surrounding him. "So I went to punch this asshole — who was disrespecting my date and, by the way," he turns his head to Frank, "also insulting your wings by saying something about Duff's being better."

Frank shakes his head and grinds his teeth. Bob blurts, "What he's trying to say is that they're not. Not even close."

"Correct," Zabka adds. "Anyway, bottom line is this — through an unfortunate chain of events, your wife's nose got in the way of my fist. Honestly, I don't see how that's my fault." He rubs the top of his right hand. "Her skull is rock hard and I was in pain for days after. Now that I think about it, you're lucky I didn't sue her face for damages."

Bob winces and tries to, but can't, deliver a countermeasure in time.

"Get out! All of you!" Frank points to the exit. "Get out before I throw you out!"

Scooter timidly asks, "Shouldn't we take that picture with our prize before we leave?"

With the calmness of a man on the edge of insanity, Frank replies, "As you can imagine, that won't be necessary anymore. Leave."

Suffering as if they've just been shot in their stomachs, the guys mope through the bar area on their way out. Zabka can feel their resentment on the back of his neck like a hot iron.

A male voice from the bar shouts, "Hey, Robert!"

Bob's subconscious makes the connection, and he reflexively turns to find the caller. He spots his friend from work sitting at the bar, sucking down a bottle of Blue. Bob waves. "Hey, Sametta."

"What's wrong? You guys look like depressed Bills fans after a loss."

"Because of this jackass." Bob points his thumb at Zabka. "Shit just hit the fan."

"I heard yelling coming from the dining area. Was that directed at you?"

"Yeah, like a guided missile," Bob replies. "So we gotta get out of here. Come with us."

"Where to?" Sametta inquires.

Zabka steps forward. "A plan is already forming in my mind. I'll tell you guys outside."

They put on their coats and exit into a numbing wind. Huddling together on the sidewalk, Scooter asks, "Okay, what's your brilliant plan, Zabka? You can't fuck things up much worse from here — or can you?"

Zabka jumps up on a cinderblock like a coach addressing his team. "Listen, you guys are overreacting to a minor setback. We've got plenty of time — over half a day to come up with tickets. Relax."

"A minor setback?!" Scooter yells. "Are you flippin' kidding me?! We had it in our grasp, until an old blunder of yours ruined everything!"

"Dwelling on the past does us no good. Concentrating on our future, well that can actually get us somewhere." Zabka thrusts his fist in the air. "Boys, I've made an executive decision. We're going to Niagara Falls!"

Bob lays into him. "And how exactly *the fuck* is that gonna get us Bills tickets?!"

"That part hasn't quite crystallized yet," Zabka replies. "But what I do know is that standing here holding our frozen dongs ain't gonna get us nowhere. We need to keep going and something good will happen."

"Astonishingly, Zabka is right," Scooter replies. He pushes Zabka off the cinderblock and takes his place on it. "Bambi told me to tell Bob — sorry, Bob, I forgot until now — that those little shits from Miami are also going to Niagara Falls tonight, to a place called Mints. Maybe we can snag their tickets from them there?"

"Perfect." Zabka taps the tips of his fingers together a few times. "Breaking news, Jed! Time to drive our asses up there!"

"Wait a sec — do you mean Canada?" Jed asks.

"Yeah, of course. All the action is on the Canadian side."

"I hate to bring this up, but that presents a slight problem," Jed informs the group. "I can't — well, technically my vehicle can't — what I'm trying to say is, my truck isn't welcome in Canada."

"What the hell?!" Bob shouts. "We can't take the Bronco?"

Jed explains, "It's a long story, but to summarize — the truck is registered to my wife, there was a misunderstanding in Cornwall, and then a minor pursuit by Canadian law enforcement. Anyway, the license plate is on file. We don't want to drive to the border and create an international incident. Trust me, once was enough."

"Jesus fucking Christ," Zabka shouts. "What are we supposed to do?"

Bob contemplates the situation for a second. "Hey, Sametta. Any way we can take your car up there? Would love for you to join us."

Sametta counts the total passengers before responding, "I suppose we could all fit, but you remember my car is a little small for five guys."

Zabka tells him, "We'll make it work."

Jed raises his hand. "I gotta cupla quick questions." He points at Sametta. "First one is — why do you keep calling him Cement-Head?"

Bob laughs. "Who? You mean Sametta?"

"Yeah, Cement-Head," Jed answers. "You keep calling him that."

Bob turns to his work buddy. "Looks like you're now Cement-Head. And oh, Bob is back! No more Robert. At least for the weekend."

"Now that we've gotten that straightened out," Jed says. "Can we get to my next question?"

"Sure, fire away," Bob replies. "But hurry up, we got places to be."

"Well, I guess it's not really a question — it's more of a 'here's what's gonna happen.' Even though we can't take my truck, I'm still gonna drive." Jed looks at Zabka. "I always drive." Zabka nods his head affirming Jed's statement like it's an unbreakable rule.

"Hey, that's fine with me so I can booze," Cement-Head answers. "I got shotgun!"

"That seems fair," Bob confirms. "Let's go!"

As they are about to leave, the Anchor Bar's metal door slams open into the wall and grabs their attention. Hope rushes out and through the guys to get to Scooter. She unzips his coat and puts her arms under it to give him a hug. She shivers as she says, "It's freezing out here. And you're such a jerk for leaving without asking for my number." She play- fully tickles him before pulling her arms out.

"I'm so sorry," Scooter replies. "I'm not sure if you noticed, but we were kindly asked to leave by ownership. Can you forgive me?"

"I'm not sure," Hope answers bashfully. "I guess that all depends on if you ask me or not." She flashes him I'm-waiting-eyes. Zabka taps his foot and looks at his watch.

"Oh, yeah sure," Scooter says. "Can I have your number?"

"Absolutely," Hope answers excitedly. "Remember this, it's easy."

"I will," Scooter insists.

"Okay, so it's 716 — Buffalo's area code. Then it's 555."

He looks at her skeptically. "Really? That sounds kinda fake."

"No, silly. That's it," she assures him. "And then the last four numbers are the same as that song by Tommy Tutone. You know, '867-5309'. It's 5309! You can't forget it!"

"Got it. So it's 716-555-5309, right?" Scooter asks.

Hope jumps. "That's it!"

Zabka pulls Scooter by his collar and says, "Great! So now we must be going. We've got important stuff to attend to."

The group starts to leave and she yells, "Wait! There's one more thing."

As Zabka drags Scooter, he walks backwards and reaches toward her. "I'll call you!"

"Please, tonight! It's important!" she cries. "I'll be close to your heart!"

—

Frozen sheets of ice hang vertically and partially hide the half-million liters of water that plunge per second over the crest of Niagara Falls. Upon pulverizing the rocks below, a fraction transforms into a cloud of mist and drifts upward. Transfixed by the thunderous sound, tourists shake as they stand next to the fences guarding the cliff. Just north of the falls, on the east side of the Rainbow Bridge, a two-door Plymouth Laser waits in line for Canadian customs.

Zabka's neck twists, as his face is smushed against the back window of their vehicle. Along with Scooter and Bob, they are stuffed in the backseat tighter than pork fried rice in a carryout container. His breath fogs the glass as he asks, "Are we almost through this damn line yet?"

"One more car to go," Cement-Head replies from the passenger seat.

Zabka crunches his beer can and drops it on the floor. "Good, because not only do I need another beer, but I gotta drain my-main-vein!"

Bob pounds the roof twice. "Holy shit! For once Zabka, didn't complain about our shitty seating arrangements."

"What can I say that hasn't been said already?" Zabka asks. "That I'm starting to enjoy Scooter's gut molding around my side? That I love driving around in a tuna fish can? Yeah, this is fucking great!"

As they roll up to the security checkpoint, Bob leans forward to address everyone. "Okay, play it cool, and obviously hide the beers. I know this is practically like entering another state, but they can deny us entry."

"*Oh, please,*" Zabka scoffs. "Our greenbacks trump their Monopoly money any day. Believe me, they want us to drop our cash and help support their single moms. It's an goddamn epidemic up here."

Scooter asks, "But they're not pregnant, are they?"

"Don't matter to me, as long as they ain't in their third-trimester," Jed comments. "I don't need flappy va-jays in my face. That's nasty."

Zabka fumes. "No! They're not pregnant! They don't look pregnant! They're hot as fuck! Guys, this is Canada, not Buffalo!"

Jed stops the car and rolls down the window. The border agent inspects the group and asks in a stereotypical Canadian accent, "Eh boys, where ya headed tonight?"

"We're going to Mints," Jed replies. "We want to take in the world-famous Canadian arts — the stuff we don't have down in the states."

The agent checks his computer. "I see. How long will you be staying in Canada, eh?"

"I'm guessing a few hours." Jed looks around the car for confirmation. "Or until we get bored, or they run out of beer. These guys like to drink."

"You bringing anything into Canada or will you be taking anything out when you leave?"

"We're bringing in alotta dollar bills — none of which we'll be bringing back," Jed answers. Zabka gives a thumbs-up through the back window. "The only thing we plan on bringing back are sweet memories."

The agent laughs, lifts the gate, and waves them though. "Alright, you guys have fun, but be safe."

"Always." Jed rolls his window back up and they cruise into Canada. "Okay, now where to?"

"I know the best way. Follow this road for a few blocks until we hit Victoria Ave and then take a left," Zabka commands.

Scooter shifts in his seat, full of excitement. "I'm pumped, guys. I can't wait to see some boobies!"

Bob yells, "You're not just gonna see 'em. They'll be smack-dab in your face!" He makes a motorboat sound, which rapidly flaps his lips.

"I'll take another beer before we get there," Jed announces. Cement-Head reaches into the 12-pack box under his legs, grabs the last two beers, and hands them to Jed and Zabka. In unison, they crack them open and take a sip.

Cement-Head gives directions, "Zabka said take a left here, Jed."

As they turn down the souvenir-shop-lined street, Jed notices something ahead. "Hey guys, see that up there?" His passengers focus down the road at red and blue spinning lights that are bouncing off a line of cars. Jed takes a large gulp of his beer, hands it to Cement-Head, and points. "This doesn't look good. I think it's a DWI checkpoint."

"Fuck, it's the cops!" Zabka urges, "Turn around and get the hell outta here."

Cement-Head tosses Jed's beer out the window, and Bob screams, "What the hell are you doing?!"

"Getting rid of evidence!" Cement-Head shouts. "What's it look like?"

"The cops might've seen that!" Bob tells him. "We don't wanna draw attention to ourselves by throwing shit out of the car or trying to make a getaway. We just gotta hide the beer and play it cool again — like at the border. If we do that, we'll be fine."

"But what if they make him take a breathalyzer test?" Scooter asks nervously.

"Don't worry," Jed replies confidently. "I usually win those contests."

"You idiot!" Cement-Head yells. "The goal here is not to *win*, like it's some bar game. It's to pass with a BAC below point zero eight." He puts his hands on his head. "And you're driving *my* car! I can't have it impounded in Canada! I'm moving to California! Fuck!"

"Great directions, Zabka!" Scooter shouts. "All in favor of doing the opposite of what he suggests from now on?" Everyone's hands pound the car ceiling as Zabka hangs his head. Slowly, Zabka raises his hand too.

"Hang on. Are we absolutely sure these are cops?" Jed asks. "I thought Canadian cops ride around on horses."

Bob slaps Jed in the back of the head and says, "No, those are the Mounties — and whatever you do, *do not* say that word to the cops. That'll not help us *at all*."

Cement-Head flips through his CD wallet. "One thing that'll get us on their good side is if we put on some Hip. Every Canadian I know absolutely loves The Tragically Hip."

"Brilliant idea. You got *Up to Here?*" Bob asks.

"As a matter of fact I do." Cement-Head pulls it out of a sleeve. "Here."

"Good." Bob tells him, "Put that bitch on."

—

Julio pulls forward to the Canadian border checkpoint and stops the limo. The border agent checks the computer inside his small office and then walks over to the limo. He leans over and taps the driver's window with his gloved finger. Julio rolls down the window, and the agent says, "I'm gonna need you all to step out of the vehicle."

Bradford pushes the button to make his window go down and sticks his head out. "Excuse me," he condescendingly reads the agent's name tag, "Agent Stewart, but we've got places to go. We're *not* getting out of our limo. It's freezing."

The agent impatiently refutes, "I'm the one who dictates how this goes down, eh. Follow our *pro*-cess and get out." As the five of them stubbornly exit the limo into the frigid night wind, he speaks into his walkie-talkie, "Send an inspection crew over."

A crackly voice on the other end responds, "10-4."

Bradford taps his foot as everyone shakes in the cold. "I'm confused. What's this all about?"

"*Surry*, did you just ask what's this all *a-boot*?" Agent Stewart looks at them with an I-know-you're-trying-to-hide-something stare. "I'll tell you what this is all *a-boot*, eh."

Bambi raises her hand. "Before you do that, can I ask you something?"

Agent Stewart examines her legs and flips the back of his hand at her. "Sure, why not, eh? Amuse me."

"Are you speaking Canadian?" The agent's mouth opens, but no words come out. Bambi continues, "I can pretty much understand you, but then sometimes your words are weird."

Agent Stewart looks at Bambi's cohorts, and they shrug in response. He tells them, "I'm gonna ignore that asinine question. I was informed that yesterday you guys had an incident in Buffalo with this same vehicle. Does that ring any bells, eh?"

Bradford replies, "Yeah, so these jackasses were next to us —"

"I didn't ask you for your version of the story. I asked if that rang any bells, and it sounds like it did. Did Officer Radzikowski give you permission to leave the United States?"

Bradford put out his arms in question. "Well, he didn't say *we can't*."

As the small team that was summoned by Agent Stewart moves the limo off to the side for inspection, he says, "Okay, I'm gonna need your identification." They dig into their wallets and purses, retrieve the requested documentation, and hand it over. "I see that all of you are from Miami, except Julio who's local. Julio, please step inside that office over there and get warm."

Juan Carlos is stunned. "I don't understand what's going on here."

"We've had a recent uptick in prostitute and cocaine trafficking into our country. Not surprisingly, it's been originating from the Miami area." He inspects their faces for any telling reaction. "So what are we gonna find when we go through your limo, eh?"

"Nothing," Juan Carlos replies defensively. "Nothing but champagne."

"I'd like to know what you girls are doing here with these gentlemen?" Agent Stewart picks a license and looks up. "I'll start with you, Summer."

Her teeth chatter as she answers, "Bradford and I are dating."

"Don't be short with me," Agent Stewart orders. "Why are you here? Where are you going?"

Summer squeezes herself tightly in her coat. "We're here for the Dolphins game and some business."

"*Really?* What type of business?" the agent quizzes her.

"It's a product for guys. Bambi and I just kinda flirt and promote it. That's our job."

"I see." Agent Stewart scratches his chin. "So, are you girls *the product?*"

"Hey, hang on a second!" Bradford shouts.

The lead inspection agent arrives and says, "We're gonna need to hold 'em for a bit. We found something in their limo."

Agent Stewart nods his head and squints his eyes suspiciously. "Yeah, I found something too."

———

Jed is temporarily blinded as the Canadian police officer uses her flashlight to inspect the interior of the car. She hums along to "New Orleans is Sinking" as the CD plays at low volume.

"Everything okay?" Jed asks.

"Not really," she replies. "Is there a reason one of you threw a beer can out the window back there?" Cement-Head shakes nervously.

"That's impossible," Jed replies. "Mine's right here." He reaches into the empty cup holder. "Oh, that's right." He looks at Cement-Head. "This nitwit tossed it."

Cement-Head tries to cover Jed's drinking admission. "He's just kidding. That beer was mine, sorry."

A crunching can emits a quick burst of noise. "Hey, what was that?" she asks. "You got more beer in there, eh?"

"Um, that was me," Zabka admits. "That's just a can of pop I had on the ride here. Nothing to see here."

"For some reason, I don't believe you." The officer waves her male partner over and addresses the car, "I'm gonna need you to hand out any and all beverages you have in there. Come on, let's go."

The guys look at each other with wide-eyes and begin to comply. One by one, the cans stream out. Some partially full, others empty or crushed. She counts them and says, "I've got five cans with remaining beer and six that are empty. If my calculations are correct — even after tossing one beer — each of you was drinking a roadie, including the driver." She knocks on the roof of the car with her fist. "Sound about right?"

Bob taps a set of knuckles on the back window to get the officers' attention. He then leans forward to address her through the open window. "What can I say? I like to double fist. I'm your math error." Bob half smiles and shrugs. "Of course our driver wasn't drinking. Look at us — we scream responsibility."

The female officer directs her full attention to Jed. "Can I get your license and registration?"

"Ah, sure, yeah," Jed replies. "It's just, the thing is, this isn't my car."

She squints at him. "I don't want any of the rest of ya to say anything while I speak to him. Is that clear?"

"Sure is, ma'am," Zabka replies.

"Keep your mouth shut when you're answering me! You should've just nodded like the rest of them." She shakes her head at Zabka. "You're not the bright one of the bunch, are ya?" She surveys them all. "If there even is one in this group." Zabka silently steams. "But that's okay. I have a mentally challenged son, so you guys like you have a special little place in my heart."

Her male partner taps his billy club on the hood and asks Jed, "If this isn't your car, then whose is it, eh?"

Jed initially looks for help and then points his thumb at Cement-Head. "Um, it's this guy's car."

The female officer leans down to get a better look at the front passenger. "Okay, so what's his name?"

Jed answers anxiously, "We, um, we call him Cement-Head."

She straightens back up and with a crooked smile, tells them, "Alright, everyone out of the car." Jed and Cement-Head open their doors and exit routinely. After the front seats are pushed forward, the three backseat passengers pop out like a jack-in-the-box. Upon discharge, Zabka falls onto the road.

"You, get up," the male officer demands. "I need everyone to hand over your identification. The vehicle registration too." The five of them comply. "I'm gonna run these and be right back."

The female officer pulls Jed away from the group to the front of the car. "What's your name?"

"Name's Jed, ma'am."

"Jed, how much have you been drinkin' tonight?" Her eyes pierce through him as she waits for his answer.

"So about that beer I reached for earlier. It wasn't there — it never existed," Jed answers. "I just want to make that clear."

"*Ahem.* Go on," she tells him.

He pauses like he's checking his memory banks for any forgotten beer consumption. "Well, I did have one, maybe two, at the Anchor Bar during dinner. But I'm the designated driver, so ya know."

"Oh, you guys were there?" She licks her lips. "I love their wings."

"Yep, me too. And now we're here to visit your lovely country. Thank you for having us." Jed places a hand over his heart. "It's an honor to be here. We worship The Hip."

"You do? I heard it in your car." Thrilled, she asks, "What's your favorite song?"

"Um, I mean, it's so hard to pick just one, right?" Jed scratches his beard. "If I had to narrow it down, I'd have to say all of them."

"Yeah, me too!" She grabs his hand inappropriately and quickly releases it.

"You like the Bills?" Jed asks.

"Of course I do. You going to the big game tomorrow?"

"We've currently got a slight snafu," he admits. "But we'll work through it. We'll be there."

The male officer walks back from his squad car. "Everyone, come here!" After they regroup, he continues, "Which of you are Robert and Kyle?" Bob and Zabka raise their hands.

Zabka answers, "Kyle's my given name, but you can call me Zabka."

"I'll call you whatever I want, *Kyle*. So I looked over your record and Robert's record, and discovered an interesting tidbit. It says that you're both restricted from coming within a hundred-yards of any church with nuns. Care to explain?"

Zabka and Bob play eye-tennis while trying to deflect answering to the other person. Bob finally gives-in and huffs. "It's a long story but it boils down to this — it was a big misunderstanding."

The female officer steps in to state her opinion to her junior partner. "I don't see any relevance between that incident and what's going on here tonight. I ran the driver through a thorough sobriety test and my judgment says our best course of action is to keep their car for a couple of hours." She turns to Jed. "And no more drinks for you." She looks back at the group. "Come back later for your car, and you guys can go."

"Sounds fair to me, don't you think?" Jed asks to his friends and quickly receives approval. He looks back at the female officer. "Cool, so one last very important question. Can you direct us to Mints?"

She laughs. "I should've guessed. It's just down the road here, only a few blocks away. Enjoy your stay in Canada!"

—

The lead inspection agent sets a large cardboard box down on the hood of the limo and pulls out a bottle of Huge Member pills. Agent Stewart takes it from him and reviews the label. He looks up at the limo passengers. "What exactly is this, eh? It appears that you're smuggling some sort of drug into Canada."

"No, those aren't drugs," Bradford tells him. "Those are supplements. Perfectly legal."

"That's the product we promote!" Summer shouts. "Like I told you."

"Bradford and I co-own the business," Juan Carlos adds.

The agent inspects the bottle further. "Dick pills, eh? You have a permit to bring them into Canada?"

Bradford shakes his head. "Um, no. I guess we don't. We didn't really think about that."

"Didn't really think about it, eh? Well, we're gonna have to confiscate the box and —" The agent looks with disdain at the mini Dolphins flags on the hood of the limo. "We're gonna have to confiscate these too." He points to the flags and another agent yanks them off.

"Why are you doing that?" Juan Carlos asks.

"It's a driving hazard to have those on your hood," Agent Stewart replies. "It could impair your driver." Another agent walks over, hands the Miami group back their licenses, and gives Agent Stewart a positive head nod. "Looks like you checked out, so you're free to go."

Julio leaves the security office with a warm cup of coffee and walks to the limo. He opens the side door so his passengers can climb in. Meanwhile, the agents have huddled and are chatting nearby.

After Julio shuts the door, Juan Carlos asks, "Hey, did any of you hear them say what I think they just said?"

"I heard something, but you'll probably get mad at me if I say it," Bambi replies.

"No, it's okay. What did you hear?"

Bambi tells them, "One of the agents said, 'squish the fish' I think."

"They did!" Juan Carlos exclaims. "Those bastards did say that! They're fucking with us!"

"Screw 'em!" Bradford punches his seat. "Julio, let's get outta here! It's ballet time!"

—

Bob leads the pack into the parking lot at the back of Mints. The quiet night amplifies the faint sound of music oozing through the cracks of the building. BAM! The side door slams open and crashes into the concrete wall. A bald man wearing a Toronto Maple Leafs jersey is spit out of the back entry and sent sliding across black ice. A large boulder-sized bouncer steps outside and yells, "That's the last time you do that to one of our girls! Don't *ever* let me see you back here!"

Bob glances at Zabka with a smirk. "Look familiar?"

"Yeah, yeah," Zabka replies with a hint of guilt. "Come on, let's go inside and see some Grade-A titties."

When they reach the entrance, the bouncer flatly says, "IDs."

Bob hands him his license. "You mind me asking what that guy did to get kicked out like that?"

"Not at all. This is a teachable moment," the bouncer replies. "That bonehead put an *unlubricated* finger in Ms. Nude Mississauga's ass!"

Startled, but intrigued, Scooter maneuvers around the guys to get closer to the bouncer. "Can I ask a few questions? I'm new to establishments like this, and I don't want to make the same mistake that guy did."

"Correct, you don't," the bouncer tells him gruffly. "Go ahead. Ask."

"I'd like to know which part of his actions specifically led to his ejection. Is Ms. Nude Mississauga considered sacred in this neck-of-the-woods? Are lady's assholes *completely* off-limits here?" Scooter holds up an index finger and sniffs it. "Or was it improper because his finger was insufficiently lubricated?"

The stare the bouncer gives Scooter strongly states, "I look forward to throwing your ass out of here later." He then nearly pokes a hole in Scooter's chest with his finger. "You're either one naive son-of-a-bitch or you're fucking with me. Either way, my advice is this — keep your hands to yourself." He finishes checking their IDs and lets them in.

At the end of the hall a man in a black suit greets them. "Gentlemen, where would you like to sit this evening? There are seats at the stage, or would you like something a little more private in the back?"

"How about the back, guys?" Zabka suggests. "We'll get some girls to bounce on us."

"The stage it is!" Scooter shouts. "The opposite Zabka move!" As Zabka grimaces, the rest of the guys wholeheartedly agree with Scooter.

As they follow their host to the stage, the drill and guitar at the beginning of Van Halen's "Poundcake" blasts around them. This triggers something in Bob and makes him go nuts. He runs at a vacant chair and uses it as a springboard to jump from. As he sails through the air, he does a split like Eddie Van Halen during a concert. "Bring on the cooter! We're gonna get fucked-up and motorboat some tit-tays!"

The T-shaped stage sticks through the horny crowd, and at its base, in the center of the room, is the main stripper pole. The host seats the guys just to the left of it for a perfect view of the spinning and crawling girls.

Cement-Head's eyes widen from the assault of visual candy. He points to the large projection screens on the left and right sides of the colossal stage. "You guys see this?! There's this year's sports highlights here, and there's porn there! Holy shit, my brain is about to explode!"

Bob slaps him on the back. "I told you, you'd have an unforgettable going away party!"

Their waitress leans down to their head level and yells over the music, "What can I get you guys?!"

"We'll take five Blue and five shots of Jäger," Bob shouts back. The waitress looks at the rest of the group for any disagreement.

Jed cups his hand and yells, "Hey Bob, I better be responsible. We still gotta get Cement-Head's car from the Mounties later."

"You know what? He's right." Bob turns to the waitress and says, "Make that five Blue and *four* shots of Jäger!" She nods and hustles off to the bar.

Zabka notices his manager is in a state of hypnosis. "Scooter! Pick your jaw off the floor! Your head is spinning!"

Scooter rattles his noggin. "I think we've died and gone to a place better than heaven."

"We absolutely have!" Jed replies as his eyes are being pulled back and forth. "It's like I'm watching ta-ta tennis!"

"The strippers here are the absolute best!" Bob yells to his crew. "You'll see when they come talk to us. They smell like flowers dipped in vanilla. Their skin is warm and silky. And they've got talent too! Once I saw one pick up a rolled-up poster with her inner labia — it was like a mini lobster claw!"

"Wow!" Scooter shouts. "Are the girls here like super-strippers?!"

Zabka pounds the stage. "Damn right they are!"

Scooter's mind drifts. *And here I always thought — you've seen one vagina, you've seen 'em all. Guess I had that wrong.* He imagines the girl on stage squatting down and clenching the poster with her clam to perform the trick. *Apparently, vaginas are NOT all created equal!*

The waitress returns with their beers and shots, and Bob takes care of the bill. They raise their drinks and Bob says, "Here's to a great night, fellas! Bottoms up!" After shooting back his Jäger, Bob stands and howls like a wolf at a full moon. An Asian stripper in lacy-red lingerie and a Santa hat walks by, and he stops mid-howl. "Ho! Ho! Ho!" he yells, and motions for her to join him.

She slides onto Bob's lap and says with a warm smile, "It sounds like you're enjoying yourself tonight."

Bob puts his hand on her thigh. "I am, and we're just getting started."

She brushes his cheek. "My name is Cherry — like cherry blossom. I'm from Japan. What's your name?"

"I'm Bob, like a woman's favorite thing to do — kneel and bob." He pauses to give her a shy grin. "Is it okay if I tell you that your eyes are beautiful?"

She giggles. "Why, of course it is."

He asks with puppy dog eyes, "Is it okay if I tell you that your body makes me tingle?"

She thinks for a second. "I suppose that's alright."

"Is it okay if I tell you —" Bob grins sheepishly. "I wanna eat your bento box and lick your fortune cookie?"

She cringes, but quickly regains her composure. "You can say whatever you want when I'm dancing for you. Let's go back to the Champagne Room." She runs her nails through his hair. "It's more intimate there."

Bob raises his eyebrows. "That sounds great to me, but I just have one last question. After you answer this, we'll go, okay?"

Cherry manufactures a smile — a skill she's perfected during her "career." *Oh god, what is this jackass gonna ask me?* She tells him, "Please, go ahead. I can't wait."

Bob signals to the guys to listen in. "This is a burning question I've had for a while, and being here brought it to the top of my mind. You ready?" Everyone nods yes. "Stop me if you disagree with anything I say." Their faces tell him they understand. "Women are the more beautiful of the two sexes, right? And one of the reasons we feel this way is because both men and women can appreciate a nice set of breasts."

While the guys wonder where Bob is going with this, the sweet smell emanating from Cherry captures Scooter's attention over the onslaught of other distractions and makes his libido do somersaults.

Bob takes a swig of his beer. "So I have a theory that at the root of this boob obsession — if I may call it that — is the fact that when we were young, we all suckled and were nurtured by the bosom. Does that make sense?" Cherry and the guys consider his logic, and then slowly begin to nod in agreement.

"Great. Now stick with me here — I'm getting to my question." Bob tips his Blue back and finishes it off. "Do we all agree that the female breast is multi-functional? On one hand, it nurtures life as a milk dispenser. And on-the-other-hand, it acts as a sexual organ — both giving and receiving pleasure."

"Yes, we agree." Cherry grabs her boobs playfully. "So let's go in the back and have fun with these puppies."

"First answer this," Bob demands slyly. "What if nature did things a little differently? What if — what if *the penis* produced milk?"

Cherry's body freezes while a scenario rushes through her head. Her face scrunches like a squeezed lemon as she thinks an unimaginable thought. "Are you really asking me this?!"

"Bare with me." As Zabka chuckles into his hand, Bob continues, "How about penis-feeding in public? Would that be socially acceptable?" He puts out his arms in question. "Would guys partially expose their dicks for sexual enticement? Similar to how women let a little boob show here-and-there?" He scrunches his shoulders, not knowing the answer. "Would testicle cleavage be a thing? Would there be push-up or padded underwear to make penises seem bigger? These are the types of questions that keep me up at night. I need answers, goddammit!"

Cherry pushes herself off Bob and stands in front of him. "So that just happened, and now I'm gonna leave. That was some fucked-up shit you just laid out." She struts towards the changing room, shaking her head.

Zabka pats Bob on the back. "Oh, man! That was hilarious!"

Bob beams. "You know how I am when I come here. I could do shit like that all night! Bring on the next one, so I can fuck with her too!"

"Pure entertainment," Jed adds. "But in addition to fucking with strippers, aren't we supposed to find those Miami dicktards? Are they here?"

"Damn, you're right." Bob stands up and scans the room. "I don't see 'em, but let's stay on high alert."

The club MC announces to the crowd, "Alright gentlemen, we have a very special treat for you coming up at the top of the hour! It is sure to *drive* you wild! Speaking of drive, now coming to the stage, coming to the stage — it's Mercedes!" He presses play on the Pebbles' song of the same name and Mercedes dances out from behind the curtain and spins around in her black satin robe.

Bob yells to her, "I wanna kiss your camel-toe underneath the mistle-toe! French style!" She dances in front of him and lets her robe fall to the floor. As Mercedes unclasps her bra from behind her back, Bob's intoxicated-iguana-eyes move in separate directions all over her body. After her breasts gently slide out of their holders, he shouts, "I wanna make a baby in your mouth!"

Meanwhile, in the elevated area in the back of the room, a couple of girls are enthusiastically rubbing their round thong-covered butts into their customer's junk for five dollars a song. In a dark corner, a woman sits alone and plays with the straw in her drink. She wasn't quite sure if it was Robert when he first walked in, but it's become clear to her that it is. The looming question she has now is — what should she do about it?

———

As the Miami group approaches the entrance to Mints from the desolate parking lot, Summer looks around suspiciously. "This doesn't look like the ballet. This looks like some sorta filthy strip club."

"Hey, I qualified it as the *Canadian* ballet, not *thee* ballet," Bradford replies. "There's a difference." He holds the door open for the girls to enter.

The bouncer says, "Ladies, you're not supposed to come in through this entrance. Management wants you to go in around back."

"Excuse me?" Bambi says in a fiery tone. "You think we work here?"

He backpedals. "My apologies. Um, you both just look like you *could* work here. No offense was meant."

Bradford steps up to the bouncer like a horse jockey about to fight a sumo wrestler. "Yeah, there better not have been!"

The bouncer laughs for a second as he towers over Juan Carlos and Bradford. "Has anyone ever told you guys that if you had a little bit of scruff, you'd look like those two cops on *Miami Vice?*"

"No, never heard that one before," Bradford replies sarcastically.

"Alright, IDs please," the bouncer tells the group. They hand them over for review. "You're from Miami, eh? Here for the game I assume?"

"You assume right," Bradford replies.

Bambi announces, "And we're gonna swa-llow the Buffa-lo!"

"Swallow the Buffalo, eh? Never heard that one, but okay. Good luck with that." The bouncer points down the hall. "Go see my man down there in the suit, and he'll hook you up with a table."

Upon arrival, Bradford asks the host for a spot near the stage, and the group is led to an empty table in their requested location. Just in front of them, they discover their 'friends' from Buffalo, each with a stripper on their lap. Juan Carlos struts over and notices Scooter sucking his finger. "What's wrong with the fat one? Does he miss his mommy?"

Scooter slides the digit out of his mouth. "No, I'm waiting for your mommy to dance. And this well lubricated finger's target is her anus." He points to himself. "Ya see — this guys understands the rules here."

Juan Carlos cracks his knuckles. "Ladies, come with me." He pulls out his money clip and peels off hundred dollar bills. "You've wasted enough time with these blue-collar hicks." The girls jump off their former cus-tomers and follow the money like rats following the Pied Piper.

Jed yells, "Hey! We may be blue-collar hicks, but you guys are white-collar pricks! Go fuck yourselves!"

Bob motions to a skinny girl near the bar. "Yeah! And it's not like we can't replenish!" The stripper walks over. "See what I mean? No big deal."

"You guys enjoy yourselves here in coach. We're going to the Cham-pagne Room." Juan Carlos puts his arms around two of the strippers. "Let's go, girls." As he leaves, Bradford and Summer follow.

Bob notices that Bambi remains behind, so he puts out his hand to tell the approaching stripper to stop, which she promptly ignores. Bambi glimpses back at her group as they disappear into the VIP area. She watches Bob try to stand from his chair, but get pushed back down by the new girl. Bambi shrugs at him and says, "I better go."

The stripper jumps on Bob's lap and lets her long, straight hair fall across his face. He pushes it aside to watch Bambi walk away and then asks, "What's your name, sweetheart?"

With a sexy squint, and in a thick Russian accent, she replies, "I'm Natasha, and your balls I wanna squasha."

"Wow! So you're a grinder, eh?"

Scooter sticks his head into their personal space. "If you don't mind, Bob, can I take the lovely Natasha? Russian women are kinda my thing."

Natasha asks Bob, "Is okay? I get 'nother girl for you. I go with chubby boy?"

Bob smiles as he hands her over to Scooter. "That's totally cool with me. I think you two look cute together. And don't worry about another girl for me, I'll find one."

Natasha eases onto Scooter's lap. "So what is your name, sexy man?"

His penis skips-a-beat. "My name is Scooter. That's the nickname my crew here gave me."

She points around at the guys. "These boys? You leader?"

"You could say that, I guess." Scooter shifts his posture to project confidence. "Yes, I'm their leader."

"So, leader man, you like dance?"

"I would, but I kinda feel weird about you, um," he puts a finger playfully in his mouth, "getting naked for me. I mean I haven't even spoken to your mom yet. Can we call her?"

Natasha playfully pokes his man-boobs. "Silly boy. I dance now?"

"But I hardly know you, and — I'm guessing — you already want to rub your bare breasts all over my face. Is that an accurate statement?"

She shifts into a facing-straddle on his lap and places her hands on both sides of his face. Her voice evokes memories of Misha-Labia. "One song, you give five dollars American. I do things to your body with my body that makes man-stuff stiff and hard like Mother Russia. Fun is had. Process repeat. More fun. Is good?"

As the song "Poison" by Bell Biv Devoe begins, Scooter nods eagerly and says, "Is good." Natasha turns around and uses her tush to caress his genitals before squishing in harder. She presses her back onto his chest, takes his hands, and puts them on her breasts over her bra. He whispers in her ear, "I'm mentally banging you so hard right now."

Natasha turns to face Scooter and straddles him again. "Your words are confused, but is cost extra for any bang-bang." She puts her hands behind her back and unclasps her bra. As she removes it, her breasts drop and dangle inches from his face. She grips her warm bosoms and places them around his nose and mouth, and slowly shakes back and forth. Scooter begins to squirm and moan, and then his groin region starts to convulse. Alarmed, she looks into his rolled back eyes. "You making man-juice in pants?! Triple price! Triple price!!"

Scooter pushes her onto the floor and jumps out of his seat. "Bathroom! Where is it?!" He does a 360-spin.

Bob points to a back corner. "It's that way!"

Scooter holds his butt and skips through the room like he's clutching something between his legs. He waddles down the hallway like a penguin, finds the men's room, and busts the door open. He scrambles into the closest stall, which is next to the bathroom attendant.

He quickly jettisons his pants and briefs, and shits a stream of Buffalo Wing lava into the innocent porcelain bowl. Sweat drips from his brow as he thanks the lord he made it. He hears an aerosol can spraying and looks down at the door gap next to his feet. There he spots the attendant's hand armed with a deodorizer, engaged in serious combat.

When the battle has ended, Scooter drops a few dollars in the attendant's tip jar, and they part ways like glory hole mates — without ever making eye contact.

When Scooter gets back, he finds his friends perched on the edge of the stage with folded dollar bills in their mouths. He observes them using that as a mechanism to distribute tips into the dancer's cleavage.

As Scooter sits down, Zabka asks, "Did she make you blow your load?"

Scooter rubs his forehead. "No, it was those wings — they really fucked with my insides. I feel like a blowtorch was stuck up my sphincter."

"Haha! That happens!" Zabka hands him a cold beer. "Drink this. It cures everything."

From her knees, the dancer removes the dollar tip from Jed's mouth with her breasts like a clapping seal. As Bob waits his turn, he looks her over closely and notices a long horizontal scar across her stomach. She slides over to him next and takes the dollar from his mouth. Bob looks at her seductively and tells her, "I wanna *fuck* your cesarean section."

With a face full of disgust, she yells, "Fuckin' asshole!" She sweeps her tips into a mound, scoops them up, and storms off the stage.

Bob turns around and notices Scooter. "Hey! You're back and in one piece! By the way, I took care of Natasha for you — if you know what I mean." He winks. "I'm just kidding, man. I paid her for your dance *and* a little extra for that bonus experience you had."

The MC announces, "It's the top of the hour and, as promised, it's time for a special *little* Christmas treat! Everybody please welcome — Mindy!" The stage lights dim while the guitar revving from Mötley Crüe's "Kickstart My Heart" shakes the room. As the strobe lights pulse, a battery-powered children's vehicle adorned with a sleigh-facade bursts through the back curtain. The driver of the car is a hot midget dressed as Mrs. Claus. She loops a couple of figure-eights at the top of the stage before driving down the spine and skidding to a stop at the pole.

Jed nearly falls out of his chair. "Holy fucking shit! My fetish wet dream!!" Mrs. Claus gets out of her sleigh, prances over to Jed, and grinds her tiny hips in a circle in his awestruck face. He begs, "Please tell me this is gonna turn into an elf orgy!" She winks back, and he tosses five singles her way. "I wanna shoot my egg nog all over you!" She runs, leaps on the pole, and spins around until gravity brings her down.

Meanwhile, the girl who recognized Robert earlier is studying the debauchery from the back of the room. While keeping one eye on Robert, she searches. *I need horny and intoxicated. And where betta ta find someone fa da night?* She watches a woman sit down next to Robert and how they interact. *Dey know each otha. Her clothes are on, so clearly she doesn't work here.* After Robert and the girl chat for a moment, they get up and head to the exit.

Her view of the two of them is partially blocked as her waitress approaches. "Can I get you another drink, Faige?"

Faige leans around her and keeps watching Robert. "Can youz gimme a few minutes? I tink I needa make a phone call."

"No problem. I'll come back in a little bit."

———

The stripper on top of Bambi — who could be her twin — pulls the bottle of Dom Pérignon out of the ice in a silver bucket, and refills their glasses. The girls on Bradford and Juan Carlos slither down to their knees and simulate oral sex. At first, Bradford refused all of the dancers and told Summer, "I just want to snuggle with you on the couch." Then, after following her to the ladies room because he couldn't "bear to be away" from her, she told him, "That's enough, I need some air. Stop stalking me." When she left, Juan Carlos convinced Bradford to join in the fun. He tried to relax, but still ended up squeezing his champagne glass too hard and breaking it.

While Prince rhythmically moans through "Erotic City", Juan Carlos revels in the sensory overload as he sits comfortably on the velvet couch. Bambi notices him drifting into the moment and forgetting about her. *This isn't good. I better do something.* She rubs his knee with her hand as his stripper shakes her butt in his face. After a sip of champagne, he firmly slaps the dancer's ass cheek.

Bambi tells her girl to take a break and Juan Carlos's girl to go sit. After the dancers find spots on the couch, Bambi stands over the girl who was just on her and says, "Relax for a sec. Now I'm gonna dance for you."

Juan Carlos's excitement builds as Bambi bends and turns like a natural. She squats and glides her hands down the stripper's thighs to her ankles. Bambi lifts and maneuvers her doppelgänger's feet behind her head, and transforms the Canadian girl into a tits-n-ass pretzel. Then, like a tidal wave, an overwhelming odor washes out of the stripper's crotch and devours the air in the room.

Bambi cries, "Oh my god! Did a fish swallow a skunk and swim into your coochie and die?!" Lightheaded, she collapses to the floor.

———

Bob opens the limo door for Summer and lets her crawl in across the back seat. He follows and shuts the door behind them. She scoots along the side seat towards the front. Along the way she runs into a half-full bottle of champagne and tosses back a few gulps. "I'm already a little tipsy, but this shit is *goooood!*"

"Here, let me have some too," Bob tells her. Summer stretches and hands him the bottle. As he drinks, he scans the limo. Upon noticing a red duffle bag lying on the floor near her, he moves in closer.

A double knock on the back door startles them. Summer whispers, "Shit. That's probably Bradford. He's turned into a stalker."

"Are you *fucking* kidding me? I didn't lock it. Shit." Bob cocks back his hand that's holding the bottle.

The door opens and nothing happens for what seems like an eternity. The person outside asks, "Is it okay if I come in?"

Bob recognizes the voice and answers, "Um, sure. Yeah, come in, Jed." He shrugs at Summer.

Jed pokes in his head, climbs through, and slams the door shut. "Hey, sorry about that. I uh, I wanted to, uh —"

Bob discerns why Jed showed up and decides to fill in the blanks in his cover story for him. "It's okay, I'll tell her. Summer, I'll cut to the chase. Jed is kind of a freak and gets off on watching other people have sex. I understand if you're not into that — but if that's the case, I think I'll have to leave. He's my buddy and I don't want his feelings to be hurt."

Summer looks back and forth at them skeptically. "Really?" She grins. "That's cool, because I'm kind of a freak myself."

Jed shoots his finger at her and winks. "She's a keeper."

"Bob, you got a condom?" Summer asks.

"Oh shit, no, I don't."

Jed tells them, "Another good reason I'm here." He pulls one out of his pocket and tosses it to Bob. "Here ya go."

Bob catches it and looks at the wrapper. "A Magnum?"

"What?" Jed smirks. "Is that not gonna work for you?"

"No, it's just I have so many questions." Bob thinks better of going down that road. "But I guess they can wait."

"Yeah, they can." Summer's eyes remain open just a slit while she tugs on Bob's jeans. "Let's go at it. The booze is really kicking in."

"I've had a lot too," he admits. "I just hope I can get it up."

"Don't worry, my pussy cures whiskey dick." Her eyes close and she sighs. "I've wanted to jingle your bells since the day we met."

Ya mean since yesterday? Bob seizes the opportunity to toss the duffle bag to Jed. As Jed rifles through it, Bob rips the wrapper and takes out the condom. He unzips his pants and looks back over his shoulder. Jed pulls out an envelope with "Buffalo Tickets" written on it and proudly shows it to Bob. Bob gives him a thumbs-up and Jed slips out of the limo.

"You gonna take off my panties and do me or what?" she asks.

Bob pulls up Summer's skirt, removes her pink cotton panties, and puts on the not-so-snug condom.

Her voice fades as she tells him, "If you find a tampon in there, just pull it out."

The circumstances force him to consider his next move. *Now what do I do?* As a sly smile takes shape, it comes to him.

———

After finishing her drink and much internal debate, Faige decided she had to call Jennifer. Now standing at a payphone at the end of a dimly lit hallway, she nervously dials the number. The music level back there is low enough that she hopes Jennifer won't hear it. Each ring on the other end of the line brings her closer to delivering the news.

Jennifer's answering machine picks up, and Faige leaves a message. "Hi *Jennifa*, it's me, Faige. Um, dis is a lil awkward, but I'm, um, I'm at

Mints. It's a club in Niagara Falls, and I — I jus' saw Robert leave wit' a woman."

The phone clicks and Jennifer screams, "He did fucking what?!"

"Hey, so I saw dis woman come up ta Robert — it was like she knew 'im. They tawked briefly and left togetha."

Jennifer yells, "That cheatin' son-of-a-bitch!" Faige feels her friend's wrath bite her ear. "I spoke with Lisa and was starting to have faith in him. Now I feel like such a fool."

Faige monitors the stage room's hijinks through the hallway as she speaks. "Wait — hang on. I actually tink I see 'im." She squints to confirm. "Yeah, dat's Robert. He's back."

"What-in-the-hell is going on?!"

Faige throws up a hand. "I don't know. He was gone fa like fifteen minutes and now he's back. I don't see her wit' 'im."

Jennifer begs, "What's he doing now?"

"I don't see 'im anymo." Faige tries to position herself at a different angle, but the phone cord is a short leash. "I'm not sure."

Jennifer urgently pleads, "Can you go find out and call me back?"

"Yeah, I can try."

"Don't let him see you."

"Okay. Bye." Faige hangs up the phone and hustles down the hall. She hides around the corner and studies Robert from afar as he rejoins his friends near the stage.

Bob gesticulates like he's on fire. "Guys, we gotta get the hell outta here!"

"Why?" Scooter asks with a long face. "I haven't even had a chance to penetrate a stripper's anus with my finger yet?"

"My sincerest apologies, but I'm sure Jed's already told you the good news." Bob looks at Jed who shakes his head no and points to the stripper on stage. "I guess he's been too preoccupied. Anyway, we got the tickets!"

"That's fucking awesome!" Zabka shouts.

"Yeah it is, but here's the thing." Bob glances over his shoulder and then squats down to their level at the table. "I kinda left a Christmas present for Bradford — and I'm pretty sure he's gonna blow his top when he sees it. There's a good chance he'll actually kill us. I'm serious."

Zabka smiles from ear to ear. "I really like the sound of this!"

Scooter's catatonic eyes stare through Bob's temple. Bob waves his hand in front of Scooter's nose, trying to get a reaction. Scooter comes back to life and asks, "Have I blacked out yet?"

"Probably," Bob replies. "Actually, there's a good chance we all have." He claps his hands. "Come on! Let's get going!"

As the four of them make their escape, Scooter grabs Natasha's hand and pulls her along. "You should come with us."

Natasha shuffles across the room in her high heels. "Can't leave. This is job. Need to make baby money."

"I don't care. I'll pay you whatever you want," Scooter begs.

She stops him and takes his other hand. "Anything?"

Bob pauses and motions back to them. "Hey! Let's go!"

"Can we fit her in our clown car?!" Scooter asks.

Bob replies frantically. "I guess we can squish her in." As he scans the room looking for Bradford, a girl lurking in the hallway shadows snags his attention. *Is that Faige? What the hell?* Faige cowers with her hand over her face. Bob turns and dashes for the exit. *I know I'm drunk-as-fuck, but I think that was really her.* He does a double-take, trips, and plunges into the bouncer at the door. *Fuck. Did that just happen?*

———

Bradford finishes his glass of champagne and tells the girl dancing for him to take a break. He says to Juan Carlos, "Hey, I think I better go look for Summer. She's been gone for a while."

"You heard her earlier. She'll go berserk if you follow her."

"At this point, I don't care." Bradford stands up. "She's been gone too long." He leaves and enters the main stage area.

Bradford's head swivels as he checks every corner. Unable to find her, he puts his hands on his hips and tries to imagine where Summer would go. *Wait a minute.* He scans the room for a second time. *I don't see those shitheads from Buffalo either. If she left with them, I'll* — As he trots to the exit, a dreadful premonition overtakes him.

Bradford bursts into the parking lot and searches frantically. The freezing cold that grips his body fails to register in his mind. A guy peeing on a tree through a chain link fence is the only person in sight.

Down to one final place to look, he sprints to the limo and is greeted by a crude portrait. Etched in the frost along the lengthy side-window is an enormous penis pointed squarely at a tiny stick-figure — and the poor bastard is clearly on the receiving-end of an epic load. "BUFFALO" is inscribed above the phallic symbol and "BRADFORD" is written above the mini-man.

Bradford's head detonates and he practically rips off the limo door. The perverse sex scene he finds inside elevates his anger to oxygen-depletion heights. His palms and forehead sweat as he crawls to Summer. Snoring softly with her dress hiked up and legs spread, her vagina stares him smack-in-the-face. Her copper aroma mixed with a tinge of sperm and latex nearly causes him to vomit. His hand lands on the torn Magnum wrapper and he flings it aside.

On all fours above her, Bradford inspects the object on her face. His head looks like a red apple and shakes as if there's an earthquake inside his skull. *Is this somebody's warped idea of a joke?!* Meticulously positioned down her forehead and the bridge of her nose like the Roman helmet piece, is a used condom.

In a fit of rage, Bradford punches the ceiling and yells, "Those mother fucking assholes! I'm gonna kill those fuckers!!"

The commotion wakes Summer into a bizarre and blurry world. Confused and frightened, she propels Bradford away with her feet and sends him onto his back. As she sits up, she notices something is stuck to her face and crosses her eyes to look. She peels off the condom and hurls it at him. "What the fuck is going on?!"

"You tell me *what the fuck* is going on!" Bradford's body shudders as he gets himself upright.

Summer jabs a finger at him. "You've been such an asshole this trip! Smothering me — I just couldn't take it!" She pulls her skirt down. "And then Bob took advantage of me when I was drunk. It's both your faults. *I'm* the victim here!"

Bradford rests his elbows on his knees and put his hands on his head. He slows his breathing until the only sound they hear are his heavy exhales. He feels every beat of his heart and wonders if it might just stop. Dumbfounded and disappointed, he turns to her and says, "I'm gonna go get everyone else. We're getting the fuck outta here."

—

Scooter stumbles while entering Bob's apartment and falls head first into the side of the couch.

"Oh shit, are you okay?" Bob asks as he helps Scooter up.

"Yeah, I think I'm fine. There was a little bit of cushion there. Hey! You know what?" Scooter snaps his fingers. "I gotta call that girl from the wings place — the Anchor Bar. She told me to. What's her name again? She was on that roast beef vagina team."

"Beats me. But I remember her phone number ended in 5309." He repeats the digits, but this time sings along to the song, "5309!"

"Okay, it'll come to me." Scooter knocks the side of his skull with the bottom of his palm. "Let me go take care of that."

"I'm sure she'll appreciate a call from you at this hour," Bob adds. "I think it's after three in the morning. Maybe four. Fuck it, do it."

As Bob staggers to his bedroom, he hears the rest of the crew bouncing off the walls as they pound up the building's hallway stairs. The apartment door bangs open and Jed, Zabka, and Cement-Head parade in like a highly uncoordinated marching band.

After successfully maneuvered his way to bed, Bob sits down on the edge. With enormous difficulty he unties his sneakers and tosses them in his closet's general direction. The picture of him and Jennifer catches his eye and he wonders how she is. The room spirals as he falls onto his back. A paper crumples, and he unwillingly rolls onto his stomach to see what it is. He finds Jennifer's note and grabs it.

The words blur in and out as he begins to read. "Dear Robert, I don't want to believe you would cheat on me, but I found Lisa's number in your trash. I don't know exactly what happened, but I need to know the truth. I understand you're mad at me, but this is something we can work through. We need to talk about it. I'm counting on you to be a better communicator. Call me. XOXOXO Jennifer"

Lisa? He shakes his head to try to clear the fog surrounding the past forty-eight hours. *Oh, yeah, Lisa. Wait a damn second. Jennifer was here? She went through my trash? What the fuck?*

Bob puts down the note and struggles to think. Beer bottles rattle and clink as someone rummages through the fridge. He attempts to recap the end of the night. *Did I see Faige at Mints?* He massages his temple with his fingertips. *Yeah, I did. Fuck. Did she see me with Summer?*

Bob gets up, walks to the kitchen, and stares at the phone. *What the hell am I gonna say to her?* He hears someone kicking cans in the living room and what sounds like a giggling girl. *Who's that?* He takes a deep breath. *Focus.* He punches in Jennifer's number, puts the receiver to his ear, and hears it begin to ring.

The Fourth Quarter

Curled up in a warm ball, Bob grins with his eyes tightly shut. Darkness fades as pink light penetrates his eyelids like he's being pushed out of a protective womb. As a hand slides over his butt, he braces for a spanking. *Where am I?*

He sniffs like a dog that's come upon an exotic odor. *What is that? Am I drunk dreaming?* As he inhales a familiar fragrance, snippets of last night's debauchery project on his internal movie screen. *Vanilla perfume!*

Bob opens his eyes cautiously. *This is my room, right?* He moves his pupils from left to right. *Yes, it is.* His back is warm from the stranger's body-heat. *Is it that stripper? What's her name? Natasha?* He slowly wiggles his shoulders to feel-up the person behind him. *Did I call Jennifer? Did she come over? Who the hell is this?*

—

Much to her pleasure, Bambi awakes to find that her wall of pillows — also known as the "Great Wall to Protect Vagina" — has not been breached. After peeking over at Juan Carlos and confirming that he's fast asleep, she gets out of bed and tiptoes to the bathroom.

Before closing the door, she checks on him once more. Satisfied, she locks the door and sits down to pee. She mentally goes over a checklist of what she's learned and what's supposed to happen next. As the last drop of tinkle falls, she grabs some toilet paper. With her cleaning pad, she wipes like her momma taught her — top to bottom. Not wanting to potentially stir Juan Carlos, she doesn't flush.

Bambi turns on a faucet to create some white noise and picks up the phone on the wall near the toilet. She punches in a phone number.

After one ring, a man picks up. "Hello," the voice says.

Bambi glances nervously at the door and whispers, "Hey, it's me."

"Good. Are you ready to go?"

"Yes. These guys are beyond clueless."

"You can relax, we're prepared. Just stay focused," he stresses.

"Okay. Gotta go." Bambi quietly hangs up the phone.

———

Bob mentally prepares himself to turn and literally uncover who his mysterious bed guest is. *It's gotta be Jennifer, but it doesn't exactly feel like her. Fuck it. Just get it over with.* He rolls around and to his horror he finds Cement-Head's smushed face in a pillow. Bob yells, "What the hell are you doing in here?!"

Cement-Head opens one eye. "I don't know." Still sedated, he scratches his scalp. "Oh yeah, I remember. I couldn't drive last night and there was no room for me in the living room."

"Yeah there is!" Bob pushes him in the chest. "Let's go out there." As they roll out of bed, Bob looks at Cement-Head. "I'm glad you at least kept your clothes on, pervert." They chuckle on their way to the living room.

To Bob, the scene is familiar. Zabka's snoring is vibrating the windows as he sleeps on the couch. Scooter's rat's nest is unchanged in the corner. The big difference is that on the floor there is an outline of Jed's body made by empty beer cans, but he's not in it. Bob squats down and feels the floor. "It's not warm. He's been gone for a while." He looks up at Cement-Head and gestures with an open hand at the clear area amongst the cans. "Welcome to your new bed."

"Funny, but don't you think we should find Jed?"

"Yeah, I suppose that's a good idea." Bob slides over to Zabka and flicks two fingers into his forehead. "Wake up, dummy."

Startled, Zabka opens his eyes. "What the fuck?"

"Jed's missing. You know where he is?"

Zabka pulls his comforter up to his chin. "I don't know. Out being a productive member of society? Whacking off? How the fuck would I know?"

"Cement-Head, can you check the bathroom?" Bob asks. "Come on Zabka, we need to find him."

"What time is it?" Zabka inquires.

Bob checks the VCR clock. "It's 8:02."

"Oh fuck, we need to get moving." Zabka sits up with newfound energy. "It's tailgate time, mutha fuckas!!"

"Jed isn't in there," Cement-Head reports. "I don't see him anywhere."

"Okay, grab your coats," Bob instructs them. "Our morning just turned into a search and rescue mission."

"Wake up Scooter," Zabka says.

Bob looks at Scooter's messy mound. "You know what? That guy's been a trooper — let him sleep. We can handle this on our own."

—

Jennifer drags her feet as she glides down the hall to her living room. A barren carton of chocolate ice cream and an empty bottle of Merlot are on the coffee table. After Faige's call concerning Robert's whereabouts last night, Jennifer decided to grant herself some "me time." She removes the pity-party casualties from the table and takes them to the kitchen.

The answering machine's blinking red light catches Jennifer's eye. She meanders over to it and gingerly presses play. The machine robotically tells her the message was recorded at 3:27 AM. "Hi, um. Dis is Bob — sorrys, I means Robert — no, dis is Bob, gawd dammit." She recoils while he struggles to form a coherent sentence. "Why youzzz lookin' through my trash? That's my trash — and it's *mine!* Lisa's a friend — a bartender. I notta cheater." She hears the phone drop and hit the floor. "An, an — you still there? An why in da hell is Faige followin' me at a strip club? Esplain dat one. *Hiccup.*" She can smell his boozy breath drift out of the speaker. "I read your note. Apology? No apologize? *You* communicate. *Burp.* Miss you." A beep ends the message.

After a moment of absorbing and trying to comprehend what she heard, Jennifer retrieves a wine glass from the cabinet and fills it to the brim with some leftover Zin. *I know what I need to do.* She pulls a knife from her 12-piece cutlery set, inspects it, and then returns it to its slot. *Like Faige said, "Do sumptin bold."*

As Jennifer sips from her glass, she stares through the window into her neighbor's backyard. A young boy in a colorful Buffalo Bills snowsuit is rolling a snowman's head. His cheeks are bright red, and gooey mucus is running from his nose. He stops and turns after sensing her presence. Jennifer smiles and waves at the innocent child. He spots her teal pajama top and, almost involuntarily like he's known to do this since birth, raises his gloved fist and extends his middle-finger. She feels a sting like a slap across the face. *Again with this shit?* She shakes her head. *That proves it. This town has cornered the market on breeding asshole kids.*

———

Bob, Zabka, and Cement-Head exit the apartment complex feeling like SEAL Team Six-Pack on a rescue mission. They stand with their hands on their hips and scan the surrounding neighborhood. The road is mostly clear and dry, with no new accumulation of snow.

Zabka observes, "It's crisp out, but not nearly as cold as I thought it would be."

"Damn it. They said the weather was gonna improve, and it did," Bob adds. "That's not good for the Bills. The shittier the weather, the better."

"What's that?" Cement-Head points. "Over there by the streetlamp?"

Bob squints. "Is that a person?"

"That's gotta be Jed!" Zabka shouts.

They sprint through the front yard snow. Upon arrival, they assess the scene with curiosity. Bob tilts his head and asks, "Why is Jed wearing Summer's panties on his head? And why — is that dog hair? Trust me, that's not Summer's. And why is dog hair all over her panties?"

Jed's hot breath actively rehydrates the dried juices encrusted in the underwear fibers. When the pungent smell hits Zabka, his nostrils clench. "Jed is one sick bastard, so I'm gonna go out-on-a-limb and guess that this is his way of fully experiencing her down-under scent."

"Personally, I think he looks spectacular in pink." Bob calls attention to the steam rising from his mouth. "And somehow he's still alive."

Zabka squats and pulls off the panties. To everyone's surprise, Scooter's face appears. It is a disturbing shade of purple, and there are ice-snot-cicles hanging from his nose. "What the?! I thought he was inside!"

Bob nudges Scooter's gut with his foot until he wakes up. Scooter's eyes open and he asks, "Where am I? Is this the Bruce Dome?"

"No, not yet," Bob replies. "But we'll be there soon."

"Speaking of the game," Zabka says to Scooter. "I seem to recall Jed giving you the tickets last night. Is that them in the envelope?"

"Yeah, he gave 'em to me." Scooter holds up the envelope. "He said I'm the most responsible, and so I should hang onto them." He attempts to toss away a bottle of Genny, but is unsuccessful because it is frozen to his hand. "What the hell?"

Bob suggests, "Just breathe on it a bunch. Eventually it will peel off."

"Okay." Scooter puts up his arms for Bob and Zabka, and they pull him to his feet. He shivers and exhales warm air onto his bottle-hand. "Can we go inside? I'm freezing."

"Yeah, you need to thaw out," Bob answers. "You know where Jed is?"

"No clue," Scooter replies.

As they begin to move to the apartment, Zabka notices something and stops. "Guys, look at this." He points to an area in the snow nearby. "Looks here like Scooter was able to piss, 'GOD HATES BUF', but couldn't manage to squirt out the end of 'BUFFALO' before collapsing. Nevertheless, nice handiwork — or should I say, dick-work, Scooter."

Scooter completes the detachment of the bottle from his palm and flings it aside. "I don't think I could've done that." He picks a chunk of frozen snot from his nose. "My dexterity was shit last night."

As they walk, Bob says, "So if you didn't do it, then someone saw you passed-out and pissed that next to you? That seems pretty fucked-up."

Zabka comments, "On the one hand, that would seem bizarre. But on-the-other-hand, it's the Buffalo. Why *wouldn't* someone piss that next to an unconscious person in the snow? I probably would."

Cement-Head shakes his head. *I can't wait to get to California.*

Bob asks Scooter, "The other question is, why were you out here?"

"When we got home, I was hammered," Scooter informs them. "Like yesterday kicked my ass on a whole new level. Thanks a lot, guys."

"You're very welcome," Zabka replies. "You can praise me later."

Scooter continues, "But the noise level coming from Jed and Zabka's snoring contest was driving me crazy. So I got a beer and went to take a leak, but some fuckhead," he gives Cement-Head the stink-eye, "was taking a record wiz. What happened next was my critical mistake. I thought I could just go outside, no problem. I remember pissing on the lamp post back there, and then I guess I fell over and passed-out."

Bob nods. "Okay, so if you didn't create the urine graffiti, then that still leaves us with the puzzle of who did?" He notices that Jed's Bronco is not in the parking lot. "Jed drove his truck back here after Anchor Bar and before Mints, right?"

"Yeah," Cement-Head replies. "I followed you guys here first, and then everyone got in my car."

"Okay, so I guess he went out to get something this morning?"

Zabka offers an alternative, "Or went to bury Natasha's body."

"Wait, did she come back with us last night?" Bob asks.

"No," Scooter replies. "She was gonna come, but that damn bouncer wouldn't let her." He groans. "I *sooo* wanted to bone her."

"Believe me, we all did." Zabka grabs his crotch. "I got a lap dance from that hot piece of Russian ass and almost Perestroika'd in my pants."

"You're lucky you didn't almost shit yourself like Scooter," Bob adds. "Natasha has that affect on men."

Down the block, they hear the sound of wheels spitting up gravel. They turn to find Jed's Bronco barreling down the road at an unsafe velocity. Jed pulls into the parking lot and jerks to a stop. He jumps out of his truck with something in a plastic bag and goes into a fit of rage. "What the fuck is wrong with this town?! All the liquor stores are closed, and the assholes at Tops fuckin' grocery won't sell alcohol until noon! I'm about to lose my goddamn mind!"

"Yeah, it's a bullshit Erie County law on Sundays," Bob tells him. "But don't we have beer inside? If my memory is correct, you guys brought several cases with you."

"Yeah we did!" Jed kicks a clump of snow and it explodes into powder. "But we drank every last beer we had! How the hell we gonna tailgate?!"

"Calm down, we'll figure something out." Bob points at Jed's bag. "What's in there?"

"I bought us a secret weapon." Jed reaches in the bag and pulls out a package. "Depends undergarments!"

Zabka looks at him sideways. "You got us adult diapers? I'm almost afraid to ask why."

"Well, my reasoning is very logical. I hate wasting time going to take a leak, so I thought why not just put a pair of these on? Problem solved."

Bob looks skeptical. "So we just piss ourselves and then walk around with a urine glacier in our pants? Is that your brilliant idea?"

"Yeah! That's exactly what I was fuckin' saying!" Jed punts the package thirty-yards across the street. "But without beer, they're just a dicktease to our bladders!"

Cement-Head watches the "adult" diapers land in a neighbor's driveway. "Alright guys, it's been fun, but I need to go home. It was a real treat waking up next to you this morning, Bob."

"Hey, that was no picnic for me! You're not exactly my first choice when it comes to spooning. Wait, so you're not going to the game?"

Cement-Head shakes his head. "Naw, I don't have a ticket."

"Scooter, look in the envelope and see if there's an extra."

Scooter pulls out the tickets. "You're in luck. Looks like there's about ten." After he reviews the first one in the pile, he crunches his brow. As he flips through the rest like a deck of cards, the earth begins to spin like a whirlpool. "Oh, shit." He collapses into a snow-covered bush.

—

Bradford's pacing has created a visible circle in the carpet of his hotel room. His view during each loop moves from the couch he slept on, to Lake Erie, to Summer sleeping in the king-sized bed. Like a bull in a ring, every time he envisions Bob's face, he sees red. A knock on the door breaks him from his cycle.

Bradford opens the door and finds his business partner. "Hey Juan Carlos, what's going on?"

"Just getting up and thought I'd check in on you."

Bradford rests against the doorframe. "I'm trying to keep my cool, but I feel like I may lose it. I'm gonna find that fucker and even the score."

Juan Carlos puts a hand on Bradford's shoulder. "Look, I know you're pissed — and rightly so — but let's go to the game, do a little business, and have a good time. We know those guys are gonna be there too, so there's a chance we run into him. You never know."

Bradford nods and glumly asks, "So what do I do about Summer?"

Juan Carlos whispers, "This is what you do. Act like you don't care about her — not one bit. Don't be mad, be indifferent to her existence."

"You sure?"

"Absolutely. I've watched your behavior and how she reacts. She's one of those girls who's repulsed by attention and attracted to neglect. It's fucked-up, but that's her in a nutshell."

Bradford digests the analysis. "Yeah, I think you're right."

"Good, I'm glad you understand. Don't break from it either — she's not even a blip on your radar. Got it?"

"Alright, thanks."

"Let's get ready." Juan Carlos leaves. "See you in an hour."

———

Scooter blinks his eyes and shakes his head. Bush branches and snow engulf his upper torso. *What happened?* He wriggles out and finds himself immersed in the midst of an incomprehensible shouting match. As his vision and hearing recalibrate, he catches Zabka scream, "We're screwed! We're so *fucking* screwed!" Scooter then watches Cement-Head's tin-can-car speeding away down the street. *Smart move.* He stands up, and inserts himself into the uproar. "What the hell's going on?"

"You forgot already?!" Zabka shakes the envelope in the air. "Jed got the wrong tickets! Can you believe this shit!?"

Bob throws his hands up. "Jed managed to steal us tickets to *yesterday's* goddamn Brewfest!"

"Whaddya want me to say?!" Jed shouts. "The envelope said 'Buffalo Tickets' on it. How the hell should I know?"

"Hum, I don't know. How about you look inside and check what they say!?" Zabka rips the tickets in half and tosses them into the wind. "Jesus Christ, we just went from the best day to the worst fucking day!" He kicks a mound of snow. "Our shit is rolling downhill picking up more shit, and now we're in one big shit-snowball!" A few neighbors peek out of their windows at the commotion.

Bob positions himself in the center like a boxing referee. "I need everyone to shut-the-fuck-up for a minute." He waits for them to listen before continuing. "You can't be mad at each other, because each and every one of you has fucked-up along the way." They hang their heads. "Scooter, it was your responsibility to get us seats in the first place. Zabka, your prize-fighting history cost us winning those Anchor Bar tickets. And finally there's you, Jed. Good lord, use your damn head!"

"So now what?" Scooter asks.

Bob looks around his circle of friends. "We can either give up. Or pull together and figure something out. What do you guys want to do?"

"Never surrender!" Scooter shouts.

Zabka lifts up his head. "Our only real option now is to try and scalp." He shrugs. "I know it's a long shot, but let's hope we get lucky."

"And maybe we'll come across a broken down beer truck and can 'borrow' a few cases," Jed says eagerly. The mood lightens as they chuckle.

"So you're saying hope is our strategy?" Scooter asks.

"Look around you." Bob smiles with his arms wide open. "This is Buffalo. We never give up. Even when we repeatedly get knocked down."

"On that note, let's get going." Zabka leads them inside the apartment.

"Can I be honest with you guys?" Scooter asks as he clutches his right side. "I think my liver jumped outta me and is hiding over there in the corner by the TV. I don't mind a booze-free day."

"Are you fucking with me?" Jed slaps himself on the forehead. "Today is the third and final round of our heavyweight title fight! Everything rides on what happens today. Do we win the weekend, or do we lose it? We've come too far to throw in the towel now. We're counting on you."

Scooter curls up in his nest on the floor. "You guys are fucking nuts."

Jed pulls deodorant out of his bag. "Trust me, once you have a little hair of the dog, you'll be just fine." He goes under his shirt and applies the roll-on to his armpits. "I'm ready."

Bob tries to fix his bed-head by pressing down his spiked up hair. "Hey Jed, do you know anything about the 'GOD HATES BUFFALO' urine bulletin that was next to Scooter's corpse in the snow?"

"Yep," Jed replies as he wanders into the kitchen.

Bob follows him and asks, "Care to elaborate?"

Jed opens a random cabinet and forages for food. "I think the message is clear. God hates Buffalo. Come on Bob, we discussed that last night."

"I know, but did you piss it? I mean, Scooter there and unconscious."

"So here's what happened." Jed slams the cabinet door shut and moves to the next. "I was about to go on my beer mission when I realized that I needed to take a leak. So I went towards the light pole to take care of business, and that's when I saw Scooter."

"So you knew it was him and you didn't do anything?"

Jed opens the oven and puts his head inside. "At the time, I had to piss like a racehorse, and so I just started writing what I thought was appropriate for the crime scene." He maneuvers to the sink and opens the door below it.

"I see." Bob closes the oven door and folds his arms across his chest. "And then?"

"And then I took off to find beer." Jed shrugs. "Clearly I had other things on my mind. Other very pressing priorities."

"Clearly." Bob shakes his head and sits down at the kitchen table. On it is a large piece of white poster paper and a couple of markers. As he begins to draw, Jed looks over his shoulder and asks, "Are you creating a sign for the game?"

"I am." Bob draws NBC vertically down the left side of the sign in bold blue and highlights the edges in red.

"What's NBC?" Jed asks.

"They're broadcasting the game, dummy." Bob continues to draw.

Jed scratches his head. "Are you trying to get us on TV?"

Bob laughs. "I don't think my creation will get us on TV, but knowing what we're gonna wear today, it might help us from getting killed."

Jed grabs the project and reads it aloud, "NBC. Nobody Blows Cox." He looks it over like it's a priceless Picasso. "I love it, but I think it needs one more thing. Can you add 'Dolphins suck'?"

"I certainly can." Bob completes the addition and they admire the finished product.

Zabka walks over to them. "Nice work guys."

"Where have you been?" Jed asks.

"I just took a four-pound shit," Zabka replies. "It looked like slimy brown soft-serve ice-cream with jalapeno seed sprinkles." He opens the fridge and looks inside. "You weren't lying. There really is no beer left."

Jed puts his hand on his chest. "Let me assure you, I would never joke about something as important as that."

"Yeah, I know you wouldn't, Jed." Zabka puts a hand on Bob's shoulder and looks at him seriously. "So as I was on the throne, I was thinking about last night. On the ride back here you said some really weird shit."

"Weird shit like what?" Bob asks. "Like funny ha-ha shit?"

"No, like disturbing shit. Like you 'really miss Jennifer' and that you were gonna call her and tell her that 'you just wanna be held.' Ya know, crazy shit like that." Zabka picks up Bob's chin to look him in the eye. "I hope you only say that type of garbage when you're drunk and horny."

Bob slaps his hand away. "Did I call her last night?!"

Zabka and Jed shrug and respond together, "Don't know."

Bob's eyes roll up and he looks at the ceiling. "I sure hope I didn't call her and say crap like that. I'm still mad at her."

Zabka over-emphasizes his pout. "Were you feeling guilty about fucking poor Summer? Please tell me you turned that pretty face of hers into a shiny glazed donut!"

"Hold on. I didn't tell you the full story?"

"No, you didn't! Give us all the juicy details. Like for example, how *juicy* is she?"

"Guys, I think you're gonna be both disappointed and pleased with what I'm about to tell you." Bob gets down on all fours like he's in the limo with Summer. "So after Jed took what his moronic mind thought were the Bills tickets — no offense Jed — Summer passed-out cold. As much as I wanted to bang her in my drunken state, I thought there might be a few things slightly wrong with taking advantage of that situation. However, I don't know what the Canadian laws are, so maybe it's not really a potential crime up there?"

"Yeah, you can pretty much do whatever the hell you want," Jed informs him. "It's like the Caucasian version of Tijuana — except instead of donkeys, they blow polar bears. We *gotta* go see a polar bear show!"

"Thanks for that insightful commentary, Jed." Bob shakes his head. "Anyway, I also thought it would be wrong to kinda cheat on Jennifer."

"I disrespectfully disagree," Zabka says.

"Why am I not surprised?" Bob asks rhetorically. "So my main motive was to really piss off Bradford, and it took me about two seconds to think of how. I hiked up her skirt, took off her panties, and put them in my pocket. At the time, I had no idea they'd be used later as an arctic ski mask and save Scooter's face from freezing off."

"Thanks, Bob," Scooter moans from his raccoon's nest.

"You're welcome, Scooter. After that I put on the condom Jed gave me and flogged the dolphin." He kneels and proudly strokes his imaginary two-foot cock. "I jerked off into the Magnum and strategically placed it on her face. I like to think of it as my personal 'fuck you, Bradford' calling card."

"Oh man, that's brilliant!" Zabka yells. "He's gotta be so pissed right now. I love it!"

Bob smiles from ear to ear. "I thought you'd appreciate that. It's the little touches that make the biggest difference." He gets up off his knees. "Jed, may I ask why a married man such as yourself is carrying around Magnum condoms?"

Jed digs a lump of crusty wing sauce out of his beard and flicks it. "Well, the Magnum part should be self-explanatory, but to be blunt, I carry them for situations like we had last night."

Bob asks, "For situations that call for someone fake-fucking an asshole's girlfriend while attempting to steal their Bills tickets?"

Jed nods. "Bingo. You hit the nail on the head."

"If we happen to run into him, there could be trouble." Zabka flexes his muscles. "Not that I couldn't single-handedly kick his puny ass and his *el dickhead* friend's ass too. However, they do have a bit more money than us, so maybe they could do something crazy with those extra resources? But I don't think it should matter."

"But what if it does?" Bob asks. "Any ideas for how to prepare for that scenario?"

Zabka thinks for a moment. "As a matter of fact, I do." He pulls a card out of his wallet. "I gotta make a quick call, and then we're outta here."

———

Summer is wearing a tight, teal v-neck shirt with a Dolphins logo strategically placed between her breasts. After putting on the finishing touches of her makeup, she examines herself in the bathroom mirror. Satisfied with her appearance, she walks into the vacant living room area expecting to find her boyfriend. Losing her nerve, she hoofs around the corner to the bedroom and calls out, "Bradford!" only to discover that he's gone.

Summer spots a note on the dresser. *There better be a good reason he's not here.* The paper reads, "Housekeeping, please take out the trash I left behind." Befuddled, she puts it back down and grumbles, "Is that fucker referring to me?" She grabs her fur coat and rides the elevator down to the lobby.

It doesn't take Summer long to spot the others in the foyer. Bambi is sporting the same shirt she is, while Bradford and Juan Carlos are wearing matching Dan Marino jerseys. Summer sees the limo pull up and scuffs her heels while racing to join them. Julio opens the back door and Bambi slides in first. Summer waves her hands. "Hey! I'm coming!"

"Did you hear something?" Juan Carlos asks Bradford.

"No, not a thing." Bradford hops inside.

Summer stops in front of Juan Carlos and asks, "What the hell is going on here?"

Juan Carlos put his hand on her shoulder and shakes his head. "Somehow you slipped our minds, but I'm glad you're here. We need our marketing staff."

"Marketing staff?!" Summer bites at him. "Don't call me that!"

"Bradford and I had a brief meeting this morning and determined that's the best way of referring to you now." Juan Carlos points inside the limo. "Now if you wouldn't mind, we've got places to go."

Summer grits her teeth and gets in. She shouts down the limo at Bradford. "What the fuck is up with calling me *marketing staff*?! I'm your girlfriend. I just sell your lame products because I'm bored!"

Bradford taps on the driver's dividing window. Julio rolls it down, and Bradford says, "To the stadium, pronto. And put on that CD."

Summer screams, "Bradford! I'm talking to you!"

Julio pushes on the disc that's sitting halfway into the CD player's slot and it gets sucked in. He starts to drive and turns up the volume as "Rico Suave" by Gerardo begins. Bradford bounces to the beat and makes wave movements with his hand and arm, while Juan Carlos plays air trumpet.

Bambi pictures Juan Carlos with a long Jheri curl and a bandana tied around his head, as part of Gerardo's crew. She rolls her eyes and wonders, which divine being thought it would be funny to bring the two biggest douches in the universe together. As the guys replicate the video dance moves from their seats, she speculates which one will mount the other first.

—

Just south of Buffalo, away from the decaying grain mills and rusted factories near the lake, is the semi-rural town of Orchard Park. Its borders hold the Mecca of Western New York — Rich Stadium — home of the Bills. Every home game spawns a monumental transformation of the community. The collection of massive parking areas and small patches of surrounding homes become one gigantic tailgate party. Front yards become parking lots, and parking lots become front yards. Tents, tables, coolers, and barbecues are transported from the garage for game day, as throngs of people in Bills gear gather in every direction.

Jed's Bronco nears the gridiron and inches forward in bumper-to-bumper traffic. Scooter points excitedly. "Is that the Bruce Dome?!"

"That's her alright!" Jed shouts.

Scooter squints. "But it doesn't look like a dome."

"It's like a domed stadium, minus a roof. Basically the same thing."

"I don't have the strength to debate, but that makes no sense."

"How shit-faced was I yesterday?" Zabka asks not really anyone. "Because I have this odd recollection of some girl flirting with Scooter."

"That's right!" Bob exclaims. "And she gave him her number!"

"I think I tried to call her last night," Scooter says. "But for the life of me, I can't remember what happened."

"Forget her." Zabka hands back a nearly empty bottle of vodka that he took from Bob's apartment. From the backseat, Bob grabs it and shakes it. "Thanks a lot. There might be one shot left in here." He unscrews the cap and puts it in front of Scooter's nose as he's resting his eyes.

After an unexpected whiff, Scooter lurches forward and almost dry heaves. "What the hell is wrong with you, Bob? You really can't wait to see me throw up, can you?"

Bob punches his shoulder. "Buddy, this is what friends do to each other. It's all in good fun."

"Okay, I know. I'm just not used to all this partying."

"We call it liver strength conditioning! You should be paying us personal trainer fees!" As a new tune on the radio begins, it catches Bob's ear. "Jed, turn this up, man!" Jed complies and "Rock of Ages" by Def Leppard blasts out of the speakers. "Listen to these lyrics, Scooter. They're words to live by." Bob raises the bottle and finishes it. "Here's to burning out! Not fading away!"

Jed pulls into the Stadium Lot 1 entrance and pays the entry fee. He follows the attendants' directions as they flag him into a parking spot. "We made it!"

"Let's see if I've got this straight," Bob says. "Our tailgating inventory consists of a bag full of potentially riot-inducing costumes, one package of underwear meant for people who have lost control of their bladder's on/off switch, and an empty bottle of vodka?" The rest of the truck can't manage a word out of their flabbergasted mouths. "Oh, I forgot what we *don't* have — tickets!"

Jed lifts a finger. "You forgot something. We gotta football."

"Yeah, Bob!" Zabka shouts sarcastically. "We gotta football!"

"Well, shit! That changes everything!" Bob jumps out of the Bronco and the others follow. "Who's ready for the best damn tailgate ever?!" Jed prepares for the cold and puts on a furry hat with earflaps.

"This is Bills country," Zabka announces. "Breathe it in. Good shit will happen." He leads them to the back of the Bronco, swings the spare tire to the side, and opens the window and hatch. He reaches inside and pulls out a plastic bag. "Jed and I painstakingly handcrafted these uniforms for you, so we would *appreciate* your appreciation." He tosses each of them an identical XXL white t-shirts. A large "51" is on the front and back, and "COX" is above the back number. The numbers and letters are in jagged teal spray-paint with orange highlights around the edges.

Bob admires his prop. "For you two dipshits, this is pretty nice work."

"Put those on over your jackets," Zabka tells them. "They'll fit."

The group follows orders and transforms into chubby Dolphin linebackers. Zabka then distributes the critical piece to complete their outfits.

"What the hell is this?" Scooter asks. "It looks like a poorly made oversized spatula, or a miniature oar."

"That, my ignorant friend, is a Bryan Cox backboard," Zabka answers.

"Backboard?" Scooter questions. "Where's the hoop?"

"There's no goddamn hoop! Jesus! Some players, like Cox, use this stupid thing to protect their necks. You put the rod part of it that sticks out of the bottom, down the back of your shirt behind your head. Like this."

Zabka puts it behind his neck and Scooter proclaims, "That blue square thing is bigger than your head!"

"Yeah, that's the point! We're mocking the shit out of Bryan Cox!"

"But he's black," Bob points out. "Should we really do this?"

"Of course we should! The color of his skin or our skin has nothing to do with it — we're a parody." Zabka adjusts his board. "Come to think of it, that difference makes us even more entertaining — which I didn't foresee as possible. The bottom line is the guy's been a prick to the Buffalo, so we're poking him with his own sword."

The rest of them properly position their counterfeit neck protectors and admire the ridiculousness of each other. A flattened beer can zips past Jed's ear and bounces off Scooter's backboard. Scooter covers his head like a bomb just went off, while the others spin around.

A Bills fan walking by yells, "Fuck you, Cox! Go back to your grandma's retirement community in Florida and bang her dentures!"

Bob grabs the NBC sign and shows it to the fan. "Hey! We're Bills fans! Read this! We're making fun of Cox!"

As the fan slowly reads aloud, "Nobody Blows Cox? Dolphins suck?" he scratches his nuts through his Bills Zubaz pants. "Sorry, guys. Let me get you a few beers to make up for it. What you've got going on there is pretty hilarious, now that I get it." He delivers a round of Budweiser and they all toast, "Buffalo!"

Zabka gulps his beer. "See, things are already starting to work out." He sets down his beer and reaches back into the bag. "To round out the game-day gear, there's one last thing. Isotoner gloves!"

Scooter asks, "What are Isotoner gloves? Are they special?" He takes a pair from Zabka. "These look thin and, sorry, a bit feminine."

"These, my bird-brained buddy, are gloves the Dolphins quarterback, Dan Marino promotes. Yeah, they actually kinda suck at keeping your hands warm, but sometimes a joke requires a little suffering."

"After you guys put those on, are you gonna join me and put on Depends?" Jed asks.

"I think I'm okay for right now," Bob replies to a disappointed Jed. "But how about this? If we miraculously run into a fountain of beer and I get a nice buzz going, I'll strap a diaper on. Sound good?"

"Better than good — it's a deal."

Zabka grabs the football. "Bob, let's throw the pigskin around."

"Sure, let's do it," Bob replies. "Just warn me if someone's about to chuck something at me or tackle me — or lord knows what else."

"I will." Zabka tosses him the football. "You do the same for me."

"Look out for you?" Bob throws a bullet into Zabka's chest. "That's probably asking a bit much, knowing how you're prone to find trouble."

"Whatever. Anyway, the vodka and beer are starting to work their magic. I'm gonna come up with a way for us to get into the stadium."

Bob catches the ball over his head. "Maybe you can try your go-to method of exchanging a hand job for game entry?"

"Ha ha, very funny." Zabka flips him the bird.

"How's that Isotoner commercial go?" Bob asks. "Something like, 'Take care of the hands that take care of you'? Work your magic, Zabka!"

"Oh, you're hilarious today, aren't ya? Come on, think. There's gotta be a way for us to get in."

"I can't think of any other option than scalping, but I didn't see any scalpers on the way in." Bob notices a few Porta-Potties behind Zabka, next to a hill of snow the size of a house. A guy with a Dolphins jacket enters the closest potty to them. "Zabka, I'm gonna go deep." Bob flips the ball to Zabka as he jogs past him. "Hit me next to the pisser." Zabka turns around and waits to properly time the thirty-yard pass.

As the Dolphins fan is relieving himself inside the latrine, the sound of footsteps crunching gravel grows louder. With the ball flying through the air, the Bills fans in line watch a cartoon version of Bryan Cox rapidly approaching. Five-yards from his target, Bob catches the perfect spiral, takes two steps — CRUNCH, CRUNCH — and catapults himself into the side of the plastic outhouse. BAM! Startled and shaken, the man inside yells, "What the fuck!?"

"That was the Bryan Cox paradox — bitch!" Bob flips off the bathroom. "See what happens when you come to the Buffalo! The Bills are gonna squish-the-mother-fucking-fish!" He jogs back to Zabka who is curled over with laughter.

"Oh shit!" Zabka yells. "That was too fuckin' funny!"

They high-five, and Bob says, "That was perfect! Nice pass!"

A man with glasses and a salt-and-pepper beard approaches them. "Son, I just watched that ridiculous performance, and I've been to a lot of tailgates over the years, but that was by far the funniest thing I've ever seen." He sticks out his right hand. "I'm Ken." They shake and introduce themselves.

Bob smiles. "We're glad we could entertain you, Ken. Just imagine what we could come up with if we had a few more drinks!"

"Yeah, we're real thirsty," Zabka confesses.

"Hell, come on over and have a few." Ken points to a blue tent with smoke rising around it. "We're right over there."

"Sounds good," Bob replies. "Can we bring our buddies?"

"Let me guess. Those other two schmucks dressed like Cox are with you." Ken chuckles. "Absolutely. Bring 'em."

"Come on guys." Zabka waves Jed and Scooter over. "And don't forget the sign." They follow Ken to the tent and find a highly unusual style of barbecuing occurring on the hood of a 1980 red Ford Pinto. People are grilling bacon on a saw, burgers and dogs on a rake, and chicken in an army helmet. The hood is charred brown and covered with grease.

Scooter remarks, "You sure have an interesting way of doing things."

"Yeah, my hood had some damage and needed to be repainted," Ken begins. "So during a tailgate I threw a grill on top because I didn't care, and well, one thing led to another, and here we are."

Jed notices the people around the car are watching suspiciously, and so he addresses them, "Just to be clear, we're Buffalo fans." He holds up Bob's sign and rotates so everyone can read it. "What we're doing here is called sarcasm." After a proper evaluation, the people carry on with their business.

Bob eyes the food being cooked. "It all looks and smells very good."

"Thanks." Ken flips over the burgers. "Go grab a beer out of the cooler." A woman smoking a cigarette, with a nose as red as Rudolph's, motions them over. She gets off a porcelain toilet and lifts the seat so they can grab a few beers.

"Wow! This is cool!" Scooter remarks.

"Hey, what section you guys in today?" Ken asks.

The four horseman in teal enemy garb fumble to respond until Bob says, "Well, the thing is, at the moment, we don't entirely have tickets."

Ken stops tending to the steaming meat. "You're kidding, right?" They sheepishly shake their heads no. "Well, that's unfortunate. It's gonna be tough to find tickets today."

"We realize that, but we're hoping for a miracle," Scooter replies.

Ken looks up at the blue sky as bacon crackles. "We gotta get you morons into this game. The crowd will love you — once they decipher your humor." He puts the bacon on a plate. "The only thing I can think of, and it's a long shot, is I have a friend who knows a guy who might be able to help you scrounge up some tickets. He'll be here shortly."

"A long shot is better than no shot," Bob says. "We'll take it."

———

As Julio nears the VIP limo lot entrance, he finds the parking attendant shaking his head and waving for him to drive past. Julio puts down the divider to the back. "Mr. Threadgold, we're not being allowed in."

"What do you mean we're not?" Bradford asks angrily. "Don't they see how important we are?"

"This guy is telling us not to turn into the lot. I don't know what to do."

Bradford slides down his window and sticks out his head. "Excuse me. Maybe you didn't notice, but we're here for the game." He arrogantly takes a sip of his champagne.

The attendant replies, "Oh, I'm sorry. I thought you were here for church."

"If church is the Bills kneeling before me and giving me head," Bradford scoffs. "Then yes, we're here for goddamn church." The cars behind them lay on their horns.

The attendant partially restrains himself. "Sir, if I wanted to lose my job, I'd tear you a new asshole. But since I like my job — and, I'm guessing, you already have a special someone taking care of your asshole — I'll kindly direct you to the bus lot where parking's still available."

"Hey! Are you trying to say I'm —" A high velocity snowball shatters Bradford's champagne glass and smashes into his face, leaving him covered in snow and Dom Pérignon. His cheek throbs as he yells outside, "I'll kill the mother fucker that did this!"

With a fuck-you smile, the attendant tells Bradford, "Sir, please refrain from using language of that sort in our place of worship. You may be here for church, but you're part of the wrong religion. Move on."

More cars lay on their horns. Without any offensive weapons available but his mouth, Bradford puts up his window before anything else can be hurled at him. He wipes the debris from his face and tenderly checks his cheek. "Just go, Julio."

—

Jed lounges in a camping chair with an overly gratified smile. Zabka takes a sip of his beer and asks, "What's going on? You look like the guy in *Ghostbusters* who's getting a hum-job from that floating spirit."

"I just had a religious experience." Jed tries to lean his head back but is denied by his blue backboard. "I just pissed myself and it was awesome. And I didn't have to move a muscle to do it — I just *relaaaaxed* my big one. That's what I call freedom! Inventions like these diapers are what makes America great!" He snags a beer from the toilet cooler.

Zabka shakes his head. "Dude, you're fucking crazy."

"I know I am, but admit it — I'm also kind of a genius."

"Yeah, in an idiot savant sort of way." Zabka looks at Bob for a comment. "Can you believe this guy?"

"He's a real outside-the-box thinker," Bob replies. "Actually, he's an outside-the-box *drinker*! Speaking of drinking, can you throw me over a fresh brew?"

"Absolutely." Jed tosses a can over the barbecues on the car hood.

Bob catches it with one hand and cracks it open. "Hey Jed, can I talk to you about something for a minute?"

"You sure can. Come on over here, cuz I ain't movin'."

Bob walks over and they tap the bottoms of their beer cans together. "Yesterday you said you can pretty much do whatever you want in your marriage. Is that entirely true?"

"Yep. Entirely true."

"Is that what made you realize you should get married? Or was it love? Or family pressure?"

Jed repeats the question slowly. "What made me realize I should get married?" He taps his head until he has an ah-ha moment. "I remember. It was when she started bitching about it."

Bob chuckles. "And what caused that?"

"Good question. I thought things were just fine like they were." Jed finishes his beer and crushes it. "Like why fuck a good thing up, right? We'd been together for about four years, and then it just came out of nowhere. Right around this time of year actually."

Bob eyes Jed with skepticism. "So nothing unusual happened leading up to her pressuring you for a ring?"

"I don't think so. I just remember not having much money for Christmas presents because of all the weddings we went to that summer." Jed fishes out a fresh beer from the porcelain potty. "Her younger sister got married too. Yeah, so nothing unusual."

"Really?" Bob laughs. "You don't see the triggers?"

"Triggers?" Jed shakes his head. "There were no triggers?"

"A bunch of your friends and her *younger* sister got married, dummy. That sets off a 'give me a ring' ticking time bomb inside a woman."

Confused, Jed responds, "Oh, I guess I missed that connection."

"Anyway, so after you got married, how's it been?"

"Meh. It's about the same as before — except my wallet was much lighter after that big marriage party."

"You mean the reception?" Bob asks.

"Yeah, that thing with the cake and music — and far too many photos. Oh, and new relatives that I don't want to ever see again. Jesus." Jed rattles the memory out of his head. "Yeah, the reception."

Bob grins. "That sounds lovely."

"Yeah, we've been married for about three years now, so that's like —" Jed performs a calculation in his head. "That's like ten years of being with the same woman."

"It's actually more like seven based on what you told me."

"No, because each year of marriage seems like two. See, this is shit you don't know because you're single."

"I guess not, but thanks for the lesson."

"You're probably wondering if there's anything I miss from before my wife and I got together."

"Actually, you're right. I do. Where's the grass greener?"

"The one thing I miss — I miss more than anything — is my arsenal of dildos," Jed admits. "Oh, the good old days. The wife eventually made me get rid of 'em." While reminiscing, he sings along to the Willie Nelson and Julio Iglesias tune, "To all the girls I've penetrated before."

"Really? That's what you miss about being single?"

"Yep. I had all shapes, sizes, and colors," Jed recalls. "Girls I'd bring home with me were frightened at first, but after a little coaching — and a few more drinks — they'd get extremely excited."

Ken walks over with another man and says, "Hey guys, sorry to interrupt what I'm sure is an enlightening conversation. This is my friend Stan I told you about earlier. He may be able to help you with tickets."

"Hi, nice to meet ya," Stan says. "You guys aren't really Cox fans, are you?"

"No, not at all," Zabka replies. "We're completely goofing on that fucker."

"I thought you were, but just wanted to make sure. So the local radio station WBEN is having a big party closer to the stadium with a band and

THE FOURTH QUARTER | 269

everything. Anyway, I know a few folks over there that might have access to some tickets. I'll take you over if you want."

"That's really nice of you," Bob says gratefully. "Thanks."

"Not a problem," Stan replies. "But before we go, you gotta have one of Pinto Ron's famous shots."

"Sorry, but who the heck is Pinto Ron?" Bob asks.

Stan looks surprised. "That's Kenny. You didn't know that? He goes to every Bills game — home and away. He's a *huge* fan."

"We had no idea." Bob turns to the former Ken, now Pinto Ron. "I assume you're named after your lovely car-grill here, but where'd the Ron part come from?"

Pinto Ron answers, "A reporter wrote an article about me and misprinted my name as Ron. My friends wouldn't let it go and so it stuck." From the backseat of the Pinto, he pulls out a bottle of mysterious liquor, a jar of maraschino cherries, and a bowling ball.

"Oh, shit," Scooter exclaims. "What the hell is this?"

"You'll see." Pinto Ron pours a shot in the thumbhole, places a cherry on top, and hands the bowling ball to Scooter. "Go stand over there away from everybody, take the shot, and then drop the ball." He grabs a red plastic vuvuzela. "You finish by blasting a note with this."

"Like this?" Scooter eats the cherry, puts his mouth over the bowling ball booze-hole, and tips it back with both hands. After sucking down the last drop, he releases the ball, almost dropping it on his foot. He grabs the horn and with Dizzy Gillespie cheeks, struggles to push out a low-pitched note. Upon completing the gauntlet, the group hoots and gives him a loud round of applause.

"What'd ya think?" Pinto Ron asks.

"You know what?" Scooter wipes booze and saliva from his chin. "That shot was pretty damn good! Was that cherry liqueur?"

"That it is," Pinto Ron replies. "I'm glad you liked it! Since you're first timers, you all get a cherry on top." He repeats the process for the rest of the guys and then finally himself, minus the cherry.

"Thanks for your hospitality, Ken slash Pinto Ron," Zabka says. "Shall we go try to wrangle up some tickets, Stan?"

"Let's do it, boys!" Stan shouts. "Follow me."

While heading to the stadium, Bob notices people gathering around one particular tailgate party. "Hey guys, check this out." He points at a Buffalo fan climbing up a ladder on the back of an RV. Once on the roof, the clearly inebriated man flexes his muscles, much to the pleasure of the hooting onlookers.

"What the hell is going on here?" Scooter asks. The crowd parts as a folding table is dragged and strategically positioned next to the RV.

Jed contributes his theory. "I bet this has something to do with tossing midgets. I heard *all* the best tailgate parties play that game these days."

"So tossing a football or playing cornhole is now passé?" Bob asks.

"Pretty much." Jed stops the group. "Let's watch what this fucker does."

Like it's a Pagan ritual, a man plunks the remains of a dolphin piñata on a table, squirts it with lighter fluid, and sets it ablaze. The mob roars, "Jump! Jump! Jump!" The lunatic on the RV raises an elbow, leans forward, and plummets toward the ground. He smashes through the burning effigy, and the plastic table collapses around him. After a few seconds of busted-rib moaning, his adrenaline kicks-in and he pops out of the wreckage. Not-giving-a-fuck, he high-fives the crowd — not yet feeling the spreading flames on the back of his Bills jacket.

"That dude's on fire!" Zabka points. "Hilarious!"

The fans around the blazing jumper douse him with beer, which he fully believes is part of the celebration. A huge woman the size of a water buffalo barrels into the man and body-slams him to the ground — smothering the flames and knocking the wind out of the aspiring stuntman.

Scooter scratches the back of his neck. "Well, that was interesting."

"That sucks — no flaming midgets." Jed sighs. "Maybe at the next tailgate?"

As they continue to the WBEN party, they receive a fair amount of heckling and boos along the way. Zabka moves to the front of the group and arrogantly leads the ass-clown parade through the surrounding circus. He holds two middle-fingers up high and chants, "Let's go Buffalo!" while his friends also join in.

After a couple of snowballs zip over their heads, Stan comments, "It seems like most of the fans aren't getting your joke."

"Yeah, they think we're Miami fans taunting Buffalo," Bob replies. "Obviously, it's quite the opposite. The whole thing is pretty ridiculous, but that's what we wanted, and I love it."

A group of attractive young women in snug one-piece winter Dolphins-getup yell from their tailgate party, "Hey Cox! We love Cox!" Without saying a word, Zabka takes a sharp right in the girls' direction, and the troops follow in stride.

Zabka checks out the girls and declares, "Cox at your service."

"Just what we've been looking for," says the redhead with dangling dolphin earrings. "A bunch of *hard* Cox — except for this one." She studies Scooter and flirtatiously comments, "Looks like girth is your winning trait, cutie. And I'm *way* into that."

The girl with teal earmuffs says to Zabka, "Hey, aren't you friends with Melissa and Stephanie?"

Zabka taps his chin with his index finger. "I'm not sure a threesome necessarily makes us friends. But sure, whatever."

Earmuffs-girl giggles and extends her arms upward, morphing into a Y-shape. "What do you guys think of our outfits?"

Zabka bends down to inspect her crotch. "Is there a little area that opens down here? If so, I'll take you into your van and do you like we'll never see each other again."

"I'm drunk and you're cute — and I'm drunk." She grabs his hand. "Why not? Just control yourself and don't *perform* like a real dolphin. They get-off really fast." With everyone's attention focused on the tailgate version of *Romeo & Juliet*, Jed stealthily pulls beers from the girls' cooler and stuffs as many as he can in his coat.

"Hey!" the redhead yells at Scooter. "What's your sign say? Nobody Blows Cox. Dolphins Suck!?" Her drunken mind spins like a tilt-a-whirl carnival ride. "What the hell? You're not Miami fans!"

Earmuffs-girl releases her grip of Zabka's hand and punches him in the chest. "You're the enemy? That's so fucking wrong!"

"Oh, screw you. You saw what you wanted to see." Zabka looks at her with disgust. "Like I'd ever really fuck you — *pfff*, a Miami fan." He turns away.

As they leave, Jed acts like a beer distribution machine for his friends. He then raises a can over his head for the girls to see and shouts back, "Thanks for the cold-ones, ladies! Squish the fish!"

———

The Miami limo enters a gravel lot and is directed between several large passenger buses. They park and find themselves at the bottom of a valley, surrounded by cliffs of black metal and shiny glass. Faces from all corners of Western New York press against the windows and glare down upon them. The limo shakes as Bambi and Summer groove to "Conga" by Miami Sound Machine. Juan Carlos refills the girls' flutes with bubbly as Bradford uses another champagne bottle to ice his bruised cheek.

"Turn it down, Julio," Bradford shouts. He addresses the cabin, "Juan Carlos and I spoke this morning and assessed our success at the Brew Festival. While we agree it could've gone a little better, and that there was some negative reaction, we disagree on how to approach today. He doesn't want to do any promoting, while I believe we should."

Bambi points to herself and Summer. "So what's that mean for us?"

"I'll tell you. We're gonna go to a tailgating event as couples — Bambi, I thought about the suggestion you gave yesterday — we're gonna socialize, and you girls will pull guys aside and tell them what Huge Member did for Juan Carlos and myself."

"And what type of story are we supposed to make up?" Bambi asks.

"Just say we got bigger — we grew a couple of inches," Bradford replies. "And you loved the results. Stuff like that."

"I've got a great idea!" Bambi shouts with delight. "We should give out before-and-after dong-rulers! That'd be a real game changer!"

"No, not today," Juan Carlos counters. "I still think any promoting is a horrible idea — specifically because of the extremely hostile environment we're in — but Bradford's been very adamant."

Bradford holds up his champagne bottle. "Yes, we're doing this! And then we're gonna watch the Dolphins win the division title!"

Juan Carlos pops open a bottle. "I need to drink more to handle the shit-show we're about to attend. Turn up the music, Julio!" He refreshes everyone's drinks while the girls wiggle and dance in their seats.

Bambi opens the sunroof, sticks her head out, and barely fits her rack through as she stands. She surveys the surrounding area like a human periscope. Through the spaces between buses she observes a zoo of human chaos — drunk girls falling over while chasing footballs, grown men wrestling into smoldering grills, and random parades of people wearing Bills gear and Santa hats. A pack of four sticks out from the rest as it confidently struts through the anarchy, side-by-side in identical half-ass made Bryan Cox jerseys. She slides back inside. "Hey, I just saw a group of Dolphins fans. Looks like we have some allies out there."

"Awesome!" Bradford shouts. "Because the war is about to begin!"

———

Stan and the Cox army march into a large party tent. It's open on one side so the band's music can project outside. On stage, an older black man with a gray beard, straight brim fedora, and a sparkly red tux moves the crowd while he sings "September" by Earth, Wind & Fire. When the song ends, the singer addresses the cheering horde, "Thank you so much, everyone! Is everyone having a good time?!" The rowdy fans throw their hands up and scream as loud as they can. "That sounds like a yes to me! I'm Lance Diamond and for our next song, we'd like to play one by our very own Buffalonian — Rick James!" The bass and drums start pounding out the funk. "This is for you ladies — give it to me, baby!"

"Holy shit!" Scooter exclaims. "This is fucking awesome! Give me another beer, Jed!" Jed complies and fishes a can out of his jacket.

"Hey guys, look at that!" Bob points at a brouhaha across the tent. "Whatever *that* is!" While being chased by security, a short, chunky woman runs through the crowd and knocks people over like a four-foot wide bowling ball striking down pins.

"This is nuts! Are all football games like this?" Scooter asks.

"Here, they are," Bob replies. "Buffalo tailgating is legendary. The fans really know how to get after it."

"Fucking A they do!" Scooter holds out his unopened beer can. "Can one of you guys show me how to shotgun this thing? We need to step up our game."

Zabka and Bob look at each other and laugh. Zabka pulls out his car keys and says, "Sure Scooter, let's do this." Zabka explains how it works, and then they all crack one back and shotgun together.

"Nice job, Scooter!" Zabka yells. "Looks like you only got half of it on your Cox jersey!"

Scooter looks down at the leakage. "Oh, fuck off. That's not too much."

Bob slaps Scooter on the back. "Screw him. You did just fine."

Stan cuts in and says, "Guys, I'm gonna go see if I can round up some tickets for you. Stay right here."

"Will do," Bob replies. "Thanks. We really hope this works out."

Scooter soaks in the pandemonium around them. "What makes this city go so crazy like this? I really like it."

"It's kinda like this," Bob begins. "This area has suffered through some pretty tough economic times. I'm sure you know this from all the history reading you've done, right?"

Scooter nods his head. "Yeah, I do."

"And there's a bunch of other shit that's happened here. The trivia contest reminded us of all that. Anyway, when people are having a rough time, they turn to a cupla things." Bob indicates two with a peace-symbol. "The first thing is, they need to believe in something — something that gives them hope. For some, that's god. For Western New York, it's the Buffalo Bills — they *are* religion. The second thing is obvious — it's boozin' and partying. You mash 'em all together, and WHAM! People have a great time and forget about life for a while. The Bills are an extension of us. If the Bills are winners, then *we* are winners — not ordinary people struggling day to day. Make sense?"

"It totally does," Scooter agrees. "But what if — what would happen if the Bills ever moved? What if they left Buffalo?"

Bob's eyes widen and he palms his forehead. "I can't even imagine — I don't *want* to imagine. It would destroy this town. It would break people's hearts."

"May I comment?" Jed asks. "Specifically on the Jesus stuff."

"Jesus stuff?" Bob tilts his head. "Yeah sure, go ahead."

"Being here — here in this tent." Jed looks up at the sagging tarp ceiling. "It feels exactly like church — minus any trace of morals. Oh, and the abundance of people getting falling-down-drunk doesn't quite fit."

"Great analogy, Jed."

Zabka hits Bob in the arm and points. "Hey, here comes Stan."

Jed remarks, "Shit, I don't like the look on his face." He studies Stan further. "Hang on. No, maybe it's good news."

Stan puts his hands on his hips. "Guys, I asked around to everyone I know and tried my best — but unfortunately I came up with nothing." The Cox crew's bodies fall limp. "I'm really sorry."

"Now what do we do? Is this it? Do we just drink our faces off?" Jed asks everyone as they stare at the ground. "If so, I'm good with that."

Zabka gulps down the rest of his beer, crushes the can, and hurls it at a Miami fan twenty-yards away. "I was really hoping that this would work out."

"Yeah, but hope is not a strategy," Scooter replies. "Hope is — hope by itself is nothing. We've got no plan, no course of action. Nothing."

Bob looks up. "Wait. Scooter, what did you say?"

Zabka summarizes for him, "He said that having hope is shit, and that we're completely fucked."

"No — Hope!" Bob's clap is muffled by his Isotoner gloves. "Hope! The girl from last night that Scooter met at Anchor Bar! Hope!!"

A light bulb flickers inside Scooter's head. "Oh, yeah. Shit, I was supposed to call her. What about her?"

"I heard her say something to you as we left — I feel like it was a clue." Bob hits his head with the back of his wrist. "Ugh! What was it?"

"I know!" Jed yells. "The clue is Tommy Tutone!"

"No, you idiot!" Bob yells. "Oh, I know! She said, 'I'll be close to your heart.' That's it!"

"How's that a clue?" Zabka asks. "That doesn't help us at all."

Bob gets restless and tells Scooter, "Check inside your coat! Hurry up!" Scooter rolls up his Cox shirt to his armpits and unzips his winter jacket. Bob feels around the inside layer and freezes when he lands on something. He reaches his hand in the inside pocket and pulls out an envelope. They look at it like it could be the Willy Wonka chocolate bar that holds the golden ticket. Written on the envelope in pristine female cursive is, "You deserve this."

Zabka jumps up and down like a child on Christmas. "Open it, dammit! Open it!"

Bob uses his finger to rip open the envelope, and he pulls out the contents. After reading it over, he looks up with a frown to their breathless faces. They wait for him to say something, and he just solemnly shakes his head. Crestfallen, they drift into a catatonic state. Bob grins and slaps their faces in one motion like they're the Three Stooges. "Look at this mother fuckers!" He holds up his hand. "We got tickets!!"

Zabka leads the charge and the three of them tackle Bob. They all yell hysterically, "Fuck yeah!!!"

"Ouch!" Bob screams. "You're squishing my nuts, Scooter! Get off me!" They scramble up from the ground and give each other bear hugs.

"We did it!" Zabka shouts. "We got the tickets!"

Scooter smiles proudly. "It turns out that *Hope* is a strategy!"

Jed adds a ludicrous claim about their tactics, "Like Hannibal said on the A-Team, 'I love it when a plan comes together'!"

Bob yells, "Let's dance, bitches!" They joyfully bounce around in circles like the dwarf court jester in the "Safety Dance" video.

"We took a year off from the Super Bowl!" Zabka screams and pounds his chest. "But this year we're going back, baby!"

—

Jennifer walks through the Rich Stadium parking lot bundled up in winter clothing from head-to-toe. Along the way she notices that literally everyone is holding a beer or red Solo cup. She passes people soaking in a miniature hot tub next to a van painted like Bills Zubaz pants.

A man grilling fish yells at her, "Hey, come have a shot with me!"

Feeling completely out of place and far too sober for her surroundings, Jennifer decides to take him up on it. "Why not? Whaddya got?"

He pulls up two bottles. "We got Jack and some cheap tequila."

Jennifer thinks it over. "Let's go with Jack." He pours two shots and they take them down. After a grimace, she asks, "How 'bout one more?"

"I like your style." He smiles at her and pours another round. "Here ya go." After tossing the shots back, he questions, "You here by yourself?"

"Yeah, actually I am." She hands her shot glass back. "It's a long story, but I'm gonna go buy a ticket now."

"Oh, I'm afraid that's not possible." He frowns. "The game is sold out."

"Fuck. Is this like a big game or something?"

He's taken aback. "You're not from around here are you?"

"No — I mean, I live here now and go to school. But I'm originally from California."

"I'm not sure what to tell you." He shrugs. "And I haven't seen any scalpers either. But maybe you'll get lucky."

"Shit, I gotta figure this out." Jennifer turns to leave.

He holds up the bottle of Jack. "One more for the road?"

She hesitates for a second. "Ah, fuck it. Line it up."

He pours two more. "Good luck." After clinking glasses, they down their third shot. "Hey, if you wanna come back and tailgate with us, you're more than welcome. I'm cooking fresh dolphin meat."

"*Eww.*" Jennifer's face scrunches as she sticks out her tongue.

"I'm joking." He laughs. "But as they say — squish the fish!"

"Oh, okay. Thanks for the hospitality." She waves goodbye. "See ya."

Jennifer spots the entrance gates and walks in that direction. About a hundred-yards into her journey, her head begins to spin like a top that's about to fall over. *Too many shots. Keep it together.* She inhales a deep breath of cold air through her nose. Upon reaching Gate 5, she looks around aimlessly, wondering what to do as people bump past her to enter the stadium. She notices an elderly man with a cane in a guest services uniform. She walks up to the fence that separates them and waves for the seventy-years-old man to come to her.

He hobbles over. "What can I do for you, young lady?"

"Hi, I kinda need your help," she tells him.

"How so?"

Jennifer bats her eyelashes. "I need to get inside for the game. It's really important."

"Just go over there." His finger shakes as he points to the gate. "Show 'em your ticket and they'll let you in."

"Well, the thing is — at the moment —" She reaches through the fence and tries to give him her hand. "I don't really have a ticket."

"Well then, I'm sorry, darling. But you can't come in."

Jennifer nibbles on the index finger of her other hand. "Isn't there something we can do about that?" She raises her eyebrows up and down a few times, attempting to be sexy, but it comes across more like Bluto Blutarsky when he's about to start a food fight.

He smiles. "I thought of something."

Still grasping at air for his hand, she asks, "What's that, honey?"

"I'll give you a hint." He uses his cane to lean closer to her and whispers, "It rhymes with blowjob."

Stunned, she pulls her hand back. "You mean, like handjob?"

His body trembles. "No, like blowjob. It's been nine years."

Jennifer shakes her head and backs up. "I just can't do that."

"Okay, fine. You're a tough negotiator." He pouts. "I'll take a handy."

"I didn't say I'd give you —" She stops and thinks, *What would Faige do?* Her mind races. *Remember Jennifer, part of Phase 2 is dedication.* She rotates her right hand in a circular motion and stretches out her wrist. *And desperate times call for desperate measures.* She tells him, "Get me inside, and you've got a deal."

The old man's head nearly explodes.

—

As Bradford leads the others through the parking lot, his head swivels as he scouts the enemy territory for potential threats. The group conceals their true colors under their coats like spies in a foreign land. As they near the tent, they hear garbled music bouncing off cars and campers.

"You guys ready to do this?" Bradford asks.

"This is stupid and a waste of time," Summer tells him. "Talking to a few people will be insignificant in increasing your sales."

"Immediately, yes. So let's call it market research then."

Bambi agrees, "I think that's a good idea."

Summer scoffs, "If that doesn't tell you it's stupid, what will?"

"Maybe you're right. I should be thinking more about your needs —" As Bradford reaches for Summer's hand, Juan Carlos elbows him. Bradford stops and recalls his business partner's advice. "No, forget that. I lead this company, so we're doing what I said — end of discussion. Let's get in there and go to work."

Bradford walks Summer into the party beehive and spots a couple having a good time. He says, "Let's go talk to them. They look like they're having fun and will be easy to talk to."

Summer disagrees. "No, they're not a good target. If we're gonna do this, let's do this right." She points. "See that couple next to them?"

"Yeah, you mean the guy that's staring at the top of the tent and his scowling wife? They look miserable."

"Yep, and that's what makes them the perfect mark. After we start chatting, let's separate them. I want to talk with her privately. Let's go."

They zigzag around people to their objective and Summer engages with the couple. "Hey, this band is really good. You know who they are?"

The grumpy woman answers, "Yeah, that's Lance Diamond. You don't know him? He's a legend around here."

"I'm afraid we don't. We're new in town."

"Oh, well welcome to Buffalo. I'm Patty and this is my jackass husband, Phil."

"Thank you, my oh-so-kind and giving wife," Phil counters. "Shit giving, that is." They awkwardly complete exchanging introductions.

"Patty, can I talk to you for a second over here?" Summer asks.

"Sure," Patty replies and they scoot over a few feet.

"I know we just met, but girlfriend to girlfriend, is it okay if I ask what's wrong?" Summer puts her hand on Patty's shoulder.

Patty looks down. "It's complicated, and I kinda feel weird telling you."

"It's okay. I've had my share of problems with Bradford too." Summer confides in Patty's ear, "Ours were in the bedroom."

"Really? Ours too."

"I know how you feel, but the great thing is we found something amazing that fixed things."

Patty gets excited. "Oh my god! You did?"

"Yes. Bradford used to be too small to give me much pleasure. But that all changed when we discovered these pills." Summer nearly has a fake orgasm as she confides, "They made him HUGE."

Patty's face squirms. "Oh lord, I don't need that. His cock makes horses jealous. It's terrifying!" Patty shakes. "I just can't have sex with him anymore. That's why he's so damn distant all the time."

Summer closes her gaping mouth before speaking. "Oh, wow. I wish I had that problem."

"You know of any magic dick-shrinking pills?" Patty asks.

"I don't think there's a big market for that, so I doubt they exist. Sorry."

Patty shrugs it off. "I didn't think so. Oh, well." The ladies move back next to the men.

"You two have a nice conversation?" Bradford asks.

"Yeah, just a little girl-talk," Patty replies. "She told me about the 'tiny problem' you used to have. For her sake, I'm glad you were able to fix it."

"Um — yeah thanks." Bradford hands her a card. "This is the supplement I used. It's called Huge Member. Let your friends know."

"Nice meeting you," Summer says to the couple. "We're gonna go find a beer." They say goodbye and leave. While walking, they notice Juan Carlos and Bambi in a deep conversation with a couple close to the stage.

Bambi's hands are up as she talks to a muscle-head with a rising temperature, "I was just communicating what your girlfriend told me. She said you could use some help in that department — not me."

The angry man barks, "Listen — first of all, she's being dramatic. And second, only because she begged me, I already tried those *damn pills* and nothing happened!" As Juan Carlos makes a move to escape, Bambi pulls him back.

"You know what? I've got an idea," Bambi says. "Juan Carlos, why don't you take his girlfriend and go get us all drinks — you buy. I'll wrap up our conversation. Sound good?" The girlfriend and Juan Carlos exchange why-not glances and walk away.

"I apologize for all that." Bambi slides her hand up his arm to his broad shoulders. "If I can be candid, I don't think she knows what she's talking about. You look like more than enough man for any girl to handle."

He smiles at her. "Thanks. I'm glad you can see that."

"I know this is a little forward, but can I get your name and number?"

He takes a peek across the room at his girlfriend. "Sure, you got a pen and paper?"

"As a matter of fact, I do." Bambi pulls them out of her purse. "Here."

He takes them from her. "Thanks. I'm Tony, by the way."

"Tony, I'm Bambi." She taps the paper. "Write your last name down too, please."

———

As Scooter exits the dark tunnel inside Rich Stadium, the field illuminates in front of him and he notices that it drops down fifty-feet lower than ground-level outside. He feels like he's entering the arctic version of the Roman Colosseum as bloodthirsty fans scramble for food and drinks, and the gladiators prepare for battle. Armed with two jumbo beers each, the guys stop and soak in the atmosphere. The Bills are running through drills dressed in their home red helmets, blue jerseys, and white football pants. The Dolphins are in all white uniforms except for teal numbers and teal high-socks. The visitors stretch and flop around on the frozen AstroTurf like fish out of water — all while a 19-degree wind chill stabs them through their helmet grills.

Scooter notices the Bills Wall of Fame behind the end zone. "Hey guys, you see that?" He points at O.J. Simpson's number 32. "The Juice is up there. That's pretty cool."

"I wouldn't say that's cool. I'd say it's more of a dilemma." Bob takes a big gulp from one of his ice-cold beers. "Hey, did you guys know that this stadium was built on an Indian burial ground?"

"Get outta here," Zabka replies.

"I'm serious," Bob answers. "Turns out there was a Wenro Indians cemetery right here that was destroyed during excavations."

Scooter reacts like he's in a spooky haunted house. "That's crazy! Does that mean this stadium is cursed?"

Bob nods his head. "Some people think that. They say that the swirling lake-effect winds are the embodiment of spirits intent on sabotaging the Bills." Bob shrugs. "Who fucking knows?"

Jed licks a gloved finger and puts it up for a test. "The wind isn't too bad today, so hopefully they're taking a peace pipe smoke break. Could be a good sign."

As they loiter in the walkway, an usher creeps up. "Excuse me, but you need to take your seats. You're blocking the flow of traffic."

"Sure, no problem." Bob points to the upper level. "Guys, our seats are way up top there. Not the best, but who cares? We're here."

"I care. So I got other plans," Zabka replies. "Follow me." He leads them around the perimeter toward midfield. As they walk in their Cox costumes, various pockets of Buffalo fans boo and curse at them.

Jed tells the guys, "Give 'em the Bryan Cox single-finger salute!" They hold one of their beers with their teeth, and raise their middle-fingers high above their heads — further aggravating the crowd.

Bob starts shouting like a vendor, "Get your gonorrhea here! Get your Bryan Cox gonorrhea here!"

Jed gets hit in the head with a plastic beer cup. "Hey! What the fuck! We're not Dolphin fans! Don't you understand gonorrhea humor?!"

Zabka screams so loud that his face turns red, "Come on, Buffalo! We're mocking Cox! You should be cheering us!"

Bob raises his NBC sign in an attempt to educate the abusive crowd. He spins around in a circle and repeatedly yells, "Squish the fish!"

As they near the 50-yard line, Jed hits Zabka. "This is it comin' up."

Zabka scans the area on the fringe of their destination and gives Jed a wink. He points down the aisle toward the field. "Boys, our seats are this way. Section 111. We've been upgraded!"

Scooter shouts with excitement, "Whatever you say, Zabka!"

They strut down the stairs like conquering heroes about to take what's rightfully theirs. Jed directs them to four empty seats on the aisle in the tenth row. "This is where we are."

"Holy shit!" Scooter does a little dance. "These seats are incredible! How'd we get these?"

"We just took 'em from the Miami dildos, that's how," Zabka replies.

"We did? But what happens when they get here?" Scooter asks.

"I'll ejaculate my awesomeness all over their faces. That's what I'll do." Zabka pokes himself proudly. "Zabka's got everything under control. Just relax and enjoy."

Spitting distance from the Dolphins bench, the guys absorb the energy that fills the stadium. Coach Don Shula looks cool and collected as he walks amongst his players while wearing sunglasses and a white ball cap. In the crowd, a few red Santas are sprinkled in a sea of blue. Different banners draped on the wall near the field read, "Batavia Party Zone" and "Hey Bryan, let's keep it positive. I'm positive you're not winning the AFC East." With five minutes left before kickoff, the guys explain their "uniforms" to the neighboring Bills fans and quickly become friends.

At the walkway above their section, Bradford reviews their tickets and then takes his group down the stairs. "Hey, look at that. There's like four Bryan Cox down there."

"Those gotta be the Miami fans I saw earlier," Bambi remarks.

Juan Carlos puts his arm around her. "Perfect, we'll be in good company."

Bambi recognizes Bob as they near. He senses her gaze behind him, turns, and they lock eyes. She feels short of breath and, without thinking, wiggles out of Juan Carlos's embrace. Her squint and subtle grin tells him, "I know what you guys are up to."

His eyebrows jump twice and silently reply, "Smart girl. Nice rack."

The Miami group stops at the tenth row. Bradford taps the first Cox on the shoulder and rudely declares, "You're in our seats."

Zabka turns and says, "Well, hello. How nice of mister-sits-down-to-pee, señor douchebag, and the butt-plug girls to join us."

Bradford's gut feels like it's been sucker-punched. "These are our seats! Get out! They're not for peasants like you!"

"Oh, yeah? I don't think so." Zabka puffs out his chest like a gorilla protecting its territory. "These are OUR seats!"

Jed shouts, "Put him in a body bag, Zabka!"

Bradford rises up on his tippy-toes and still falls short of reaching Zabka's stature. "*Pfff,* you guys can't afford tickets like this! *Please* — look at yourselves. You put these funny little costumes together with spray paint and duct tape from K-Mart. You're pathetic Buffalo losers!" Like a magnet, the attention of the surrounding Bills fans is pulled their way. "Go ahead. Show me your tickets then. You know you can't do it."

"We don't have to provide evidence." Zabka crosses his arms. "We ain't showing you shit. We're here, and we ain't moving unless *you* can prove otherwise."

From the far end of the Cox line, Bob waves Summer's pink panties. "*Hiii Bradford! Hiii Summer!* What did they say in the O.J. trial? If the condom doesn't fit, you must acquit?"

Bradford jumps at Bob. "You mother fucker!" Zabka quickly moves to his left and uses his chest to deflect Bradford before he can get by.

Juan Carlos tells Bradford, "Just show him the tickets. Heck, show everyone the tickets. This'll be over soon." As Bradford stews, Juan Carlos motions to security to come down.

With a smug expression, Bradford pulls out their tickets. "Here they are! It says right here — section 111, row 10, seats 1 through 4. These are our seats! Now get the hell out!"

"Hey, Summer!" Bob yells. "You wanna go out to the limo — *again?* Or are your lady-bits still sore? I know your tonsils must be!"

Steam emanates from Bradford's forehead as he triumphantly holds up the tickets. "I'll kill you, you tonsil fucker! Remember when we took all your strippers? Women wanna be with guys with money, like us. We made it rain then, and we'll make it rain now." Bradford throws the tickets in Zabka's face and crawls between his legs to go after Bob. He makes it halfway through the wickets before Zabka grabs the top of Bradford's pants, pulls him up, and dangles him like a suspended skydiver.

Bob laughs at Bradford. "Pussy didn't do you any favors just now!"

As a stadium security guard and a police officer approach, the adjacent sections buzz and rise to their feet. The enforcers move Bambi and

Summer aside to reach the bickering. The security guard asks, "Alright, what's going on here?"

Bradford swims in the air. "Make him put me down!"

"Say please," Zabka teases. "Oh, forget it." Zabka releases his grip and Bradford slams onto the concrete.

The security guard asks again, "I said, what's going on here?!"

"I'll tell you." Bradford stands up and holds his elbow in pain. "These losers thought they could just waltz in here and take our seats!"

"I'm sorry, but I beg to differ." Scooter hands to the security guard the tickets he picked up from the ground.

"*Nooo!* Those are our tickets," Bradford cries.

The police officer steps up and says to the Miami group, "That's it. You need to leave and go to your own seats."

Bradford stomps his foot. "We're not going anywhere! We're already at our seats!" He tilts his head while looking at the officer. "Wait a minute. You're that same cop from Friday! What's going on here?!"

Officer Radzikowski smirks. "Either you exit this area or we'll escort you from the game. Do you understand me?"

Bradford can't speak as he rapidly seesaws between rage and rationality. Each sensible swing makes it clear that the deck is stacked against him and tips him back to rage.

"Can I make a suggestion? Just kick 'em out of here," Jed proposes.

"Oh, because they were verbally and physically harassing you?" Radzikowski asks. "Is that what you're telling me?"

Jed shrugs and answers, "Um, yeah?" Bob elbows him. "I mean yeah, that's what they were doing!"

A woman in the row behind them yells down, "Officer, I witnessed the harassment if you need any statements. And so did my husband."

"Alright, let's go." The officer signals for them to start walking. "You can do this the easy way or the hard way. Your pick."

Summer asks, "Bambi, isn't that your sign to say, 'it's *easy* for me to make you *hard*' or something that might help us get out of this?"

"Are you propositioning me?" Radzikowski asks.

"Um, no." Summer veers her eyes to implicate Bambi.

"I advise you not to pull that type of shit." The officer stretches out his arms and drives them up the stairs from behind like a cattle dog.

"The Bills are all you have to live for, aren't they?!" Juan Carlos yells. "You've got nothing else!"

Radzikowski pushes Juan Carlos in the back of the head. "Keep your mouths shut, and *maybe* I'll be generous and not kick you out of the stadium!"

As they leave, the crowd cheers. Zabka jumps up on his seat and yells, "I don't mean to gloat, but go fuck yourself!" Bradford turns to spit a venomous comeback, but thinks better of it.

"That was brilliant!" Scooter shouts. "Unbelievably brilliant!"

Zabka high-fives the circle of hands around him. "I told you I had this shit under control! Now it's time for the Bills to kick some ass! *This* is the year we go all the way! *This* year we take home the Lombardi Trophy!"

———

As the National Anthem plays, Jennifer marches around the stadium's lower walkway for the second time. It's become clear how difficult it is to find someone in the midst of 80,000 drunk people. As she rubs her left thumb into the palm of her sore right hand, she shudders while thinking about the extra long time it took to stroke-out her admission.

A thunderous roar fills the stadium as Steve Christie kicks off for the Bills. After watching Irving Spikes receive the ball for the Dolphins on the 3-yard line and run it back 24-yards, her mouth starts to water for a beer. On the Dolphins first play from scrimmage, Dan Marino hands it off to Bernie Parmalee who tries to cut through the defensive line. Bruce Smith slams into Parmalee at full speed and drops him for a 1-yard loss. The crowd cheers and yells, "BRUUUUUUCE!!!"

Jennifer leaves for the concession area. *If I were those morons, where would I be?* While waiting in line, Jennifer thinks it over. *Of course — the cheap-seats.* After purchasing a beer, she asks one of the ushers to direct her to the nosebleeds. Following a long trek upward, she exits a section tunnel to a full view of the stadium. She senses that the level of intoxication in the atmosphere has increased equally with the elevation.

An elderly woman with a cigarette hanging from her mouth presses into a railing that protects her from toppling over to the lower level. Spit foams around her mouth as she rabidly and rapidly fires obscenities. "Fuck my dry pussy and suck my hairy left nut!" As she continues a tantrum that would rival the vilest of Tourette's outbursts, a father scrambles to cover his young son's ears. After watching the next play and catching her breath she yells, "My vagina tackles better than you!"

Jennifer takes a large, brain-freezing gulp from her beer. *Now what?* As she walks the upper perimeter, she does her best to scan faces and look for anything recognizable like *his jacket or that weird dance he does.* She notices a number of people attempting to get on the TV broadcast by holding NBC acronym signs. Everything from "Not that Bloody Cold" to "Nothing Beats Canadian fans". One crazy woman is even flashing her knockers — much to the delight of her fellow Bills fans. *How are her nipples not freezing off?*

As Jennifer reaches the opposite end zone, the crowd cranks up the decibel level. She pauses to see what's happening and watches the action from above. It's 4th and 1 for the Dolphins on the Buffalo 35-yard line, and Miami decides to go for it. The two lines crouch down across from each other and, like heavy breathing horses, white steam heaves from their helmets. Marino hands off to Kirby and he runs to the left and into a mountain of players for no gain. The crowd erupts as the Bills take over the ball on downs.

The game is just noise to Jennifer as she comes to terms with her needle-in-a-haystack stalemate. Mired in frustration, she thinks, *There's no way I'm gonna find him.*

On the first play of Buffalo's possession, Kelly fakes a handoff to the left and then gives it to Steve Tasker on an end-around. He dashes to the right for a 12-yard gain to the Buffalo 47-yard line. After cheering, a fan tells his friend, "With the Bill's offense banged up and Reed out, Tasker's gonna fill in all over the place. We need a big day from him."

Meanwhile, Jennifer taps her foot on cold concrete — its frigid sting permeating through the soles of her shoes. As her mind almost exhausts solutions, she snaps her fingers. *If I can't find Robert, maybe he can find me?*

———

Bunched together in the entrance of a lower-level tunnel, the Miami crew searches for open seats. On 3rd and 1 from the Miami 3-yard line, the Bills fake a run and Kelly drops back. His pass to Cline in the end zone is low and into the ground. Bambi observes the others clapping and follows along. With it now 4th down, coach Levy decides to try to put some points on the board and sends in the field goal unit. Christie easily knocks it through the uprights to draw first blood and delight the crowd. That gives the Bills a 3-0 lead with 3:39 left in the 1st quarter.

"Fuck!" Bradford shouts.

Juan Carlos consoles him, "Chill, it's a long game. At least we stopped them from getting seven."

"This game is confusing. Why was that 3 points and not 1?" Bambi asks. "Can someone explain?"

"No, absolutely not. We don't have time for this," Juan Carlos replies.

"But you just said it's a long game," Bambi informs him. "So how can we not have time?"

Juan Carlos answers impatiently, "Because we need to find seats."

Summer drops her empty beer on Bradford's foot. "Yeah, we need seats, beer, food — and real men to take care of us."

Juan Carlos holds up a finger. "Hey, what the hell are we thinking? We've got plenty of money to get us whatever we want."

"Yeah, you're right." Bradford swivels around and spots an usher. "Let's talk to her. I bet she can help us out if the price is right." He waves and grabs her attention.

The usher waddles over and scolds them, "I realize the view from the 50 is nice, but you can't stand here all game."

Bradford flashes his seductive eyes. "We know that, and that's why we'd like to upgrade our seats."

"And *where are* your seats?"

"That's irrelevant." Bradford takes out a money clip stuffed with hundred dollar bills and pulls one off. "We'd like — oh I don't know — access to one of your suites." His fake smile badly masks his pompous aura, and patches of teal under the girls' fancy coats poke the usher in the eye.

"*Hmmm,* I see. So you asked *me* because I'm black, and you think you can buy me?" She takes the hundred from his hand. "That's for me listening to this blatantly racist request. But by all means, continue."

Bradford puts his hands halfway up. "Hold on, this has nothing to do with that. We'd just like to upgrade our seats, like I said. If anyone's racist here, it's those four white Bryan Coxes. Have you seen them?"

The usher nods. "As a matter of fact I have. *Shiiit,* they ain't racist. They're funny as fuck."

Juan Carlos steps in. "I swear, we just want to work out a deal, and we've got the cash to do it. Help us, okay?"

"So again, you expect me to let some white southerners — yeah, I see your Miami colors — tell me what to do? Is that it?"

Bradford gulps. "Um, no. Not at all."

"Well, then you'd be wrong." She checks for onlookers and pulls Bradford closer by his collar. "Gimme three hundred more and I'll help ya."

Summer commands Bradford, "Give it to her, stupid."

Bradford stuffs the cash in her palm. "Let's go back over to the other side of the field. There are some jackasses over there I'd like to piss on from our luxury suite."

The usher feels the crisp greenbacks in her hand. "Sure, follow me."

—

Jennifer returns to a viewing area in the upper level with a fresh beer in her hand. *I'm gonna need a little more alcohol to keep this up.*

As she combs lower level of the stadium in search of Robert, a cluster of white pops out at her like a pimple on an otherwise blemish-free face. Under closer inspection, she notices hints of teal and some large blue objects sticking up behind their heads. *Where have I seen that before? Robert's?* She chugs half her beer and belches out a smile. *Yep, Robert's.*

The crowd behind Jennifer roars and she turns to see what the commotion is. What she finds is a happy guy with his face buried between the flashers bare breasts. *That girl sure likes attention.*

—

Bob and Zabka gingerly walk down the stairs to their seats like a four-armed beer delivery robot. They sip as they go — staying hydrated and trying not to spill. When they arrive, Jed and Scooter greet them like they brought water in the desert.

Jed grabs a beer. "Thanks guys! What took you so long?"

Bob shuffles sideways into his seat. "The men's room was crowded. It was so bad, that people were pissing in this circular sink. I thought it was some sort of bizarre community toilet until I saw you can press your foot on this bar to make water come out like a fountain. Anyway, the beer line took forever too."

"I don't mean to brag," Jed boasts. "But I hope it's becoming clear how flawed your process is, and how efficient mine is."

"You mean the process where we go get you beer while you watch the game and piss yourself?" Bob asks.

Jed smiles like a happy baby. "Yep, that's the one."

"I put one on too so I can pee right here." Scooter grins like Jed's mentally challenged twin. "This is life changing."

Bob tells them, "You two are the illegitimate children we never asked for." Bob and Zabka look at each other and shake their heads like disappointed parents. "Don't ever ask us to change your diapers."

"Hey, what about the game?" Zabka glances up at the scoreboard. "We're now up 6-3. We missed seeing a cupla field goals?"

"Yeah, no big deal really," Jed replies. "Ours was from a short distance and was partially blocked, but luckily still knuckleballed through. They kicked a 50-yarder that just made it over. Now we've got the ball back."

The crowd's volume level increases and refocuses the group on the game. From midfield, Kelly unleashes a bomb down the middle that sails deep into Miami territory and within reach of a sprinting defensive back. As if he's the intended receiver, the D-back outstretches his arms and dives forward. The ball hits his fingertips, but he can't intercept it. A yellow flag is thrown away from the play, and the crowd cheers.

Bob jumps and points. "Yes! They saw it! That fucker grabbed and knocked over Tasker! This is gonna go our way!" The referee announces that the Dolphins are being penalized 24-yards for defensive pass interference, which places the Bills 17-yards from the end zone.

Zabka adds, "Hey, they're putting Thurman Thomas back in to run after they rested him." The ball is handed off to Thomas who runs it for a minimal 2-yard gain. The Bills wait for the halftime two-minute warning and go back to the sideline to strategize.

"What are the Bills gonna do here?" Scooter asks.

"They're gonna score a fucking touchdown. That's what," Jed replies.

Zabka huddles up the guys as if he's their coach. "So Thomas missed the game in Miami this year because of a pulled hamstring. And the media's been saying he's injury prone — that he's at the end of his career. But that's all bullshit. I don't think Cox and their shitty defense can stop him today. It's time for the Thurman-ator to pound it in!"

Kelly takes the ball from under the center, hands it to Thomas, and he runs it up the middle for a 4-yard gain. Bob watches the time tick down to 1:40. "We gotta get a touchdown and burn the clock — no reason to leave Miami any time. Makes sense to keep running it here if we can."

"Yeah, but now it's 3rd and 4," Zabka replies. "I don't care how we do it, we at least need a 1st down."

The ball is hiked to Kelly. He drops back and avoids a sack by throwing the ball away out-of-bounds near the end zone. However, a flag was thrown because a defensive end for the Dolphins jumped offside. Instead of it being 4th down, the 5-yard penalty gives the Bills a 1st down on the 6.

"Yes!" Bob shouts. "I can't believe he did that! We'll take it!"

Zabka tells them, "Time to pound, baby, pound!"

The crowd thunders as the teams get in position for the snap. Kelly hands it to Thomas who runs the counter trey misdirection play to the right. He finds a hole and shoots forward before being tackled near the sideline at the 2.

Bob yells, "Yeah, boys! Here we go!"

Kelly gets under the center, Thomas stands behind him, and Brooks runs in motion to the left. Kelly takes the snap, hands the ball to Thomas and he bashes up the middle into the opposing line. Thomas is grabbed by his feet, but is able to generate enough force to push forward as he's falling and put the ball into the end zone. The crowd's throats burst with joy, and the "Buffalo Jills" cheerleaders dance and shake their pom-poms.

Zabka leads his friends in a trampoline-like jumping celebration. "Yeaaah! Muthafuckin' Buffalo!!"

Some after, Christie knocks home the extra point to put the Bills up 13-3.

Zabka tells Jed and Scooter, "Alright, tinkle-twins, time for you guys to go buy a round of beers."

"Yeah, and be efficient about it," Bob commands. "I'm thirsty!"

Jed whacks Scooter on the back. "Alright, let's roll."

With 38 seconds remaining, the Dolphins receive the kickoff and run it back to their 35-yard line. On the next play from scrimmage, Marino drops back and passes to wide receiver Irving Fryar over the middle for a 9-yard completion. The Dolphins take a timeout, and two players help Fryar hobble to the bench after being hurt on the play.

On 2nd and 1, Marino looks deep but can't find anyone open, so he throws a shovel pass to Kirby behind the line of scrimmage. Kirby takes it to the left for 16-yards and runs out of bounds in Buffalo territory. The clock stops with just 15 seconds left in the half.

Now on Buffalo's 40, and with one timeout remaining, the Dolphins are not only fighting the Bills, but also the clock to get at least within field goal range. The crowd yells as loud as they can to help their defense by making it difficult for the Miami players to communicate. From the shotgun, Marino takes the snap and the defense quickly surrounds him. He moves to his left and Hansen wraps his arms around his chest. While trying to escape, Marino slaps Hansen's helmet with his left hand, and as he's about to go down, throws the ball a few yards away to the turf.

"That's intentional grounding!" Zabka shouts.

Bob adds, "Yeah, and Marino is hurt!"

"Yep, they're taking him off the field," Zabka points out. "Looks like he hurt his hand — maybe his left hand?"

Bob gets excited. "Oh, wow! If Marino *and* Fryar are injured, that would be very good for us."

The Dolphins use their final timeout as Bernie Kosar quickly warms up to replace Marino. Because of the penalty, they are moved back to the 50. Kosar takes the ball from the shotgun and tosses a weak, 10-yard Hail Mary looking pass that is 40-yards short of the end zone. Hill makes the reception near the sideline, but can't make it out of bounds before being tackled and time expiring.

"Where are those assholes?" Zabka asks. "I need a halftime beer."

"Who? Scooter and Jed?" Bob turns around and pokes his head in the aisle. "Oh, here they come."

"Gentlemen!" Jed shouts. "We bring you libations!"

"That was pretty quick." Bob takes the beer Jed hands him. "Your game day drinking strategy is growing on me — diapers equals speedier beer delivery. I like it!"

"Hey, you guys see the chick who's flashing everyone?!" Scooter asks.

"What? No, where?" Zabka scans the crowd behind him.

Scooter points to the upper level. "She's up there."

Bob puts his hand above his eyes like a salute and looks in that direction. "I don't see her. Shit, maybe we missed her."

Scooter continues, "I overheard some people talking about her in line. They said they saw her showing off her cans down here earlier."

"Sounds like a serial flasher, so there's a good chance she'll be back," Bob concludes. "Gentlemen, keep your peeping eyes on alert."

—

The second half of the game has begun, and a hot-air balloon floats at a low altitude just outside the perimeter of the stadium. As a frigid gust of wind sweeps across the upper deck, Bradford buries his head in Summer's chest for protection and looks like a baby searching for a milky snack. From their perch, four rows down from the highest part of the stands and even with the 10-yard line, Bambi comments, "I'm not sure who has better seats. Us or that balloon?"

"Yeah, this whole weekend has been a mess," Summer complains. "Could we have ended up with shittier seats? I don't think so."

Bradford puts his arms out. "Hey, I tried to get us into a suite, but this is the best that usher said she could do."

Summer pushes him away. "We shouldn't even be up here in the first place! You got all hot-headed down there and fucked us!"

"Stop your arguing for a second," Juan Carlos tells them. "We're about to kick a field goal." They watch the teams get down in formation as fans wave flags and banners behind the goal posts. The ball is hiked to the holder, who places a pointed-end on the turf, and Stoyanovich boots it through the goalposts for another 3 points.

Bradford claps as a minimal portion of the crowd cheers. "Hey, now we're only down by a touchdown."

"Big deal," Summer whines. "I need a beer."

Bradford tells her, "Well, go get one then."

Summer's glare at Bradford says, 'Did you really just say that?' She replies, "No, that's your job. I shouldn't have to tell you these things. You dragged us to this hell hole and now you want me to go get my own beer?" She shakes her head. "I don't think so, mister."

Bradford regretfully concedes, "Fine, I'll go get a couple after I finish this one."

"I got a question," Bambi says.

"Dare I say, what is it?" Juan Carlos responds.

"Is it a thing at these games to take off your top?" Bambi points down and one section over. "See that guy standing up — the one with no jacket and a hairy gorilla back. Are the people mental here? It's like negative 50 degrees out or something!"

"They're crazy," Juan Carlos explains. "You'd have to be to live here of your own free will. That's the only explanation I can come up with."

"Yeah, and it's not just that guy," Bambi says. "Earlier, I saw a woman flashing too. I'm not jealous, but I would be if I was Summer. The woman's got a hell of a rack — grade A natural double-Ds."

Bradford's head pops up like an erect nipple in Buffalo winter. "Oh, yeah? Where is she?"

Summer hits Bradford's arm and shouts, "You shut your hole! And you too, Bambi!"

The crowd's volume level turns up a notch as Buffalo fans groan and swear furiously. Juan Carlos yells, "Oh shit! We intercepted it!"

Bradford screams, "Fuck yeah!" He stands up and mocks the crowd. "Who's squishing who! The fish are squishing!"

Bradford feels cold beer pouring on his head and jerks around to find a 6'3", two-hundred-and-seventy-pound man towering above him. The giant says to him, "Fish like to be wet, right?" Frightened, Bradford accepts the rest of the liquid in his face as the man continues, "How about when you go get your sexy lady here a beer, you get one for me too." He shakes his empty cup. "Seeing as how I'm fresh out."

Bradford wipes his face with his sleeve. "Um, I'll see what I can do."

Summer punches Bradford. "You're such a pussy."

The Dolphins get in formation for their first play after taking the ball from the Bills. Marino's finger was dislocated at the end of the first half, so his middle and ring fingers on his left hand are taped together. He takes the snap on Buffalo's 25 and drops back. Green runs up the middle of the field for the Dolphins, and Marino puts it perfectly over his shoulder and in his hands. He runs 5-yards to the goal line where Darby hits him at full steam and knocks the ball out. The officials hesitate at first, but then the side judge rules the ball crossed the line for a touchdown.

Bradford feels warm breath on the back of his neck as the behemoth behind him says, "I wouldn't cheer if I were you." Bradford and his pack decide it's for the best to celebrate on the inside. After the extra point sails through, the score is tied at 13 each with 7:51 left in the third quarter.

"Okay, I'm gonna go get those beers now," Bradford announces to the group. "Juan Carlos, you wanna give me a hand?"

The girls look at each other with a bit of unease at the thought of being left alone. "How about we join you," Summer suggests. "We can get more beer that way. And maybe find some binoculars too."

Bambi says, "Yeah, plus I need to do something — I mean I need to go tinkle."

Bradford stands up. "Yeah, let's go." As they all walk down the stairs, "Rock and Roll All Night" plays over the loud speakers and keeps the fans loose and rowdy.

—

After Thomas is tackled at the Miami 12-yard line, Scooter stands and scans the crowd behind him. Like an excited boy seeking a peek at his first nude centerfold, he points to the upper level. "She's up there! I see her!"

Zabka turns and follows the invisible line from his finger to its target. "Oh yeah, there she is!" The guys' eyes focus in on the well-endowed woman who's literally letting it all hang out. Different pockets of fans hoot and holler when they notice. Large reflector glasses and a furry winter hat hide the top half of her face.

Scooter leans his head back and pushes out his groin. *"Daaamn!* She's got some *niiice* titties! Those suckers must be freezing!"

"Yeah, they could use some warmin' up!" Bob frantically waves his arms to grab her attention. Once they lock eyes, he holds his heart and tilts his head like he's in love, and then gestures for her to come down. In response, she points at her crotch and motions for him to enter the tunnel below her — the symbolism of which is not lost on Bob. He smiles and gives her a thumbs-up. To tie-a-bow on their public display of foreplay, she yanks up her sweater and wags her breasts.

Bob elbows Scooter and brags, "You see that?! I just set up a date with the flasher!"

"You dog, you!" Scooter shouts. "I should be learning from you, not Zabka! None of his lines work."

Zabka's chest balloons. "Hey, who's the only one here who's gotten laid all weekend?"

"Yeah, by a total nut-job," Bob replies. "Who, by the way, you've had sex with before. So that doesn't count."

"The hell it doesn't!" Zabka shouts.

"So if I had sex with Jennifer, would that count?" Bob asks.

Zabka rubs his earlobe. "Well, no. She's your girlfriend — or whatever she is now."

"See — doesn't count."

Zabka brushes-off Bob and crows, "Whatever, man. I got laid."

Jed pushes Zabka into Bob. "Hey, while you dickwads are having your sword fight, the Bills are close to scoring. Pay attention." They refocus on the action on the field. "There was a holding penalty on us, and then Kelly threw one for 7-yards."

Zabka looks up at the scoreboard. "So it's 3rd and goal on the 11. We gotta get a touchdown — no more of this field goal shit."

"Yeah, Marino and the offense are starting to get it together," Bob adds. "We can't afford not to get 7 this time."

From the shotgun, Kelly takes the snap and gets good protection in the pocket. As Thomas races across the back of the end zone, Kelly zips a low bullet passed a Dolphin defender's outstretched arm. Thomas falls on purpose to catch the ball in his chest for a touchdown. The Bills fans thrust their arms skyward and erupt. As Kool & The Gang's "Celebration" plays, it accurately describes the mood of 99% of the dancing crowd. Zabka howls, but also thinks, *It's way too early for them to be playing this song.* After Christie kicks the extra point, Buffalo's lead ticks up one more to 20-13 at the close of the 3rd quarter.

"This game is fucking awesome!" Bob shouts. "But please excuse me. I must go meet up with a sweet pair of knockers. See you guys in a bit!"

—

After a fifteen-minute wait in line, Bradford, Summer, and Juan Carlos move to the side so the drunk couple in front of them can leave with their foamy top beers. Bradford reaches the counter and says to the person at the register, "We'll take eight beers."

The concessions manager yells, "No more alcohol sales! End of third quarter!"

Bradford whines, "You've got to be fucking kidding me!"

The concessions manager overhears Bradford's complaint and steps up to him. "No sir, we are not. Perhaps I could interest you in a few pops instead?"

"Fuck this place." Bradford huffs and turns around to his group. The line that had been behind them has evaporated. "It can't get any worse than this. Where's Bambi?" He scans the sparsely populated concession area. "Not that I really care."

"She said she had to take a leak," Juan Carlos replies.

"The rocket scientist is down there." Summer points down the large, poorly lit area under the stands. "Who's she talking to?"

Juan Carlos squints and says, "It's hard to tell with the outside light behind her. Let's walk over." Bambi, a few police officers, and a couple of other men come into focus as they approach. He asks her, "Hey, what's going on? Everything alright?"

"I'm afraid I have some bad news for you, gentlemen." Bambi flashes her credentials. "My real name is Barbara, and I'm with the Food and Drug Administration. My colleagues and I have been investigating The Growth Firm and your Huge Member product for several months."

The two business partners react as if they've just woken up from a blackout and discovered 'the woman' next to them has a mismatched set of genitals. Juan Carlos moans, "You cannot be serious."

"Oh, I am. And you Juan Carlos were the perfect mark. I played a role that I knew would lure you in. The information you shared with me will come in very handy during the trial."

"Trial!? I never said —" Juan Carlos nearly faints.

"This is ridiculous," Bradford says flippantly. "We want our lawyers."

Barbara squares up to Bradford. "I've been monitoring your financials, collecting consumer complaints, and compiling a list of the falsehoods you knowingly market. The FDA has a very strong case against you."

"I had nothing to do with all this," Summer petitions. "I was bored and came for fun this weekend. I don't even work for the company. Plus, they told me this stuff was legit."

"Summer, even though you acted like a real *cunt*, that's not legal justification to detain you. And even though I know you knew damn well what you were peddling, technically you aren't an employee. However, we will be bringing you in for testimony. For now, you're free to go. Bradford and Juan Carlos, you're coming with us."

As the officers move to apprehend them, Bradford shouts, "Suck my taint!" He grabs Juan Carlos by the jacket and pulls him backward. As the culprits sprint away, the officers follow in hot-pursuit.

———

Bob enters the tunnel to rendezvous with the flasher. Inside, he rounds the corner, continues through a smattering of people, and nearly steps on an over-served Santa lying on the ground. He peruses the cavernous hall until a girl that's slowly weaving her way through traffic like a cautious drunk driver catches his eye. As fate would have it, that girl happened to be the exact one he was looking for.

A clamor behind Bob echoes down the hall and turns his attention. Two men are sprinting like they're being chased by hungry tigers, as three policemen follow in hot-pursuit. As the fleeing prey nears, Bob zooms in on their contorted faces. *That's fuckin' Bradford and Juan Carlos.* Adrenaline pumps as he puts on an imaginary Bills helmet and makes a calculation using their speed and trajectory. His feet take over and he rushes toward the estimated collision point. As he's running, he hears the voice of a German female yell, "Hôlt!" and watches a flying mustard-covered hotdog bounce off his target's faces. Blinded by grease and yellow condiment, they never see Bob coming as he dives through the air. His outstretched arms crush their Adam's apples, and momentum sweeps their legs — slamming their backs onto the concrete. The Miami suspects writhe in pain as the officers nab them.

Bob looks for the woman who chucked the hotdog, and to his surprise, discovers it was Dr. Cramps. She snickers while he tells her, "Great aim! Thanks for the assist!" She gives him a few heavy claps of approval and leaves.

Officer Radzikowski helps Bob to his feet and says, "Thank you. That was incredible! You and your buddies are amazing!"

"No need for thanks." Bob grins. "Clotheslining those douchebags was my pleasure." He glances back at the flasher. "But if you'll excuse me, I have another pleasure to attend to."

Bob struts over to the flasher. Without a word, she takes his hand and pulls him into the nearest ladies' room. Her nonchalant attitude coupled with his healthy buzz lessens his jitters. His condition chimes in and informs him, *You haven't a clue what you're doing.* Women in the restroom shoot him dirty looks, not because of his presence, but because he's dressed like Bryan Cox. As they move from stall to stall and check under, they're disappointed to find them all occupied. To their relief, the last one is not only open, but it's also handicapped and roomy. As they step inside and close the latch, Bob's excitement isn't the only thing growing.

The woman, still wearing her sunglasses and winter hat, pulls up her sweater with one hand and yanks Bob's head between her breasts with the other. Her warm flesh-earmuffs bring a smile over his smothered face. She then grabs his crotch and, after a satisfactory status check, turns around, drops her pants, and bends over like a dog in heat.

Bob's jeans are around his ankles before he can comprehend what's happening. *Is this for real?!* As he removes his boxers, his little camper springs out of its tent like it just heard a grizzly bear, and quickly slips into her cozy sleeping bag. *Carpe vajayjay!* For stability, she grabs the handicap railing attached to the partition dividing them from the neighboring stall. While his piston is popping, the metal wall shakes like there's an earthquake. He notices the neighbor's foot through the floor space and closes his eyes to remove the distraction and enjoy the ride.

A harsh bang on their door diverts his attention once again. A voice from outside yells, "Hey, I'm in a wheelchair and need to pee badly! Stop your gallivanting and get outta there!"

The flasher reached back between her legs, gently tickles his chilled Rocky Mountain oysters, and sends him into orbit. After a simultaneous release of endorphins and DNA, his hips come to rest, and they both pull up their pants. In ecstasy, Bob tells her, "That was incredible. I apologize for not being more of a gentleman — I forgot to ask you your name."

Her crooked mouth frightens him, and she shouts in a very familiar tone, "What the hell do you mean by that?! You don't know who I am?!" As she tears off her hat and glasses, Jennifer reveals herself.

Realizing his biscotti just got caught in her cookie jar, Bob stammers, "Oh, no, um. Of course I knew it was you — and once I was inside you, I knew for sure." He winces and waves meekly. "Hi honey."

"You mother fucker! You didn't know it was me!" Jennifer's scream echoes off the walls. "You just cheated on me!"

"What are you talking about?! This is a 'Piña Colada Song' type of situation here." Bob scrambles as if he's trying to defuse a ticking time bomb. "You know how it goes with that couple, their personal ads, and when they meet up — now's that moment — that moment we laugh!" He begins humming the catchy tune.

"Asshole!" Jennifer's face boils red as she pulls her hair back. "I did something bold and different to spice up our relationship! I came into your world! And you go and *cheat* on me?!"

"Bullshit! You stalked me here!" He leans in at her with his arms out. "And how the hell did I cheat on you?! I had sex — WITH YOU!"

"The facts don't lie! You had sex with some random woman! Someone you thought wasn't me!" She looks at the filthy floor and huffs. "I'm such a fool. And to think that I was gonna give you an expensive couple's massage for Christmas — it literally makes me want to vomit."

Bob steps back. "A couple's massage?! Really?! I don't even like massages! That gift has everything to do with you!"

The handicapped woman pounds on the door. "Are you two freaks about finished? I'm close to pissin' in my damn knickers!"

"Yeah, we're finished." Jennifer crosses her arms as she stares Bob down. "Finished for good!"

He looks at her cross-eyed. "What? You've got to be kidding me."

"You're dead to me, Robert." She rips open the door and storms out.

"Good!" He yells at her backside. "Because Robert's dead to me too! I'm fucking Bob now!"

The woman in the wheelchair looks at him and laughs. "Enjoy fucking Bob. I'm sure you two will make a lovely couple." She then proceeds to whack him in the nuts with her cane, which curls him over in pain. "Now get the hell outta there before my bladder explodes!"

After a much needed recovery period, Bob arrives back at his seat and says to Zabka, "You're never gonna believe what just happened."

304 | SQUISH THE FISH

"No, you're never gonna believe what just happened." Zabka points to the scoreboard. "Goddamn Dolphins ran one in for a touchdown and tied it up 20-20."

"Shit, that sucks! But I've gotta tell you something crazy."

Zabka's attention remains on the field. "Let's wait 'til later. We're halfway through the 4th quarter — time to focus on the game."

"Yeah, you're right."

After Miami's fair catch on their own 9-yard line, their offense prepares to attempt a long drive down the field. Marino takes the snap from under center and drops back close to the goal line. Looking down field, Marino fires a pass at Fryar as he hooks back from the 25-yard line. On defense, David White makes a gigantic leap at the 20, twists around, and picks off the ball high above his head. He turns 180 degrees and runs it back to the 11 before getting tackled. The crowd goes bonkers as Marino hangs his head, and the Bills players jump for joy.

Zabka goes crazy. "Holy shit! That's so huge!"

"Yeah! Fuck yeah!" Scooter screams.

Zabka pounds the top of Scooter's head. "That guy White that made the interception — he didn't even play last year. No team wanted him. Unbelievable!"

"I just pissed myself!" Jed yells. "I love *the* Buffalo!"

"Alright, guys." Zabka shakes with adrenaline and nerves. "We gotta get this bitch in the end zone."

The Dolphins defense plays tough on the next two plays, only allowing 3-yards as the Bills run with Tasker and Thomas. On 3rd and 7, the Bills huddle before the critical play.

"We gotta penetrate here!" Bob screams violently. "Give it to 'em! Stick it in hard! Find a hole and pound it! Pound the shit out of it!"

Jed leans over to Bob in front of Scooter and says, "This might not be the right time to ask, but are you watching football or directing a porno?"

Bob laughs. "Midget porn, of course. Now shut up and watch the game."

From the shotgun, Kelly takes the hike and pitches it to Thomas on his left. The ball arrives a little behind him, so he slows and catches it with one arm. Thomas looks for a hole, but with the timing of the play thrown off, he's only able to run a yard before getting tackled on the 7. It's now 4th and 6.

"Shit!" Zabka yells. "We blew a golden opportunity!"

"I know! Dammit!" Bob stomps his foot. "This is gonna come back and bite us in the ass — I just know it! Marino has more than enough time to drive for a touchdown — or a field goal at the very least."

"Let's not get ahead of ourselves, we still need to kick this one in first. Here comes Christie."

Bob shares his analysis, "This *should* be a gimme from this distance. But with the Bills, nothing's a gimme."

The holder for the field goal attempt sets one knee on the 15-yard line. He takes the snap, places the ball down perfectly, and Christie swings his right leg through the ball. The ball sails through the air, between the yellow sticks, and into the net, putting the Bills up by 3 points. As the score changes to 23-20, the crowd bounces and sings, "The Bills Make Me Wanna Shout!" a remake of the Isley Brothers' classic, "Shout".

The crowd shows no sign of calming down as the ball is kicked off to the Dolphins. Spikes returns it to the 22-yard line, putting them in position to try to make a long push downfield with 6 minutes left.

Zabka turns to Bob and says, "Okay, so back to what you were saying earlier. What was so crazy? Was the flasher kinky?!"

Bob begins his story, "Well, a couple of things happened when I went to meet her. First thing was I saw those Miami guys being chased by the police, and so I tackled them."

Zabka gives Bob a high-five. "That's amazing! I wonder what those dickheads did."

"I don't know, and I don't care," Bob replies. "I laid them out hard, and they were taken away in cuffs. I couldn't ask for a better ending for that whole debacle."

"Yeah, *fuck* those guys." Zabka rubs his hands with excitement. "So what about the flasher?"

Bob shrugs. "Nothing much happened. She just took me into the ladies' room and I banged her in a stall."

"No fucking way!" Zabka pounds Bob on the back. "Shit, I'd take a stall-fuck over a dumpster-fuck any day. It's much more romantic."

"Ha ha. I agree."

"So, I guess this means you're over that messy thing you had going with Jennifer?"

"Here's the part you're not gonna believe. Are you ready?" Bob asks. "That flasher was Jennifer!"

"What!?" Zabka yells. "Those tits are yours for the taking? Those suckers are amazing! I've never been jealous of you — actually I've never been jealous of anyone — but I am now!" He shakes his head. "Damn, I really don't like this feeling."

"Well, sadly, those beautiful breasts aren't mine anymore."

Zabka squints and cocks his head. "I'm confused — you just banged her. Explain."

"Basically we fucked and I didn't know it was her. Then she accused me of cheating and broke up with me."

"What?! That's the most ridiculous thing I've ever heard!" Zabka replays the scenario in his head. "You know what? Who cares? She was no good for you anyways."

"I don't know." Bob thinks it over. "Yeah, maybe."

Zabka leaps into the air and pecks his finger rapidly at the Dolphins sideline. "Cox is coming our way!" He makes a megaphone with his hands around the edges of his mouth and shouts, "Hey Cox! Don't get all-mad because you suck and do something stupid again! Hey, over here!" Zabka holds up two middle-fingers and so do his fellow mockers. "Look at what it looks like when four of *you* give *you* the finger!" Cox walks away in the other direction. "Yeah, I knew you were a pussy!"

"Watch the game, goddammit!" Scooter shouts. "I can't take this, I'm so nervous!"

"If we can put pressure on Marino and stop the pass, we'll be fine," Zabka says. "Their running game has been shit all day, and they've got one of the best quarterbacks of all time. That spells pass, pass, pass for them. Should I run over and let our defensive coach know?"

"Something tells me he's way ahead of you," Bob replies.

"Holy shit, this place gets loud!" Scooter yells.

"Shut up and scream!" Bob shouts.

On 2nd and 6 from the Miami 38, Marino sends a pass over Fryar's head and into Buffalo's sideline area for an incompletion.

"What did I tell you?" Zabka proudly states. "Pass. And another one's coming. We gotta stop this 3rd down!"

Everyone in the crowd is on their feet, including the disabled who are lifted up by friends and family. With the crowd volume at jet-takeoff decibel levels, Marino waits in the shotgun. After the hike, he has good protection and time to look for an open receiver. With McDuffie in his sights 20-yards down field, Marino throws a dart at his chest. Bennett, who's standing watch in the middle of the field for the Bills, reads Marino's eyes and hastily moves to his right. Just before the ball reaches McDuffie, Bennett practically extends his arm out of its socket and deflects the ball with his fingertips. Like cocaine to a crazy rock star, the wild crowd cranks it up to eleven. The Miami offense drags to the sideline and their punt team trots on the field.

"Our defense is playing off the charts!" Zabka shouts. "I feel really good about this!"

"Yeah, but there's still four-and-a-half-minutes left to play," Bob replies. "That's a lot of time."

"There's no way we can lose this, right guys?" Scooter asks.

"I've watched a lot of Bills games, and far too many have ended in heartbreak," Bob confides. "This is part of their curse — they lead you to believe you're gonna win and that leaves you exposed. I, for one, am

308 | SQUISH THE FISH

gonna protect the family jewels." He puts his hands in front of his crotch. "Because, like it or not, you have to be prepared for a groin kick."

———

Jennifer walks through a parking lot jam-packed with cars but devoid of people. As the stadium roars behind her, it pains her to picture Robert enjoying himself during her time of misery. After reaching the edge of the lot, Jennifer beelines it across the street to the Big Tree Inn. Desperate to find a phone to call Faige, she enters. At the bar there are a handful of patrons watching the end of the game on TV. The bartender notices her and waves a white bar towel. *Do I know him?* She squints and approaches. *He's kinda cute.*

"Hey, Jennifer," he says. "What are you doing here?"

She tilts her head. "Um, sorry, where do I know you from?"

Disappointed, he answers, "Law School. We're in Advanced Legal Research class together. I'm Joe."

"Oh yeah, that's right. I'm so embarrassed, Joe. How are you?"

"I'm good, thanks. Just working here part time to help pay the bills." He points at the taps. "Can I get you a beer or something? On me."

"Oh, that's okay. I'm really not in the best of moods and need to make a call. Is there a phone in here?"

"Yeah, it's around the corner by the bathrooms." Joe points and hooks his finger. "I hope you'll reconsider a drink after you're done." He grins at her. "Bartenders are known to be easy to talk to."

The pain of what happened with Robert permeates through her mind and she forces a smile. "I'll think it over."

She walks to the back, drops a quarter in the payphone, and dials Faige's number. After several rings, the answering machine picks up. On the verge of sobbing, Jennifer leaves a message, "Hey, it's me. I did what you said, *sniff*, I was bold. I went to the game, found Robert, and, *sniff*, he cheated on me." As tears roll down her cheeks, Robert's protein-tears roll down her leg. "He —"

Faige picks up the phone. "Dat scumbag!"

"Oh thank goodness you're there."

A muffled moan and a high-pitch "*uuuh*" travel across the wire and into Jennifer's ear.

"Are you okay?" Jennifer asks.

"Oh — *OH* — yeah. Sawree, *oh god*, come ova in a ow-a and we'll tawk. I gotta — *uuuh* — go."

Jennifer hears a click, looks with confusion at the receiver, and hangs-up. *What the hell?* She returns to the bar area and says to Joe, "Ya know what? I'm gonna take you up on that beer. Plus a shota whiskey."

Joe grins. "Great, I'll join you! Let's do this!"

Meanwhile, back in Faige's apartment, she's on her couch, spread-eagle and naked from the waist down. As a tongue goes-to-town between her legs, she grabs a tuft of the scalp's short hairs and pushes down. Faige arches her back — her mouth wide-open — and squeaks like a mouse with its tail caught in a mousetrap. After a half-dozen groin spasms, she slowly collapses like a balloon losing air.

As the head rises from its dining area, Faige glows. Her female carpet-munching companion wipes away the glossy ring of secretions that circle her mouth and says, "You taste like chicken... chicken of the sea."

"Tanks." Faige's eyes roll up and to the side. "I tink."

"I knew at the OUTLaw dinner, this moment would come."

"I knew it would come too." Faige grins. "And girl, did I cum."

"Happy to be of service. Was that Jennifer on the phone?"

"Yep. I tink she broke up wit' her boyfriend. She's on 'er way ova."

"Perfect." Faige's new "friend" licks her lips. "Let's get her on our team."

—

Back inside Rich Stadium, Thomas is tackled on the Miami 46-yard line, and the officials blow their whistles and wave their hands. The Dolphins have taken their third timeout of the Bills possession with 2:38

remaining in the game. Still down by 3 points, the Dolphins are fighting to get the ball back with enough time to score.

"Burn baby, burn!" Bob shouts while giving a few Travolta *Saturday Night Fever* pointers in the air. "That was their last timeout and we've done a hell of a good job running time off the clock."

Zabka runs some calculations in his mind. "I think if we can manage to get one more 1st down, we can burn the rest of the clock."

Down on the field, Jim Kelly surveys the stadium and absorbs the energy as "Enter Sandman" pumps up the crowd. He smiles as he walks over to his players near the 50-yard line where painted on the turf is a large red helmet with a blue Bills logo. "You guys see the numbskulls in the stands behind the Dolphins bench? They're all dressed like Cox."

Thomas looks over and spots them in the crowd. "Oh yeah, I see 'em." He laughs and shakes his head in his helmet. "White people do the funniest shit."

Gardner, the fullback, asks, "Where?" He jumps up and down. "I'll murder 'em!"

Kelly ferociously responds, "Take it out on the real Cox! Those guys are a joke. Cox is a joke! Miami's a joke! Now let's put this game away!!"

The Bills and Dolphins line up across from each other on 2nd and seven. Kelly takes the snap, gives it to Thomas behind him, and he cuts up the middle through the defense for a 5-yard gain. Buffalo lets the clock run down to the 2-minute warning.

Zabka says to the guys, "This will pretty much do it if we can get 2-yards for the 1st down."

"Yeah, but if we don't, it'll be 4th down and we'll have to punt. Then they'll have about a minute thirty left to work with," Bob adds. "And my balls don't like thinking about that possibility."

"I know, you know, and the Dolphins know we're gonna give it to Thomas," Zabka says. "It all comes down to who punches harder. Here we go!" He pounds his hands together.

Everyone's attention in the stadium is on the play. Kelly gives the ball to Thomas — he cuts left, rushes forward, and slams into Cox near the line of scrimmage. Cox grabs Thomas around the waist and stops him in his tracks. As Cox falls backwards to the ground, he tries to pull Thomas with him. Thomas's second-effort temporarily slips him away from Cox's grip, allowing him to jut ahead close to a 1st down before Cox finally pulls him down by his ankles.

Cox and Gardner jump up and yell at each other. Their teammates' attempts to restrain them are futile as Cox loses his temper, grabs Gardner's helmet, and lands several haymakers. Gardner counter-attacks by throwing a few retaliatory punches. The altercation is finally put to a stop when the refs pull the boxers away from each other.

As Zabka gets up on his seat, the rest of the Cox quadruplets follow his lead. They give Cox an eight-barrel salute and Zabka yells, "You just blew the game, dumbass!"

Cox moves to his respective corner on the Dolphins sideline and takes off his helmet. White steam bursts from his gasping lungs as he faces the field, full of rage with his arms on his hips. Fierce spit expels from his mouth and freezes before reaching the ground.

The referee comes out and indicates a personal foul against Buffalo and a personal foul against Miami. He announces, "Number 35, Buffalo, is ejected. Number 51, Miami, is ejected. We'll have a measurement."

This sends an angry Gardner off to the Bills' locker room. As Cox struts off the field, he removes the tight white insulation garment from around his head and neck. He spits profusely in multiple directions at the stands and enters the tunnel surrounded by screaming Buffalo fans. As he's ushered through, trash rains down upon him.

The officials run out the chains to measure if the Bills picked up a first down. They stretch the chain and put down the orange marker, which indicates the Bills made the first down by the length of a football. The crowd goes ape-shit with happiness and relief.

"That first down was so clutch!" Bob yells.

"Thomas is the fuckin' man!" Scooter bellows.

Bob and Zabka react with amusement to Scooter's comment. "Damn right!" They bark in unison and pound Scooter's back.

Cornelius Bennett hops down Buffalo's sideline and joins in with the elated crowd. As he howls, stomps, and waves his arms up and down, the fans scream with pride.

Buffalo gets in victory formation, hikes the ball, and Kelly takes a knee to end the play but keep the clock ticking. With 24 seconds left, they repeat this for a third time and are able to let the clock run out.

Kelly bounces around and puts the ball up over his head. As the players exchange friendly hugs and handshakes on the field, confetti flies in the stands. Along with 80,000 of their closest friends, the four Coxes sing with their arms around each other, "Hey ey ey ey! Hey ey ey ey!" to the Bills "Shout" song.

"They *all* said the Dolphins are going to the Super Bowl this year!" Zabka yells. "Well, look at who just won the *mother fuckin'* AFC East!"

Bob leans back and screams, "The Bills are back, baby!" He borrows a red Bills hardhat from the fan in front of him and puts it on Scooter.

Scooter yells until it hurts, "Squish the fish!!"

Jed pounds Scooter's head. "Time to RAGE!!!"

Postgame

The crowd flows out of the stadium gates and into the parking lot like a school of fish. As the Cox squad marches, they sing, "I gotta feeling, Buffalo's going to the Super Bowl!" Then, out of nowhere, a large slobbering man wearing a furry, blue, Flintstones Water Buffalo hat grabs Scooter in a reverse bear hug.

Zabka rips the guy away and throws him to the ground. "You stay the fuck away from him! Nobody messes with us!"

From the dirty snow, the man shouts back, "He's a Cox loser and so are you!" He rolls onto his back and thrusts up his arms. "Buffalo!!"

"Goddammit! For the last time!" Bob holds up his torn sign with beer-streaked lettering. "Look at this, asshole! We're Bill fans!"

Jed grabs Zabka and Bob by their shirts, pulls them sharply to the left, and yells, "Hey, Scooter! Over here!"

Scooter scurries to join them. "What are we doing?"

"See that small bus there with the tall flags?" Jed points over a few rows of cars. "The one with people funneling beer on the roof."

"Yeah, can't miss it," Bob replies. "Oh, I know who they are."

"Me too," Zabka says. "Those fuckers know how to party."

Their party vehicle is a short school bus that's been painted white, with a large Bills logo on the side. On the back is a sign that reads, "Bills Army". People nearby are pounding beers and dancing merrily.

As they near, Scooter asks, "You think they'll let us party with 'em?"

Zabka restrains himself from slapping Scooter in the face and shouts, "Blasphemy! Have you not learned anything today? Bills fans are friendly-as-fuck and love to party — they live for it!"

"Yeah, you're right. The Buffalo is pretty awesome."

Zabka adds, "I hope you've learned that god doesn't hate Buffalo. At least not today." He thanks the sky. "Today we were blessed."

A teetering Bills fan in the direct path to the party presents them with an upside-down bird. The man can only manage to screech, "CAAA!" to express his disapproval of their Dolphins attire.

Zabka mumbles, "I'm about sicka this shit," and starts bouncing at the tormenter like a gingerbread man with his arms up and legs out. As he approaches striking range, the man is paralyzed like his feet are in blocks of ice. Zabka jumps in the form of his caricature and slams his chest into the Bills fan's face. The man topples over and loses his Gore-Tex mittens, while Zabka continues on to the party without ever looking back.

Bob chuckles. "That, my friends — that is how you take care of a drunk heckler."

Scooter points at some girls participating in a keg stand contest. "Check 'em out. Is —" Arms strangle his neck, and his eyes practically burst out of their sockets. He bucks like a bronco, twirls around, and collapses onto the gravel. With his face a new shade of purple, he rolls over and discovers his assailant is Hope, the girl from Anchor Bar.

"Hey, asshole!" Hope screams. "Thanks for calling me last night!" Scooter wheezes while struggling to respond.

Jed yells, "Scooter! You let a woman take you down like that?!"

"Jesus Christ!" Scooter shouts. "Couldn't we have handled this in a different way?" He puts his arms out. "I swear I was just about to call you."

"Oh yeah?! It looks to me like you were about to go party!" Hope exclaims.

While Bob and Jed stealthily leave to join the Bills Army, Scooter and Hope continue their discussion on the ground.

"Well, yeah. I mean, I was gonna call you right after we had a few celebratory drinks." Scooter puts his hand on her cheek and looks her in the eye. "I wanted to thank you for the tickets. That was very sweet of you."

"You're welcome." Hope smiles. "I'm glad you found 'em. I secretly put them in your jacket so you'd be the hero."

"It worked out that way." He flexes his biceps. "I'm now officially cool."

"I'm sorry for attacking you. I just really wanted to see you again." She lightly pushes him away. "Don't leave a girl hangin' like that."

He gets up off the ground. "I really like you, and I want to see more of you." He gives her his hand and helps her stand.

"I really like you too. Can I tell you something?" she asks bashfully. "And you promise not to laugh?"

Scooter scratches the scab on his face. "You can tell me anything."

"This is kinda embarrassing, but here it goes." Hope places her hands on her chest. "I haven't had a penis inside me in two years." Scooter's heart stops pumping for two full seconds, before it starts racing at full speed. She continues, "And part of the reason is, I'm not-that-kind-of-girl. I don't sleep with a guy unless I'm in a relationship with him." She looks down at her feet. "I guess what I'm trying to say is." Her eyes move back up to his. "Do you want to be in a 'relationship' with me?"

He feels woozy as the blood in his head rushes like Niagara Falls to his junk. He stutters, "I — I — do."

"Good." Hope gets closer and grabs his crotch. "My mouth's been craving your dick from the moment I saw you."

Scooter works out a reply, "Oh — well my dick's been craving your mouth since I first saw you."

"Oh, yeah?" She moves her face an inch away from his. "Well, my mouth's been craving your dick's craving of my mouth."

His eyes spin. "Oh, yeah? Well, my — hey, if it's cool with you, can I just stick it in your mouth now?"

She nods her head, takes him by his belt, and pulls him towards the Bills Army bus.

—

As overjoyed Bills fans pour inside the Big Tree Inn for the postgame celebration, the crowd rapidly grows. Jennifer slides an empty shot glass across the bar to Joe and sucks down the last drops of her beer.

"One more round?" Joe asks.

"One more fuckin' round!" Jennifer shouts with her glass in the air.

"Looks like someone is feeling much better." He smiles at her and chuckles. "This is a pleasant turnaround."

She reaches for his face and swipes a finger down the bridge of his nose. "No, you turn around. I wanna see whatcha got back there."

Joe rotates his hips in a circle like a hula dancer and flaunts what's packed in his tight jeans. "So whaddya think?"

"I think I wanna jump over this bar and doing something I'll regret in the morning." Jennifer pushes her hair behind her ear. "That's what I think."

His initial instinct is to survey the bar and calculate the chances of pulling something like that off. "I'm not gonna lie." He replenishes her beer and shot. "I really like the sound of that." The impatient stares of patrons waiting for drinks at the bar involuntarily pull his attention. "But I need to take care of these customers first. Let's put a bookmark in that for now."

She jokingly pouts and gulps down her shot. "Well, I ain't going no-where."

He returns a reassuring smile, and shakes his head playfully. "Who knew you're fun like this? You always seemed — forgive me for saying —

a bit standoffish at school. I don't know, I guess I had the wrong impression?"

"Well, I know what will make an impression." Jennifer points to her bulging bosom. "These suckers."

"Goddamn." Joe's eyes pop. "I seriously need to quit this job. Let me go sling some drinks, and I'll be right back."

As Joe leaves for the other end of the bar, the chair next to her is vacated, and an elderly man slithers through the dense mob to take it. After he saddles up, he does a double-take at Jennifer and says, "Hold on, I know you from somewhere."

She turns to him and her wrist begins to ache. "Oh my god." Horrified, she struggles with what to do. "I mean no. No we don't know each other."

He inspects her smooth hands and grins like when he was a young man fifty-some-years ago. "Oh, yes we do. Did you enjoy the game?"

"Okay, we're not having this conversation." Jennifer chugs half her beer and wipes her chin.

"Why not?" He scratches his chin. "We're gonna have a playoff game in a couple of weeks and perhaps you'll need entry into that game too?"

Jennifer puts her dizzy head in her hands and closes her eyes, hoping to be delivered safely out of this dreadful day. The commotion of her surroundings fades away, and she spends the next minute in her own peaceful world. A tap on her skull brings her back into the chaos of the bar. Much to her surprise and relief, she finds Joe standing before her, and the old man from guest services has mysteriously vanished.

"I've got great news," Joe says. "My replacement has arrived, so my shift is now officially over."

"That's great news!" Jennifer scans the bar room. "I'm not really into crowds this big, so how about we get outta here? Maybe we go somewhere, I don't know, more intimate?"

"I like that sound of that." He comes around from behind the bar and grabs her hand. As he leads the way to the exit, they bounce off people and come to a stop several feet from the door.

She tries to peek around his body to see what's happening but the crowd is too crammed. "What's going on?"

Joe spins back to face her. "Before we go, I want to introduce you to somebody special." From behind he pulls the same old man from the bar around to Jennifer. "This is my grandfather."

Jennifer's jaw drops, as her handjob nightmare continues to be inescapable. "He's — he's your grandpa?"

"I am. Nice to meet you." The grandfather grabs her hand and shakes it. "Oh, she's got a nice firm grip, Joe. What every man needs, if you know what I mean." He winks at Jennifer.

"Oh, gramps," Joe says. "Always the joker." An intoxicated college kid caroms off them. "Anyways, good to see you. Sorry, but Jennifer and I must get going. She's not a fan of crowds like this."

"Yeah, we gotta roll," Jennifer adds with a touch of urgency.

As they slide past the old man, he says, "It was a *stroke* of good luck meeting you, Jennifer! Hope to see you again at that playoff game!"

———

As Scooter and Hope walk to the Bills Army bus, they pass by the keg where everyone else is hanging out. Scooter notices that Zabka is talking to Summer, which he finds unusual. Bob and Jed are nearby drinking from red Solo cups, which he finds not unusual.

Zabka asks the approaching lovebirds, "Hey, where you guys going? You wanna beer?"

"No," Scooter replies. "We're going to have mouth sex." Scooter points at Hope. "Her mouth."

Zabka shakes his head in disbelief. "You literally just fell into pussy. Unbelievable! But you know what?" He grabs Summer's ass. "We're joining ya." Jed and Bob shrug and toast the four of them as they leave.

The two couples climb on the bus and move to the back. Summer picks a seat, lies down, and tells Zabka, "It's a good thing you stopped acting like a pussy, because that was the only way you'd get in *this* pussy."

"You're not a stalker, right?" Zabka stops with his belt half off. "Because after we bang, I better not find you outside my place at 4 AM."

"I don't know where you live, and I don't care. You're hot — that's what this is about." Summer slides down her pants. "That work for you?"

"Does a priest fuck underage boys?" Zabka unzips his jeans. "It sure-as-shit does work for me. But first I want to apologize for calling you a Miami bimbo the other day. I —"

"Don't be stupid and cock block yourself." Summer positions herself spread-eagle and points at her bald beaver. "Just shut up and fuck me."

"That sounds like a better plan." Zabka begins following orders and pulls out a couple of condoms. "It would be my pleasure to split your uprights." He hands one to Scooter.

Hope follows the handoff and says, "He doesn't need that. We're in a relationship."

"You're in a what?" Zabka asks. He studies the blank look on Scooter's face. "Oh, never mind."

Two seats away, Hope lies down and takes off her jeans. She leaves on her crotchless Bills Zubaz panties and asks Scooter, "Which orifice would you like to penetrate?"

Scooter grins like the pizza delivery guy in a porno. "I think the mouth thing we talked about would be cool, but how about all of them?"

"Unless you've got multiple penises — which could be fun but weird — you're gonna have to choose one to start." Hope watches his mind spin and decides to speed things up by unzipping his pants. While doing that, she discovers his adult diaper. "What the hell is going on down here?"

His hard-on, which siphoned blood from his brain, has left him mentally impaired and incapable of giving her an answer.

In the heat of the moment, she doesn't really care and is undeterred. "How about this? Let's do what I want — and what I want is —" She puts her ankles on top of the neighboring seats and with a snarled upper lip tells him, "I want you to *squish my fish.*"

Scooter jumps on her so fast, it's as if he's saving his platoon from a live grenade — except the grenade is a magnificent vagina. He and Zabka thrust in-and-out in harmony like two Olympians going for gold in the synchronized-fucking competition. Scooter thanks the alcohol he's had for the extra stamina as Zabka hums *The Karate Kid* theme song, "You're the Best Around".

Zabka notices a tall man spying on them from beside a pickup truck that contains the corpses of two deer. "What the fuck is that guy doing?" The man extends his neck to peer over the cabin for a better view.

"Who?" Scooter asks while in mid-stroke.

"That creepy giant out there with the long neck." Zabka points at the guy with the jiggling head. "I'm pretty sure he's watching us and playing with himself."

Scooter inspects the man. "What a loser."

Hope's pupils roll back and her eyes turn white like an attacking shark. She pounds the seat with her fist and cries, "Shut up and squish me, baby!"

Scooter gives Zabka a high-five. "Dude, I'm actually fucking her!"

"Thanks for the update — I can see that," Zabka replies.

"On top of that, she's not that prickly *and* she might be wetter than my balls!" Scooter tilts his head back and howls, "The juice is loooooose!!!"

"If I may share a piece of advice — switch to internal dialog." Zabka steers his eyes away from Scooter's contorted sex-face and then smirks. "However, I do think now's a perfect time to discuss a raise."

"For once this weekend, you're right." Scooter wipes the sweat from his brow as he pumps away. "I'll start the paper work tomorrow."

Meanwhile, Bob and Jed are outside drinking from the keg. Bob notices the shameless masturbator with the giraffe neck and nudges Jed. "Hey, look at that guy." Bob squints. "Holy shit, I know him! That's Janks!

I work with that psychopath and he's whacking off! Dale's never gonna believe this!"

"Fuck! Even *The Deer Hunter* gets more action than us!" Jed cries.

"Yeah, with himself. Which I'm pretty sure that doesn't count."

Jed becomes a play-by-play announcer. "Look at Janks go! His eyes are squeezed shut and his face is beginning to spasm. Christ! His puckered mouth looks like a dick hole about to explode!"

"It does!" Bob adds as the color commentator. "Let's hope ejaculate doesn't squirt out and nail somebody in the face!"

"That's disgusting, Bob." Jed looks behind them. "There might be fucking kids walking around here. Think before you talk."

Bob chuckles. "Sure, buddy. I'll try to be more aware."

"Looks like he finished his business, but now what's he doing?"

They observe Janks as he climbs up into the bed of the truck with the deer. He reaches down with both hands and grabs something. Bob exclaims, "Oh lord, he's got the axe from work!"

Like they're watching a horror film, they recoil as he chops into the belly of the deer's carcass. Whack! After a few more precision cuts, Janks pulls out a chunk of venison and tosses it to his friend next to their grill.

Bob slams down the rest of his beer. "That settles it. I'm not going into the office tomorrow."

Jed begins with a creepy laugh. "Ha, ha, ha. All work and no play, makes Janks a dull boy."

Bob refills his beer and continues watching the postgame chaos with Jed. To their surprise, Bambi appears out of the crowd streaming by and says, "Hi guys. Can I join you for a beer?"

"Hey, Bambi! Sure, why not." Bob grabs a cup and pours her one.

"Bob, I want to thank you for what you did in the stadium."

"I'm not sure what you're talking about?" He looks at her curiously. "Something's different about you. The way you're talking."

"You stopped Bradford and Juan Carlos from getting away," she reminds him. "Officer Radzikowski told me about it. Pretty awesome."

"Oh, yeah." Bob brushes imaginary dirt off his shoulder. "That was no big deal. Actually, do you know why the cops were chasing them?"

"As a matter of fact, I do," she answers. "I'm an undercover agent for the FDA, and I was leading a sting operation investigating their bullshit business."

Bob shouts, "You're what?! Holy shit! Fuck those guys!"

"Hold up," Jed says. "No offense, but you're not an idiot?"

"No, of course not. That was a role I was playing." She winks at Bob. "My real name is Barbara. I'm glad I was convincing."

Bob remarks, "I had a feeling you were up to something. Hot and crafty is my kind of combination."

"Thank you," she replies with a curtsy. "You don't even know how happy it makes me to hear that."

Jed asks her, "So what's gonna happen to those two fuck-nuggets?"

"They'll go to trial, and if convicted of fraud — which they will be unless our lawyers royally fuck it up — they'll spend a few years in a minimum-security prison."

"I bet Bradford and Juan Carlos will beg to be someone's bitch in the slammer," Bob adds. "They just seem like the type."

"Hey, get this," Barbara tells them. "Bradford's full name used to be Peter Short before he legally changed it. How funny is that, considering the scummy business he's in?"

Bob laughs. "Damn, that is funny. I wonder if that's how he came up with the idea for their cockamamie product? Pun intended."

Barbara giggles and chugs the rest of her beer. "Switching topics — I have a question, Bob." She squints at him. "You didn't really have sex with Summer, did you?"

"Um, no. Actually I didn't," Bob admits. "How'd you know?"

"The ol' sniff test never fails. I smelled the condom and, as I expected, found no feminine traces."

"I guess Bradford was too stupid to try that." Bob smiles. "But why would you do that? That couldn't have been part of your investigation?"

She answers bashfully, "I wanted to know if we could, ya know, hang-out in the future. So I checked to make sure you didn't *go there*."

"Oh, I see." He cozies up against her with his eyes glued to her chest. "Well, in that case, I advise you not to smell my junk at the moment." He laughs like he's joking, and Jed uses his cup to cover his chuckle.

Barbara twirls a hair. "And you don't really have a girlfriend either, right?"

Bob pauses for a drink and shakes his head as he swallows. "No, of course not." They toast with their plastic cups. "Yeah, let's hang out."

"I'd like that." She grabs his hand. "Plus I really feel like celebrating."

Bob instinctively checks in Janks's direction for any impending threats. As he looks, he sees Lisa walking by and gets excited. "Hey, Lisa!" She looks around for her caller. "Lisa!!"

She spots Bob and walks over with a grin from ear to ear. "Hey! That was one hell of a game, wasn't it?" She gives him a hug.

"Sure was. You wanna drink?"

"Yeah, thanks." As he starts pouring her a cup, she adds, "I like this. Finally, the tables have turned and you're the one serving me."

He hands her the beer. "My pleasure."

Lisa looks at the others and says, "Hey Bambi. Hey Jed."

"Oh, Bambi's not her real name — it's Barbara. Long story short, she's not a dimwit, and the Bambi-thing was all an act. She is, however, still very hot."

Lisa tilts her head and looks at Barbara in a different light. She grins while raising her eyebrows. "You got that right."

"Thanks." Barbara fixes Lisa's wind-blown hair by pushing it behind her ear. "You're pretty hot yourself."

Lisa gets lost in Barbara's eyes for a noticeable amount of time before turning to Bob. "So I gotta tell you something. Your crazy girlfriend came into the Base last night."

Bob gasps. "She did what?"

"Hold up," Barbara says. "You just told me you *don't* have a girlfriend."

"Well, *I did* — but, um, now I don't. We broke-up today." Bob pouts. "Cheating was involved —" He chokes-up and wipes a fake tear from his eye. "So I'm extremely vulnerable at the moment."

Both girls melt with an "aww," like they're looking at an adorable puppy, and engulf Bob with their warm bodies.

Jed stares from the sidelines and mumbles to himself, "*What-in-the-hell* is happening over there?"

Lisa says to Bob, "You poor thing — but you're really much better-off without her."

Barbara slides her hands down Lisa's back and squeezes her butt firmly. "We need to take care of this boy."

Lisa returns the favor to Barbara's tush. "I agree."

"You up for that, Bob?" Barbara asks.

Lisa feels a poke from Bob's massive erection and answers for him, "Oh yeah, he's definitely up for it."

Bob nuzzles his face into a bouquet-of-breasts and feels blessed to be in his "happy place." While the chorus of "Some Guys Have All The Luck" plays from a nearby car, he wiggles his head energetically and buzzes his lips to sound like a motorboat.

Meanwhile, Jed is pumping the keg at such high-velocity, that it looks like a he's finishing a self-pleasure session. He slows and sighs while finishing his pour. "And so the story goes —" Foam runs over the lip of his cup. "In the end, the married guy is always the one left with his dick in his hand.

As the Bills Army bus shakes from carnal pleasure, Jed glances again at the Barbara-Bob-Lisa sandwich and rolls his eyes. "Forget dating — or whatever *that* is." He looks at his beer with adoration. "We'll always have each other. You never let me down." He thrusts his drink to the sky. "To debauchery!!!"

Epilogue

While the fans in the Rich Stadium parking lot were engaging in the type of debauchery normally only found in the Grotto at the Playboy Mansion, Gardner was still steaming-mad inside the stadium. He attempted to go after Cox in Miami's locker room but was derailed by stadium security before he could enter. Gardner then went to the Dolphins' bus twice and tried to bait Cox to come off and finish the fight. Gardner later denied both of these postgame claims and instead spoke about what happened on the field, "What [Cox] did was totally uncalled for because I was just blocking on the play."

Miami managed to win a wild card spot that season with a victory in their last game, which set up a rematch against Buffalo in the first round of the playoffs. The Bills hosted the game and again defeated the Dolphins — this time 37-22 on December 30, 1995. As events currently stand, this is the last time Buffalo has won a playoff game. The Bills ended up losing the following week in Pittsburgh 40-21.

Buffalo made it back to the playoffs in the '96, '98, and '99 seasons — each time in a wildcard spot. The last Bills playoff game was on January 8th, 2000, barely squeaking them into the new millennium. With just 16 seconds left in that game against the Tennessee Titans, the Bills kicked a field goal to take a 16-15 lead. On the ensuing kickoff, Neal received the ball for the Titans and handed it to Wycheck. He then threw a lateral across the field to his teammate Dyson — a Titans' special-teams play called the "Home Run Throwback." Dyson caught the ball and ran it 75-yards down the sideline to score the winning touchdown. Bills fans to this day swear the lateral was actually an illegal forward pass. The resulting 22-16 Bills loss is known as the "Music City Miracle." Tim Russert, a Buffalo native and moderator of NBC's *Meet the Press*, said after the game, "It's not a miracle, it was a crime. It was a fraud, perpetrated on the streets of Nashville."

Since then, nearly two decades have passed, and Buffalo and Miami have sunk into mediocrity. Meanwhile, their division foe, the New England Patriots, have become one of the most dominant teams in the league. During that time, pretty boy Tom Brady and alleged head-cheater Bill Belichick have also transformed the Patriots into the most loathed football team in the country. While New England has gone to seven Super Bowls and won five since 2000 (thank you, New York Giants, for delivering the two losses), Buffalo has had more drunk fans fall from the upper deck of their stadium (one) and more dildos thrown on their field (one) than they have playoff appearances (zero).

In 2014, the Bills were put up for sale after Ralph Wilson, Jr. — the Buffalo Bills founder & owner, member of the NFL Hall of Fame, and WWII Navy veteran — passed away at the age of 95. Most fans feared the team would leave Western New York when competitive offers were made by both Donald Trump and a Toronto-led group that included Jon Bon Jovi. If one of them had successfully purchased the franchise and taken the team elsewhere, it would've decimated the loyal fans in Western New York. Thankfully, those fears were alleviated when the Buffalo Sabres owners, Terry and Kim Pegula, purchased the Bills for $1.4 billion and kept them in Orchard Park.

Now Buffalo's goal is to return to the Super Bowl and win for the first time in their history. When that happens, you'll want to be in Buffalo because it will be the biggest and craziest party you've ever seen — I can guarantee that. Just search the Internet for "Bills Mafia" or "Buffalo Bills tailgating videos" and you'll be amazed.

Oh, and if you're wondering what happened to Juan Carlos and Bradford — they were convicted and sentenced to five years in a white-collar 'country club' prison in Florida. One evening they escaped through a sewage pipe and got lost in one of the surrounding swamps. There, unbeknownst to them until it was too late, they became gator bait and were never heard from again.

As for what happened to Bob, Zabka, Scooter, and Jed — well, that story is too unbelievable and lengthy (that's what she said) to be summarized here. Perhaps someday, someone will write a book about it.

SONGS IN ORDER OF APPEARANCE

"Crazy Train" by Ozzy Osbourne
"I Touch Myself" by Divinyls
"Big Poppa" by Notorious B.I.G.
"Slide It In" by Whitesnake
"Hazy Shade of Winter" by The Bangles
"I'm Coming Out" by Diana Ross
"Hip Hop Hooray" by Naughty By Nature
"Used to Love Her" by Guns N' Roses
"Have a Drink on Me" by AC/DC
"Let's Talk About Sex" by Salt-N-Pepa
"Loser" by Beck
"Gin & Juice" by Snoop Dogg
"The Christmas Song" by Nat King Cole
"Chicken Dance" by Werner Thomas
"Fat Bottomed Girls" by Queen
"Man in the Box" by Alice In Chains
"New Orleans is Sinking" by The Tragically Hip
"Poundcake" by Van Halen
"Poison" by Bell Biv DeVoe
"Kickstart My Heart" by Mötley Crüe
"Erotic City" by Prince
"Rico Suave" by Gerardo
"Rock of Ages" by Def Leppard
"Conga" by Miami Sound Machine
"September" by Earth, Wind & Fire
"Give It To Me Baby" by Rick James
"Rock And Roll All Night" by KISS
"Celebration" by Kool & The Gang
"Escape (The Piña Colada Song)" by Rupert Holmes
"Enter Sandman" by Metallica
"Buffalo Bills Shout" by Scott Kemper
"You're the Best" (from *The Karate Kid* Soundtrack) by Joe Esposito
"Some Guys Have All The Luck" by Rod Stewart

329

"Squish the Fish" Lyrics by Dave Lundy

When I first saw her, I grabbed my fishing pole.
She gave me that look, to slip it in her watering hole.
Advance down her field, to penetrate that vertical line.
No block below the waist, now it's time to dine.

Oh girl from Miami, there's one thing I gotta do.
For this boy from Buffalo, it all ain't nothin' new.
Inhale your ocean breeze, goddamn it smells dee-lish.
Time to do my favorite thing and, squish, squish, squish the fish.

Entering your end zone, you're as excited as me.
Your eyes rolled back, no way ya can possibly see.
Excessive celebration flags, the refs just made the calls.
Yeah, yeah, caress me there, and deflate my balls.

Oh girl from Miami, there's one thing I gotta do.
For this boy from Buffalo, it all ain't nothin' new.
Was it good for you? To fulfill my wish.
Ya want me to do it again? To squish, squish, squish the fish.

It was great at first, couldn't imagine nothin' better.
Got soaked in a hurricane, and you were much, much wetter.
Tired of dolphin free tuna, at your tailgate party.
Hey there goes a school of snapper, I don't wanna be tardy.

Oh girl from Miami, there's one thing I gotta do.
For this boy from Buffalo, I'm off to catch something new.
Don't care what her name is, don't matter if it's Trish.
My clock's at high-noon to, squish, squish, squish the fish.
Squish, squish, squish the fish.
Squish, squish, squish the fish.
Squish, squish, squish that fish.
Squish, squish, squish the fish.

(Purchase or stream the song from every music store and app on the planet!)

ABOUT THE AUTHOR

Dave Lundy was born a devious prankster, raised in upstate New York, and voted "Class Clown" in high school. After graduating college at UB and working in Buffalo, he followed his girlfriend west to Las Vegas (alas, she wasn't a stripper) and then on to California. When their cross-country fairytale ended, he moved to San Francisco where he currently resides. While Dave's crazy adventures are often the spark of his hilarious stories, it's his clever imagination that takes them over-the-top.

For more "Squish the Fish" and Dave — like, follow, and whatever:
Facebook: www.facebook.com/squishthefish
Cafe Press: www.cafepress.com/squishthefish
YouTube: tinyurl.com/lundytube
Instagram and Twitter: @DaveLundyAuthor

47388225R00204

Made in the USA
Middletown, DE
25 August 2017